D0515214

DEMOCRACY IN
THE THIRD WORLD

DEMOCRACY IN THE THIRD WORLD

SECOND EDITION

Robert Pinkney

LYNNE
RIENNER
PUBLISHERS

BOULDER
LONDON

Published in the United States of America in 2003 by
Lynne Rienner Publishers, Inc.
1800 30th Street, Boulder, Colorado 80301
www.rienner.com

and in the United Kingdom by
Lynne Rienner Publishers, Inc.
3 Henrietta Street, Covent Garden, London WC2E 8LU

© 2003 by Lynne Rienner Publishers, Inc. All rights reserved

Library of Congress Cataloging-in-Publication Data
Pinkney, Robert.
  Democracy in the Third World / Robert Pinkney. — 2nd ed.
  Includes bibliographical references and index.
  ISBN 1-55587-972-1 (alk. paper)
  ISBN 1-55587-997-7 (pb. : alk. paper)
  1. Democracy—Developing countries. 2. Developing countries—
Politics and government. I. Title.
JF60 .P56   2002
320.9172'4—dc21   2002073435

British Cataloguing in Publication Data
A Cataloguing in Publication record for this book
is available from the British Library.

Printed and bound in the United States of America

The paper used in this publication meets the requirements
∞ of the American National Standard for Permanence of
Paper for Printed Library Materials Z39.48-1984.

5 4 3 2 1

Contents

Tables

Preface

To search for democracy in the third world is to pursue a moving target. Indeed it was a near-invisible target for much of the 1970s. By the time the first edition of this book was published in 1994, extreme pessimism on the part of democrats had given way to optimism, as military and single-party regimes had been removed from much of Africa, Asia, and Latin America. Like many of yesterday's luxuries, democracy appeared to have become one of today's necessities, available to rich and poor alike.

By the millennium, the mood had become more cautious. The total number of democratic countries had continued to increase, in the sense of countries enjoying relatively free elections and the protection of basic civil liberties. However, there was concern that the increase in quantity had not been matched by improved quality. This did not necessarily imply that the democratic performance of every country should be measured along some arbitrarily imposed scale, but most people would agree that there is something lacking in democracies where the ruling party is invariably able to manipulate resources to ensure its reelection, where many political decisions reflect the wishes of foreign donors rather than the popular will, and where the basic rules of competition for power are still in dispute.

The questions that scholars are asking about democracy have begun to change. In the early 1990s, there was much emphasis on the conditions necessary for a transition to democracy and a widely held belief that a successful pincer attack had been launched on authoritarianism. Opposition groups had articulated growing popular discontent, while foreign powers had transferred their allegiance from authoritarians to democrats, so that the path could be smoothed to free elections. Since then, there has been a growing realization of the complications. Many opposition movements were a nine days' wonder and had shallow bases of support, and ruling politicians have found ways of making only minimal concessions to democratic demands. More questions have been asked about the adequacy of civil societies to sustain democracy, and economic decline has left the victors in democratic elections with few resources with which to carry out their chosen policies. Western influence is now less likely to be seen as benevolent, as stringent conditions are imposed on economic aid, and countries are valued more for their strategic importance than their democratic credentials.

For all these reasons, a revision of my 1994 book seemed overdue, and I was delighted when Lynne Rienner invited me to write a revised volume. Although much has been written on democracy and democratization since 1994, I feel there is a need to return to some of the simple questions about how and why democracy emerges, survives, deepens, or regresses. The background history and the ideas in the classical literature obviously remain important, but we also need to think more about the nature of civil society, external pressures, and specific actors. Democratization is not just a matter of assembling the right ingredients such as economic development, tolerant attitudes, or foreign backing, but of subtle interactions between a variety of individuals and institutions with a variety of resources. These interactions, in turn, take place against internal and global backgrounds that may encourage or impede democracy. This revised volume takes the reader through some of the highways and byways in the search for democratic successes and failures. The paths are seldom straight and the view is not always clear, but I hope the journey is always interesting and stimulates further exploration.

* * *

Many people have made the completion of this book possible. I was guided through the maze of literature by Maimie Balfour and Austin McCarthy at the University of Northumbria Library. Lecturers and students at the university provided many helpful comments when I tested my ideas on them. Stephanie Clements and Sharon Metcalff retyped the first five chapters after I discovered that the original disks had been lost. My wife, Mary, eliminated many of the typing errors and much of the inelegant prose from various drafts. Vicky Randall of the University of Essex offered many helpful criticisms of the original draft. David Brading of Cambridge University kindly answered my queries about race relations in colonial Latin America. More recently, Katharine Adeney of Balliol College, Oxford, and Andrew Wyatt of the University of Bristol helped to clarify my understanding of South Asian politics. I am grateful to everyone who helped, but I take sole responsibility for the opinions expressed and for any errors that remain.

—*Robert Pinkney*

Introduction

In 1994 I noted that a book on democracy in the third world written twenty years earlier would have been a very short book. Competitive elections and civil liberties had survived since the achievement of independence in India, the Gambia, Botswana, Mauritius, and some of the islands in the West Indies, and, since the ending of civil war, in Costa Rica. But these were oases in a desert dominated by military governments, one-party regimes, and personal dictatorships. Today, virtually all the governments of Latin America have been chosen by means of competitive election. Asia, South Korea, Bangladesh, Thailand, Nepal, the Philippines, and Indonesia have all emerged from authoritarian, military, or personal rule, and single-party domination in Taiwan has ended with the main opposition party winning a free election. In sub-Saharan Africa the vast majority of countries have held competitive elections since 1990, even though many authoritarian tendencies still persist and political violence continues. This leaves Myanmar (Burma), Pakistan, and much of North Africa and the Middle East under authoritarian rule, with question marks over whether the dominant one-party systems of Singapore and Malaysia can yet be regarded as democratic. The transformation of so much of the world in so short a time is remarkable by any standards. Why should democracy have emerged, or reemerged? What is its significance, and what are its future prospects?

To use the terms "democracy" and "third world" in the same sentence is to provoke immediate arguments about definitions and the utility of particular concepts. The term "third world" is probably no more illuminating than the terms that preceded it, such as "developing countries," "underdeveloped countries," or "emergent countries," yet it has come into common usage for want of anything better. One can argue about where the third world ends and where the first and second worlds begin, but I shall accept the common usage and take it to include the countries that are characterized by greater poverty—compared with Western Europe, North America, and

I

the Antipodes—though they have not had their political systems transformed by membership in the communist bloc. The poverty can be measured not only by narrow material indicators, such as per capita income, but
also by illiteracy, low life expectancy, high infant mortality, and unsafe
drinking water. It is these social and economic circumstances, together with
an unequal relationship with the developed world outside and, in many
cases, a recent experience of colonial rule, that help to give third world politics its distinctive flavor, even though there is much diversity among the
individual countries. In particular, it has frequently been argued that these
countries are the ones least likely to be able to sustain democracy. Politics
is more of a life-and-death struggle, in which those who possess a disproportionate amount of the meager resources available are not likely to risk
losing these resources by permitting free elections.

How, then, can one explain the emergence and survival of democracy
in such a hostile climate? When the first edition of this book was published,
much of the academic debate centered around the relative importance of the
preconditions for democracy as compared with the skill of political actors
in achieving transitions from authoritarianism to democracy. The former
approach has been concerned mainly with explaining why countries in the
West enjoyed the right preconditions, such as material prosperity, urbanization, cultures that encouraged tolerance and participation, and political
institutions that had developed accepted ways of resolving conflicts. Third
world countries lacked most of these preconditions and were therefore
much less likely to be able to establish or maintain democratic political systems. The transition approach, in contrast, acknowledged that many countries were developing democratic systems and sought to explain such developments in terms of the ability of different political actors, whether inside
or outside government, to reach sufficient consensus on a new set of rules
of the political game.

These two approaches continue to provide invaluable insights and
enable one to test hypotheses about why democracy has succeeded or failed
in a particular country, but they do not tell the whole story. One could argue
that a "developed" country like Singapore enjoys many of the preconditions
that would favor democracy but that democracy has failed to materialize
because insufficient actors or actions have been present to initiate a transition, whereas Benin has achieved a transition despite the absence of most
of the generally accepted preconditions. Democratic setbacks in the Gambia and Pakistan might suggest that the foundations of democracy remain
shaky if many preconditions are absent, whereas the survival of democracy
in much of Latin America in the face of economic decline might suggest a
triumph of political will over hostile conditions.

Yet a discussion of preconditions and "transitology" alone leaves us
with many unexplored areas. At least three aspects of the subject have

become more important and the subject of greater debate since the publication of the first edition of this book: relations between the state and civil society (discussed in Chapter 5), external influences (Chapter 7), and democratic consolidation (Chapter 9). Civil society tended to be neglected in the earlier literature because it was frequently assumed that most transitions involved negotiation between government and opposition, or elite and counterelite, with the wider society having little more than a walk-on role in the occasional riot or attempt at communal self-help. It is now widely acknowledged that there is a significant new relationship between state and society. Society has shown its willingness to challenge the state as it pressed for the ending of authoritarian rule, and the state has been forced to accept a more modest role as it suffers diminished resources for economic development, social provision, and the maintenance of order. More human activity now takes place away from the shadow of the state umbrella. Not all of this will be conducive to democracy, but the general effect is to establish a more pluralist political process.

The importance of external influence was acknowledged in the past to the extent that one could see the impact of major events and decisions such as the collapse of communism, the ending of the Cold War, the withdrawal of Western support for authoritarian rulers, and the insistence on good governance as a condition of aid. But we now need to look at more subtle influences. External support for authoritarianism or democracy is not simply something that can be switched on or off at will but involves a range of intended and unintended influences running through a variety of channels. Third world countries may respond to these pressures in a variety of ways, sometimes bowing to Western demands, sometimes putting their own interpretation on them, and sometimes rejecting them. And beyond links between governments, there has been the growth of global forces that have been seen sometimes as an aid to the transmission of democratic values and sometimes as damaging democracy by reducing the ability of elected governments to carry out the popular will.

The concept of democratic consolidation became more important as the focus of interest shifted from the ability of countries to achieve transitions to democracy to their ability to sustain and deepen it. If it is accepted that there is more to democracy than holding periodic elections, questions arise as to the extent to which governments are accountable and responsive to public opinion, the extent to which there are adequate means of participation and representation for civil society, and the extent to which there are adequate constraints to prevent the arbitrary exercise of authority, especially by the armed forces. This requires us to build on the discussion of the relationship between the state and civil society but also to pursue the more traditional concerns of political scientists about the adequacy of institutions.

In addition to exploring these new areas, Chapter 6, which focuses on continuous democracies, has been expanded to include a fuller discussion on India. Although that discussion still cannot do justice to such a vast country, it seems important to explore the reasons for the survival of democracy in a poor, heterogeneous, and heavily populated country. Scholars are rightly skeptical of any suggestion that the experience of one country necessarily provides a model for others to follow, but if democracy is ever to be established in China or consolidated in Indonesia, the Indian experience might be more relevant than that of smaller states.

Chapter 10, a new chapter, explores the question of whether there are distinctive African, Asian, or Latin American factors that influence the shape of democracy. It is suggested that while each individual country is obviously unique, there are similarities of history, culture, institutional patterns, and external relations within each continent that may explain some of the variations in democratic patterns or, indeed, some failures to establish democracy at all.

For the rest of this book, all the themes of the first edition are preserved.

We begin by looking at the various definitions and forms of democracy in Chapter 1. Although we are no nearer than the ancient Greeks to arriving at a universally agreed definition or deciding which form of democracy is best, there has been some process of elimination. People's democracy, as practiced until recently in Eastern Europe, is out of favor, and the practicability of socialist democracy, at least in the old-fashioned sense of the common ownership of the means of production, has come increasingly into question as the limitations of the capacity of the state have come to be recognized. The focus has thus narrowed, at least for the present and the immediate future, to variations on liberal democracy, with free competition for elective office complemented by a "free economy." Many advocates of democracy might want to go beyond this stage to a more participant, egalitarian system, but most would still accept liberal democracy as a necessary stage along the road, and it is therefore this form of democracy that occupies much of our attention. But even the minimal definition of liberal democracy is too generous a description of some third world democracies. The term "electoral democracy" is often used to characterize political systems in which relatively free elections are held but with few of the traditional checks and balances and with few opportunities for public participation.

Whether it is a staging post or an ideal in itself or even the final destination marking the end of history, liberal democracy offers third world countries something that is in stark contrast to the alternatives most of them have experienced. At the very least, it implies an absence of arbitrary arrests, tortures, and executions; of costly decisions taken by arrogant rulers whose fallibility no one could question; and of demeaning personality cults that encouraged sycophancy in place of informed debate. Even the achievement of such practical objectives as stability, order, and development has generally eluded authoritarian rulers. And, although democracy has seldom been canvassed primarily as a means of achieving these objectives, it can help to contain the worst excesses of corruption, prestige spending, or individual shortsightedness through the checks and balances it provides. What, then, are the opportunities available for, and obstacles in the way of, achieving the democratic goal?

Following the discussion on the meaning of democracy, Chapter 2 examines the debate on the conditions conducive to its emergence. Although much of the debate is centered on developments in the West, we consider the extent to which the theories can be adapted to the third world and the extent to which new explanations of democratic development need to be added. Most of the third world countries were colonies of European powers before they attempted to develop democratic institutions, and the varied effects of colonial rule are considered in Chapter 3. The majority of countries established some form of pluralism after achieving independence, although this involved a lengthy time interval in Latin America, but these eras generally proved to be false dawns, with incipient democracies superseded by authoritarianism. The explanations of this eclipse of democracy are discussed in Chapter 4.

Chapter 5 looks at relations between state and civil society, as already explained, and Chapter 6 considers the exceptional countries that have preserved democracy continuously since independence. Chapter 7 discusses external influences, and Chapter 8 offers a revised discussion of the processes of transition to democracy. It takes into account the arguments about preconditions and then examines the different perspectives from which the different political actors can be viewed. Whereas the earlier literature saw actors largely in terms of government versus opposition, I suggest that they may also be perceived as members of social classes, elites, or groups or simply as influential individuals. We then look at the context within which the interaction between them takes place, including the underlying political cultures, economic conditions, and the roles of particular institutions.

Chapter 9 examines the successes and failures of attempts at democratic consolidation, as explained above. It looks backward at the circumstances in which democracy was established and forward at the ability of countries to develop democratic institutions. Chapter 10 explores the variations in the experience of democracy between the African, Asian, and Latin American continents.

The concluding chapter may seem more pessimistic from the point of view of democrats than the conclusion in the first edition, though that is for the reader to judge. Since the early 1990s, apartheid has been dismantled peacefully in South Africa, and the remaining one-party states have gone. In Indonesia the longest-serving military ruler has had to step down. Equally remarkable has been the way in which nearly all the bridgeheads gained for democracy have been held. Very few countries have reverted to authoritarianism. Yet according to expert observers, only one of the many countries emerging from authoritarian rule is deemed to have achieved democratic consolidation. If the shallowness of democracy was simply a matter of inexperience that could be overcome in the fullness of time, that would not be a matter of any great concern, but there are reasons to believe that the problem is much more deep-rooted.

There has been little improvement, if any, in per capita income in most third world countries, and little if any reduction in poverty or debt. Even if extensive poverty is not an insuperable barrier to democratization, it is likely to do little to stimulate democratic participation or to increase the commitment of the masses to a political system that is bringing them few benefits. Competitive elections continue to be held, but many rulers are learning how far they can go in ensuring their own reelection without provoking too much resistance at home or abroad. Western powers continue to proclaim their belief in democracy, yet their own practice of democracy has not always provided a model that is conducive to democratic consolidation in the third world. Their growing acceptance of market forces reduces the scope for democratic control over economic policy, and democratic choice in the third world is limited now that social democratic alternatives are deemed to be ideologically incorrect. Western acceptance of the permissive society gives third world rulers a pretext for associating Western democracy with moral decadence, and a growing willingness by Western governments to make generous concessions to big business makes it difficult for them to urge other governments to combat corruption.

None of this means that any further democratic advance is impossible in the third world, but we should at least be aware of the rocky terrain to be negotiated. Democratization in the West in the nineteenth and early twentieth centuries generally occurred against a background of economic growth and a political order in which governments were willing to use the machinery of state to expand social welfare and redistribute wealth. The justification for democracy has never been simply that it offers a better means of material advancement, but unless it can give voters something in return for their votes, no amount of philosophical argument about liberty, human rights, or political choice will ensure its survival. That is the challenge facing both third world governments and Western governments that proclaim a belief in democratic values.

1

The Nature
of Democracy

There is a growing belief that authoritarianism in the third world served people ill, in terms of failing to provide material prosperity, stability, order, the protection of human life, or the pursuit of goals that in any way reflected the wishes of the majority. Occasional exceptions can be found, such as the rapid rate of economic growth in Brazil and South Korea and the relatively benign nature of one-party rule in Tanzania. But the vast majority of third world citizens, whatever their degree of political influence or perception, have had little reason to favor the continuation of military governments, single-party regimes, or personal rule.

The obvious alternative to authoritarianism is democracy, but democracy is elusive both as a concept and as a feasible objective. We shall consider feasibility later and concentrate for the moment on the varied conceptions of democracy, the ideologies underlying them, and their implications for the state, society, and the citizen. The classification of the democracies is as old as political science itself, and we have an embarrassment of typologies to offer the aspiring third world country. For our purposes, the works of Dodd and Sklar help to illustrate some of the more obviously relevant types (Dodd 1979: 176–178; Sklar 1983: 11–24). After eliminating Dodd's "direct democracy," which is hardly feasible in any but the smallest communities, and Sklar's "participatory democracy," which seems to overlap with the other categories, Table 1.1 offers a fivefold classification and summarizes the features of each type of democracy in terms of objectives, perceptions of society, the role of the state, the political process, citizen participation, citizens' rights, and the actual and potential problems to which each type gives rise. Each category is, of course, an ideal type, and most countries claiming to be democracies will contain elements from more than one category, but we shall begin by looking at each category in its abstract form.

7

Table 1.1 Types of Democracy

	Radical Democracy	Guided Democracy	Liberal Democracy	Socialist Democracy	Consociational Democracy
Objectives	Enabling undifferentiated individuals to exercise their rights and protect their interests	Achievement of the general will	Representation and protection of diverse interests	Equality; social justice	Consensus between diverse groups
Perception of society	Aggregation of individuals	Organic whole with common interests	Aggregation of diverse individuals and groups autonomous from the state	Potentially organic whole but requiring transformation through state action	Aggregation of diverse groups autonomous from the state
Role of the state	Executor of the will of the majority	Executor of the general will	Referee	Redistribution of resources and guide to action	Referee
Political process	Provision of arena for pursuit of individual interests	Unchecked pursuit of objectives proclaimed by the ruling elite	Checks and balances to prevent tyranny of the majority, or its representatives, or of powerful minorities	All citizens given an equal voice by reducing inequality of wealth and resources	Recognition of the diversity of interests and identities by bringing leaders of all major groups into the governmental process

(continues)

Table 1.1 Cont.

	Radical Democracy	Guided Democracy	Liberal Democracy	Socialist Democracy	Consociational Democracy
Citizen participation	Active participation is encouraged; electoral contestation	Mobilization by ruling elite; no elections to key institutions, or only noncontested elections	Permitted but not actively encouraged; electoral contestation	Popular participation to offset elite power; may involve mobilization or coercion; electoral contestation possible, sometimes only intraparty	Participation within constituent groups and by group leaders in the allocation of resources; electoral contestation
Citizens' rights	Individual interests are subordinate to the interests of the majority but are protected by equality before the law	Individual interests are seen as synonymous with state interests; rulers decide on the extent of equality	Constitutional safeguards of individual rights; equality before the law	Attitudes to civil rights ambiguous; objective of social equality	Variable; may be safeguarded by state or within constituent groups
Actual and potential problems	Tyranny of the majority	Tyranny of the elite	Elite domination on account of unequal distribution of resources	Extent of coercion required to achieve objectives	Reinforcement of social divisions; immobilism

Radical Democracy

Dodd traces the ancestry of this type of democracy from the ancient Greeks through Tom Paine and Thomas Jefferson to the utilitarians (Dodd 1979: 176–178). Society is seen as an aggregation of undifferentiated individuals, without the allowance made in subsequent literature for the existence of people as members of groups with common interests and resources that distinguish them from other groups. The democratic ideal is to enable these undifferentiated individuals to exercise their rights and protect their interests as active participants in the political arena. Citizens' rights are protected to the extent that all are equal before the law, but there is not the same emphasis as in liberal democracy on protecting the individual against the power of the state, for the will of the majority is paramount and the state exists to execute that will. Even if the method of establishing the will of the majority is impeccably democratic, problems remain with regard to the position of minorities, whether they be permanent minorities such as a particular ethnic or religious group or more transient groups such as residents living close to a proposed hydroelectric dam that is purported to be in the public interest.

The complexity of group interests and the need for governments to retain the support of these interests in order to survive make this form of democracy unusual in the modern world. Elements of it may survive in the United States, where political decisions in many states are taken by referenda, and governments at all levels are regarded as executors of the popular will rather than means by which corporate bargains are struck between groups enmeshed in the political process. But in practice, the sanctions that various groups can wield (including votes) and the checks and balances written into the constitution prevent a crude majoritarianism. In the third world, the network of influential groups is generally less extensive, and the assertiveness of citizens wanting to safeguard their rights against the "tyranny of the majority" is lower. Some governments have thus been able to claim a mandate from the majority to pursue radical reforms, even if this meant riding roughshod over the wishes of minorities or imprisoning subversives who stood in the way. Ghana under Kwame Nkrumah, Guinea under Sékou Touré, or Sri Lanka under successive leaders might be cited as examples. Yet experience suggests that a country will not approximate to the radical democratic category for long. The democratic element is suspect, not only because "first past the post" elections can give extensive power to rulers who have not received a majority vote but also because the absence of checks and balances may tempt them to retain power through elections and referenda that are increasingly unfree, with opposition groups harassed or banned altogether. If democracy is not to degenerate into authoritarianism in this way, or if people want to restore democracy after authoritarianism has already been imposed, they may demand more checks and balances to restrict the power of those claiming to represent the majority.

Guided Democracy

Guided democracy also borders on authoritarianism and on the people's democracies recently in power in Eastern Europe. Society is perceived as an organic whole with common interests, unlike the aggregation of undifferentiated individuals in radical democracy. Leaders claim to know what these interests are (the general will), and the state exists to execute the general will without being inhibited by constitutional checks to protect minorities or—as in radical democracy—by majorities who have a false perception of their real interests. There are therefore no individual rights that might obstruct the execution of the general will, and citizens only enjoy equality, whether politically or economically, to the extent that their rulers deem this desirable.

One could ask whether the term "democracy" should be used at all to describe such a system. Yet, unlike totalitarian systems, contested elections are permitted as long as they do not threaten the power of the executive. Kenya and Tanzania allowed a choice between parliamentary candidates of the same party, and military governments in Brazil and Indonesia permitted rival parties to compete for seats in the legislature. General Ayub Khan openly proclaimed his system in Pakistan to be one of "basic democracies," in which competitive elections were held at a local level and provided the base of a pyramid for the election of higher authorities. (Colonial rule might be regarded as a form of guided democracy, in which people were not given rights for which they were not yet considered ready.) Such arrangements may be regarded as long-term political solutions that avoid the divisive effects of interparty competition or threats to the presidency. Why should Africa follow the Western model when it did not have the class divisions of the West and did not want a more rigid polarization along ethnic lines? Why should Pakistan tolerate competition between corrupt party politicians whose dishonesty and incompetence had been clear for all to see?

Supporters of guided democracies have been more on the defensive in recent years. Like radical democracies, they can easily degenerate into crude dictatorships, but if some opportunities for dissent and participation survive, people may question the legitimacy of those who claim to rule in the public interest without allowing the public to pass judgment on them through the ballot box. Brazil and much of East and Central Africa have already moved from guided democracy to a form of democracy in which the top political offices depend on popular election, though the current rulers of Pakistan may claim that they preside over a guided democracy.

Both radical and guided democracy therefore exist as ideal types that have a philosophical claim to be regarded as forms of democracy, but they are not forms to which politicians or reformers outside a small privileged elite are likely to aspire. Even in their pure form, they leave the governed with only limited control over the government, and in their corrupted form they may be little more than a cover for crude dictatorship. To understand the aspirations of those who seek an alternative to authoritarianism, let us turn to the remaining three forms of democracy cited in Table 1.1.

Liberal Democracy

Liberal democracy is more willing to recognize society as an aggregation of diverse citizens acting as both individuals and members of groups. It aims to secure the representation of these individuals and groups as well as to protect them from other groups and the state. There is thus a notion of a clearer separation of the state from society than in radical and guided democracies. The state does not exist to execute the general will, whose existence is denied on the grounds that people's interests conflict with rather than conform to an organic whole, or the will of the majority, which may be incompatible with the rights of minorities. Rather, the state exists as a referee to ensure the representation and protection of diverse interests. Citizens enjoy equality before the law, but not necessarily social equality, and their rights are protected by constitutional safeguards, whether enshrined in writing or by convention. Citizen participation is permitted but not actively encouraged, and the main democratic emphasis is on representative government chosen through competitive elections rather than on direct participatory democracy.

A frequent criticism of liberal democracy is that it merely allows political competition between nominally equal citizens without taking into account the unequal resources that citizens possess. Elites enjoying superior wealth, contacts, education, or political skills in general may be able to perpetuate their privileges at the expense of the majority by manipulating the key political institutions and the media and influencing public opinion so as to minimize public debate on issues that bring their privileges into question. This can been seen clearly in many Western countries, where the wealthier sections of the population are numerically overrepresented in executive and legislative bodies. Sources of inequality are perpetuated, such as inherited wealth, private profit from land, and profits from capital that owe more to imperfect markets than entrepreneurial skill. These are seldom subjects of debate between contenders for power. Nationalist politicians in the third world who have experienced foreign exploitation may seek not merely a set of rules to govern political competition but also a means of achieving greater social and economic equality. To them, liberal democracy may offer an inadequate solution to their perceived injustices.

Socialist Democracy

Socialist democracy is concerned more explicitly with equality and social justice. Like the advocates of guided democracy, its supporters see society as a potentially organic whole with common interests, but only after society has been transformed. This is to be done through the actions of the state, which exists to redistribute resources, generally through greatly increased public or cooperative ownership and extensive welfare provision, and to provide a moral guide to political action. The greater equality of wealth and resources enables the political process to operate without the built-in advantages that are enjoyed by privileged groups in a liberal democracy, and the threat of elite power is largely offset by the popular participation of the masses, though it is not always clear whether this activity is purely voluntary, a process of mobilization in which social pressure is put on people, or even compulsory in some instances. Democratic socialists generally insist that they have no objection to electoral competition, even if they do not treat it with the same enthusiasm as liberal democrats, but they face a dilemma in deciding how much electoral freedom to give those who want to restore capitalism. Nicaragua and Tanzania both conceded that freedom, with the result that their membership in the democratic socialist camp eventually lapsed.

Socialist democracy's attitude toward citizens' rights, like its attitude toward electoral competition, is ambiguous. Its supporters may insist that democratic socialists are as keen as any liberal to protect the citizen, but if the pursuit of equality and social justice takes precedence, this may heighten conflicts between the state and the individual, often to the detriment of the latter. This leads us to one of the central dilemmas of socialist democracy. How far can the ideals it enshrines be achieved without considerable coercion? This is not merely a matter of progressive taxation or the appropriation of private property (possibly with compensation) but also of policing a variety of activities that might detract from the egalitarian, socially just ideal. How does one respond to private education or medical care, varied forms of entrepreneurship, or the importation of goods that upset the government's economic plans? If the material progress necessary for the well-being of society is not to be achieved through the profit motive, what part will state compulsion play in securing an efficient use of resources? At the extreme, there is even the danger of censorship to prevent indigenous minorities or foreign publishers from spreading bourgeois values.

Much of this has to be in the conditional tense because the countries that can be regarded as socialist democracies, unlike guided and liberal democracies, are few in number. Democratic socialists would disown the former people's democracies as undemocratic. They would have doubts about many of the African and Asian leaders who claim to be socialists but rule over countries in which widespread inequality and capitalist ownership continue to predominate and in which electoral competition continues to be restricted. Nicaragua and Tanzania in the 1980s might qualify as members of the democratic socialist camp, but for the most part socialist democracy remains an ideal that has yet to be tested in the real world. The age-old question of how far the pursuit of equality requires a sacrifice of liberty, or even economic efficiency, has yet to be resolved.

Consociational Democracy

The term "consociational democracy" was first used in relation to the third world by Apter to describe the way in which a culturally diverse country such as Nigeria ensured that all significant groups were incorporated into government without any being frozen out by a crude majoritarianism (Apter 1961: 20–28). The system recognizes society as consisting of these distinctive groups, based on language, race or religion, and autonomous from one another and the state. The state exists not to promote any utopian ideal such as socialism, the will of the majority, or the general will but to act as a referee in the process of intergroup conflict. Although groups based on social class may blur into each other and there is normally some mobility between groups, people cannot change their race and only infrequently change their religion or principal language. The exclusion from power of a social class is thus seldom total, because people with working-class backgrounds may be recruited into the elite, or governments with mass bases may be leavened with intellectuals from higher up the social scale, whereas the exclusion of Catholics in Northern Ireland, Tamils in Sri Lanka, or Africans in South Africa under apartheid represents a much sharper break between the "ins" and "outs." The object of consociational democracy is to seek consensus between the different groups through a political process that brings all their leaders into the governmental process, whether through carefully tailored forms of proportional representation or federalism or by specifically reserving offices of state for members of the different groups. In these ways, each group will have an ultimate veto power over the others, though it will normally be retained only as the ultimate deterrent if the system is to work smoothly.

If the cleavages between the groups are sharp, citizen participation will be mainly within each group, with the respective leaders then negotiating with each other over the allocation of resources. Electoral competition is open to all, as in liberal democracy. Voters may polarize between monolithic groups, but in Europe there are often divisions within the groups, as between working-class and middle-class Calvinists or radical and conservative Flemish speakers. In culturally diverse African states such as Kenya and Nigeria, the divisions within each group are less marked (at least in terms of voting behavior). Each group has a geographical area in which it predominates and may gain representation in the legislature proportionate to its size, even without a formal system of proportional representation. Citizens' rights may be safeguarded specifically by the state, or the state may leave the constituent groups to fill in much of the detail. Hence, the degree of freedom to deviate from Muslim orthodoxy in Malaysia may depend heavily on social pressures within the Malay community.

One obvious problem created by consociational democracy is that of immobilism, with political change moving at the pace of the slowest, and possibly the most privileged, and with the political system reinforcing cultural divisions that might otherwise wither away. In rejecting crude majoritarianism, consociationalism may go to the other extreme of giving minority groups influence (and enabling them to retain resources) disproportionate to their size. Thus, the solution of consociationalism canvassed as an answer to South Africa's problems might be supported on the grounds that it is preferable to either violence or a mass exodus of Europeans whose skills and capital are vital to the economy, but it could still leave the political system a long way short of "one vote, one value."

There are also practical questions of whether the conditions that have sustained consociationalism in European countries, such as Belgium, Holland, and Switzerland, are so readily available in the third world. The normally accepted requirements of the legitimacy of ruling elites—respect for well-established institutions and procedures, a spirit of compromise, and an overarching sense of national loyalty—may be less strongly developed in the third world (Berg-Schlosser 1985: 95–109; Tindigarukayo 1989: 41–54). Many elites have lost their legitimacy as a result of their performance in government, institutions are generally new and ill-developed, a winner-takes-all attitude often prevails over one of compromise, and national loyalty—though developed in the struggle for independence—is often less deeply rooted than in European countries that have spent centuries asserting their identities in the face of hostile neighbors. If the preconditions for consociationalism remain inadequate, a country may be left with a loose marriage of convenience rather than a durable form of democracy.

Democratic Forms: Pure and Perverted

The above discussion suggests that each of our types of democracy has a "perverted" form into which it can degenerate. The ideas and perverted types are suggested in Table 1.2.

Table 1.2 Ideal Democratic Types and Their Perverted Alternatives

Type of Democracy	Perverted Form
Radical democracy	Populism
Guided democracy	Totalitarianism
Liberal democracy	Electoral democracy/Formal democracy
Socialist democracy	Paternalism
Consociational democracy	Immobilism

Radical democracy can degenerate into populism as the will of the majority, real or alleged, is used as a pretext for ignoring or persecuting minorities, and rulers maintain their legitimacy by exploiting the prejudices of their supporters. Guided democracy can degenerate into totalitarianism, or crude authoritarianism, as a benign interpretation of the interests of society is replaced by any arbitrary interpretation of the public interest that suits the convenience of the rulers. Socialist democracy can become paternalistic as the state squeezes out civil society, and consociational democracy can lose its democratic edge as controversial decisions are avoided in the search for the lowest common denominator. For liberal democracy, which is the model now most frequently sought, the perverted versions have long been recognized. Haynes sets up a model of "substantive democracy," which looks like a polished version of liberal democracy. In a substantive order, citizens enjoy individual freedom, interests are represented via elected public fora and group participation, and all citizens have easy access to the governmental process and have a say in collective decision-making. Equity, justice, civil liberties, and human rights prevail. In contrast, most third world countries that have escaped from authoritarianism enjoy only "formal democracy" in the sense of democratic rules existing on paper. A shift to substantive democracy would enable the powerless to have a real say "in the direction of the nation" (Haynes 1997: 85). "Electoral democracy" is another term frequently used to characterize the system prevailing in many third world countries, with citizens able to vote in elections that are conducted under varying degrees of freedom and fairness but enjoying few opportunities to influence, or seek redress from, governments between elections.

These analytical refinements are important not just to academics but because the focus in the real world of politics has shifted since the early 1990s from transitions to democracy to its consolidation. Most authoritarian governments have yielded to pressures to hold competitive elections and to allow at least a degree of freedom of expression and association. Indigenous dissidents, sometimes supported from abroad, now demand something closer to substantive democracy. In Chapter 9 we shall look at some of the problems in achieving consolidation, in the sense of ensuring that the letter and spirit of democracy are respected.

The Democratic Melting Pot

The purpose of the discussion above is not to offer third world countries a consumers' guide to the forms of democracy available but to present a range of ideal types in order to show the range of theoretical possibilities and dangers inherent in taking any one form of democracy to extremes. The practical problems in achieving any form of democracy are immense, let alone in achieving one unadulterated form. What is interesting is the way in which different blends of the different types are being canvassed or attempted, not as a means of achieving perfection but as alternatives to hitherto undemocratic systems that have frequently produced tyranny, social inequality, the plundering of public resources, or plain incompetence. Just as Aristotle urged the Greeks to develop a synthesis of different types of political systems, so modern political scientists have sought to learn from the failures of those who have peddled their own exclusive brands.

Sklar sees signs of the emergence of "developmental democracy," which accommodates the goals of social reconstruction implicit in socialist democracy, the resistance to authoritarianism implicit in liberal democracy, as in the struggle for trade union autonomy in Zambia, and the recognition of cultural diversity implicit in consociationalism, as in federal experiments in Nigeria (Sklar 1983: 19–21). Glickman sees a convergence not only between different types of democracy but also between left-wing and right-wing ideologies, which are both rejecting authoritarianism in Africa (Glickman 1988: 234–254). Table 1.3 attempts to spell out, and perhaps extrapolate, some of Glickman's ideas. A growing body of opinion on both left and right, he argues, rejects authoritarianism, apparently on the grounds that it has proved both harsher and less efficient than was once anticipated. The distinction between left-wing and right-wing authoritarianism in Africa has, perhaps, been rather blurred, with right-wing governments like those in Kenya and Côte d'Ivoire using the mechanism of the one-party state once associated with Leninism, while nominally left-wing governments have used international capitalism to bolster their authority, as in Ghana or Zambia. One can nonetheless make a broad distinction between left-wing authoritarianism based on the state control over the economy and political patronage—with political competition and dissent explicitly suppressed—and right-wing authoritarianism based on the power of economic elites who use the machinery of the state to protect their privileges but without necessarily imposing a monolithic political structure. One can see the distinction more sharply in Central America and the Caribbean, where left-wing authoritarianism is

Table 1.3 Left-Wing and Right-Wing Democracy and Authoritarianism

Left-Wing	Right-Wing
Democracy based on:	Democracy based on:
Development to reduce economic dependence	Self-reliance
Popular control of government	Reduced government control of the
Government more responsive to the	economy
popular will	Individual rights
Authoritarianism based on:	Authoritarianism based on:
State control of patronage	Class exploitation
Repression of political competition and dissent	

preserved in Cuba through one-party exclusiveness and extensive state penetration of the economy and society, while right-wing authoritarianism survives in Guatemala and El Salvador, despite the existence of nominal party competition, because economic elites ensure that no effective political force challenges their domination.

At one time most of the opponents of left-wing and right-wing authoritarianism had little in common. Opponents of right-wing dictatorships, including colonial regimes, sought an end to economic exploitation and poverty without generally being concerned with democratic rights. Fidel Castro, or even Ho Chi Minh, was more likely to be a hero than politicians who had won contested elections. Opponents of left-wing dictatorships, such as the opponents of Nkrumah and Jerry John Rawlings in Ghana, were more concerned with restoring or establishing pluralist competition and civil liberties than with building an economic base or maintaining a degree of social justice that might sustain democratic government. But Glickman suggests a growing convergence of views, or even a search for similar solutions under different names. Hence, the left speaks of reduced dependence, the right of self-reliance; the left of popular control of government, the right of reduced government control over the economy; the left of government more responsive to the popular will, the right of individual rights. One can still detect elements of socialist democracy and liberal democracy in these different approaches, but the gulf between them is not unbridgeable. Points have been conceded on both sides. Few people on the left still accept the practicability or desirability of an omnipotent state controlling the economy and of dispensing patronage to the extent that few groups in society are left with political or economic autonomy. In 1988 Glickman saw prospects for the emergence of "nonliberal democracy," with the general retreat of the state, intraparty elections in Zambia (subsequently followed by interparty elections in 1991), the development of the ruling party as a watchdog over the government in Tanzania, the search for greater political participation in Ghana, and the growth of such groups as cooperatives, trade unions, and professional bodies (Glickman 1988: 241–250).

The collapse of the Soviet bloc and the limited achievements of third world governments that attempted to insulate themselves from world capitalism have hastened support for a less centralized, more participatory brand of socialism. And if socialism based on coercion is deemed impracticable or morally undesirable, it is a short step to accepting that socialists must win power through pluralist elections, or even risk losing it through such elections as in Nicaragua in 1990 and Zambia in 1991. The line between socialist democracy and socialism within liberal democracy becomes blurred.

At first sight the right does not appear to have traveled as far as the left along the road to democratic convergence. The notion that economic liberalization is a precondition of political liberalization, to which we shall return in later chapters, is not a new one, and the demand for individual rights in the face of state encroachment has for centuries been the battle cry of privileged groups that do not want their privileges attenuated. But a more populist strand has come into right-wing thinking, with the emphasis on self-reliance. If it came merely from the well-established elites, it might be dismissed as a new version of "let them eat cake," but if it comes, however inarticulately, from small entrepreneurs who see more future in working out their own social or economic salvation than in relying on a corrupt or inefficient state, then we may be witnessing a strand in pluralist development that complements the left-wing emphasis on reduced economic dependence on the outside world. Chazan suggested that the growth of autonomous economic groups was helping to strengthen conditions for democracy in Ghana (Chazan 1989: 349–350), while much of the literature on social movements in Latin America, covering such groups as shantytown dwellers, relatives of victims of political persecution, or the unemployed, suggests a comparable autonomous base for political participation (see especially Lehmann 1990: 149–186).

Another way in which the right may be yielding ground is in its greater reluctance to shelter behind the military in preserving its privileges. The obvious contrast between past and present is in Chile, where right-wing politicians who were part of a democratic system in 1973 either actively supported the coup to overthrow President Salvador Allende or offered little resistance. By the late 1980s, most politicians and elites on the right had rejected the military solution on the grounds that it was no longer practicable in the face of the public resistance at home and external pressure, or desirable in view of the human suffering and economic devastation that military government had created—an indiscriminate sledgehammer to crack a left-wing nut that might now be cracked more easily through electoral competition. Other right-wing military governments may have been less extreme than that in Chile, and the extent of right-wing conversion from authoritarianism to democracy less remarkable, but a comparable trend could be seen in most of Latin America as well as Pakistan and, somewhat earlier, in southern Europe. Capitalists, like socialists, were less willing to impose their ideas without democratic consent.

Skeptics might argue that it was the right who got the better of the democratic bargain and that nominally democratic systems can sustain privileged elites as effectively as military governments, especially if parties demanding radical change are banned or harassed by authority or if it is made known that votes for them may provoke military reintervention. Jonas calls for "real democratic transition," which requires structural changes to reduce inequality, working-class involvement, and mass participation (Jonas 1989: 150). The point is reinforced by a study of Central American republics such as Guatemala and El Salvador, where the change from military governments to elected civilian ones has done little to widen political choice or participation, let alone tackle the inequalities in a society that many people would regard as inimical to the democratic process.

In contrast to Jonas's search for real democracy, Karl prefers a "middle range definition" of democracy, which requires a set of institutions permitting the entire adult population to choose leading decisionmakers in competitive, fair elections within the context of the rule of law, political freedom, and limited military prerogatives (Karl 1990: 2). More rigorous requirements for democracy, such as nondiscrimination against any party, equality, or active involvement of the subordinate classes, would, she argues, restrict unduly the number of countries qualifying as democracies.

Such conflicting views could take us back to the arguments about whether liberal democracy is preferable to socialist democracy or even whether some of the real-life approximations to liberal democracy are really democratic at all. There is also the dynamic question of how democracy, in its various manifestations, evolves. Is liberal democracy, or still more the crude form of limited political contestation found in Central America, a blind alley that enables elites to retain effective control of the polity and the economy without the embarrassment of having to be sustained openly by brutal military dictators? Or is democracy something to be valued not only because it is less repressive than military government or personal rule but also because it provides a relatively peaceful means of responding to changing pressures and ideas in society? Does it, in other words, provide potential openings for those who would pursue their own versions of equality, social justice, and mass participation, just as in the West it facilitated a transition from oligarchy to universal suffrage, and responses to the social and economic demands of the newly enfranchised middle and working classes?

This chapter has concentrated on the nature of democracy and has noted the diversity of the groups that prefer to strive for a pluralist order rather than pursue their more exclusive goals by less democratic means. But is the mere desire for a particular political solution sufficient to guarantee its adoption? We must now look more closely at the forces that shape the evolution of democracy and at its potential for meeting new challenges.

2

The Conditions
for Democracy

The question of whether democracy existed in the precolonial third world is an interesting one, but of limited relevance to this study. Although decisionmaking in some communities undoubtedly involved widespread participation and a search for consensus, the link between decisionmaking in such communities and in the modern state is a tenuous one. The greater size of the modern state, the heterogeneity of groups within its boundaries, the range of functions it attempts to perform, and the resources at its disposal make even the poorest modern state a much more complex entity than the political systems of most precolonial communities. Different types of political skill are required if the loyalty and compliance of diverse groups are to be achieved and maintained, and delicate decisions have to be taken that can make enormous differences to the wealth and lifestyles of the winners and losers: Does village A obtain a new school at the expense of village B, with the result that children in village A grow up literate and acquire new opportunities for employment while children in village B are deprived of these? Does the proprietor of firm C obtain a large government contract that can enrich him overnight while the proprietor of firm D goes hungry? Is the currency overvalued to the benefit of urban elites consuming luxury imports while peasants find it difficult to sell their crops in world markets? Will a devaluation of the currency increase the wrath of the urban elite, who then persuade the military to displace the politicians responsible so that new groups can gain access to government patronage while former rulers and their clients are thrown back on their own resources?

Whatever the nature of precolonial politics, the political skills displayed will be of limited value in coping with the intricacies of modern government, even if traditions of tolerance and experience of containing conflict offer some cultural bases for democracy. It is not, therefore, for reasons of ethnocentricity that we begin our search for democracy in the West. Rather, it is because one modern nation-state, however poor, may learn more from another modern nation-state than from its distant ancestors who were generally concerned with the administration of much smaller areas and with a much less complex range of functions.

Democracy is clearly not part of the natural order of life. For most of human history, rulers have ruled without being chosen by the majority of their subjects and with, at best, only limited opportunities for subjects to make their views known on decisions affecting them. This remained the situation in virtually all the countries of the world, from the demise of ancient Greece and Rome until well into the nineteenth century. Why, then, did the situation change?

In searching for clues, we can note what is different in the countries where democracy now prevails, compared with the days when it did not. In most of these countries, industrialization has been accompanied by such developments as migration to urban areas, vast educational expansion, longer life expectancy, and improvements in material well-being and increased leisure time, which have enabled people to think more of requirements and aspirations beyond mere survival. Society is also different from pre-democratic times in terms of the social groups that exist and the ways in which they interact with one another. While the earlier relationship between lord and peasant could remain largely static for generations, the relations between different sections of the middle and working classes today are less bound by tradition and are more likely to be characterized by conflicting demands that governments will be expected to resolve. This leads us on from the nature of the groups to their political attitudes and actual behavior, which again imply an expectation of governmental responsiveness rather than fatalistic acceptance, especially if the groups have the means of articulating their demands and of threatening sanctions if they are not met. Such articulation—and the governmental responses to it—is possible because of the existence of a complex network of political institutions both within the formal state structure and in the political subsystem of groups from the wider society interacting with it. Finally, it follows that if society, the economy, and the political structure are different from those existing in pre-democratic times, a variety of changes must have occurred over time to bring about this transformation. Nowhere was there a big bang, which immediately ushered in industrialization, urbanization, new social structures, and new political institutions simultaneously.

My attempt thus far has not been to prove that democracy has been the result of a process of cause and effect but merely to note that there is a correlation between democratic developments and the other developments, and even here there are exceptions. Countries in Eastern Europe achieved many of the other developments without democracy, yet a country such as Botswana, with few of the developments described, has sustained a pluralist system. And where democracy and other developments have gone together, the pace of each has been uneven. Consider, for example, the way in which economic development outstripped democratic development in Germany before 1945. In attempting to generalize, it is possible at least to enumerate the ingredients that are commonly found in the democratic cake, even if we are not yet in a position to specify the proportions in which they may be best combined or to offer a recipe to show how they should be processed.

To search for a causal relationship between other developments and democracy, several explanations of democracy can be offered, as indicated in Table 2.1. As in Chapter 1, each variable is taken as an entity in itself for the sake of simplicity, without implying that the authors cited necessarily accept one explanation of democracy to the exclusion of all others.

Economic Development

One of the pioneering explanations of democracy was made by Lipset in 1959. Lipset noted the correlation between the existence of democracy and such variables as per capita wealth, industrialization, urbanization, and the level of education. With increased wealth, he argued, the question of who ruled became less important, because governments had less power to affect the crucial life chances of the most powerful groups—who now enjoyed sources of wealth independently of the state—while poorer groups could secure some redistribution of wealth relatively painlessly without the rich having to make any great sacrifice. Such redistribution need not be seen purely in terms of the size of pay packets but in terms of, for example, sacrificing private sector investment to expand education and social welfare or permitting trade unions to pursue demands for better working conditions. In such circumstances, the lower classes would be less likely to turn to extreme ideologies and would be more likely to be integrated within the polity (Lipset 1959: 84)

To be fair, Lipset did acknowledge the possibility of a legitimacy crisis if rising social groups were denied political access or if new class divisions reinforced older divisions based on ethnic or religious affiliations (Lipset 1959: 87, 97), but the general implication was that economic development was the main driving force for democracy, albeit a rather narrowly conceived democracy in which opportunities for constitutional changes of government were given greater prominence than political participation or social equality. It is certainly difficult to refute the fact that virtually all the countries of Western Europe, North America, and the old Commonwealth have achieved substantial economic development and arrived at the democratic destination despite different starting points, different problems along the road, and the different beliefs and responses of political actors—but the question of causality is still not resolved.

Table 2.1 Conditions Conducive to Democracy

Conditions	Supporting Authors	Arguments	Problems
Economic development	Lipset (1959)	Correlation exists between wealth and democracy; increased national wealth makes competition for resources less desperate	Correlation is not the same cause; greater wealth may strengthen the resources of authoritarian rulers; process and rapidity of economic growth are not specified clearly
Political attitudes and behavior	Almond and Verba (1963)	Democracy requires a willingness to accept government by consent as a means of resolving conflict	Attitudes may be shaped by social and economic circumstances
Interelite relations	Rustow (1973) Valenzuela (1999)	Democracy emerges when elites agree to the rules of the political game rather than risk national disintegration; these rules can subsequently be adapted to accommodate nonelites	Why is a point reached where national unity is preferred to violent conflict or disintegration? How can elite attitudes be ascertained?
Social structures and interaction between social groups	Moore (1967)	Democracy is most likely to evolve where the monarchy checks the power of the nobility, and the aristocracy goes into commerce	How to explain the existence of democracy in countries with a diversity of social antecedents?
Political institutions	Heper (1991); Stephens (1989); Valenzuela (1999)	Democracy requires the development of institutions (especially pressure groups and political parties) that can filter public demands and thus facilitate compromise	Danger of historical determinism; role of economic changes, external influences, and even society not clear
Sequences in development	Binder et al. (1971); Dahl (1971)	Democracy is easier to establish if political competition precedes mass participation and if major conflicts over the role of the state are resolved one at a time	Danger of historical determinism; problems of recognizing and quantifying the variables
External influences	Green (1999)	Foreign governments, institutions, or individuals may supply ideas, offer inducements, or apply sanctions	Influence can only be indirect; democracy cannot be imposed

Did the industrial revolution in Britain produce the wealth that enabled elites and the masses to achieve consensus on the right to electoral participation and the benefits that flowed from it? Or was the industrial revolution only possible because elites who had dissipated their resources in civil war in the seventeenth century were now able to agree on a political settlement that was conducive to both economic growth and the co-option of other social groups into the political process? And if we even concede that industrialization then produced the wealth that lubricated democratic evolution, we can point to countries such as Germany, Japan, and Russia where industrialization was fostered by authoritarian governments and, at least in the short term, helped to strengthen these governments by providing them with more resources for repression. Democrats might seize on the phrase "in the short term" to argue that a wealthier, more educated population will eventually find authoritarianism intolerable. Other things being equal, that might be true, but democracy has been helped by quirks of history that were not economically determined. What if the twentieth century's greatest totalitarian rulers, Adolf Hitler and Joseph Stalin, had preserved their nonaggression pact instead of turning against each other, or if another authoritarian regime had not provoked the United States through the bombing of Pearl Harbor into supporting the Western European democracies in World War II? Would we still be boasting about democracy as the end product of economic development, or would many of George Orwell's forebodings have proved more accurate? A Europe dominated by Hitler or Stalin might have enjoyed substantial economic prosperity (especially if it had been spared the ravages of a costly war), but the achievement of even the limited form of democracy envisaged by Lipset might have had to wait for several generations.

For the third world specialist, there is also the phenomenon of the existence of many very poor countries that have become democracies since the 1980s, at least to the extent of holding relatively free elections and extending civil liberties. The withdrawal of external support for previous authoritarian rulers helped, but so did the inability of the authoritarians either to buy off or to coerce potential opponents as the resources available diminished. Przeworski et al. suggest that democracy may survive in poor countries on account of education, a balance among political forces, or the existence of the "right" institutions. The creation of democracy in poor countries is not a major problem, but its survival is (Przeworski et al. 2000: 137, 273).

Although democracy may survive economic or political upheavals in wealthier countries for the reasons enumerated by Lipset, democracies in poorer countries may be more vulnerable to military intervention or to the machinations of leaders with authoritarian tendencies, such as Robert Mugabe or Alberto Fujimori. Just as Jackson wrote of poor states enjoying "negative sovereignty" in the sense of surviving only because the international community was willing to underwrite them (Jackson 1990), so we might think of the survival of democracy in poor countries as depending on external support for democrats against authoritarians. If that support is reduced or withheld, democracy will be in trouble. This is not the whole story, and democracy has survived against the odds in countries such as Botswana, India, and Jamaica for indigenous reasons that we shall consider later, but a combination of poverty and external hostility will make democracy difficult to sustain.

Political Attitudes and Behavior

Almond and Verba's *The Civic Culture* shifted the focus from material wealth to the willingness of people to accept government by consent as a means of resolving conflict (Almond and Verba 1963). There is no obvious reason why such willingness should require a high per capita income. The ancient Greeks managed to sustain such a culture, whereas relatively wealthy people in modern Cyprus or Northern Ireland have been unable to agree on who should rule over whom or by what means. Greater wealth may help to take the rough edges off political conflict because, as Lipset argues, differences between winning and losing are less a matter of life and death. However, whether one is willing to compromise with one's adversaries—and to concede advantages to them as a result of majority decisions or the working of constitutional checks and balances—will depend on a variety of cultural and historical factors. If a rival group is seen to enjoy particular privileges or to threaten aspects of society or the political system that another group holds dear, consensus will clearly be difficult. But the existence of such attitudes and perceptions may have to be explained in terms of either inflexible elite domination (the preservation of apartheid or of landed elites in Central America) or the impact of particular historical events (the partition of Ireland, the colonization of Cyprus). Yet we are still left with the question of why key groups in some societies eventually arrive at a consensus, despite previous intractability, while groups in other societies do not.

Interelite Relations

Rustow, like Almond and Verba, puts the emphasis on a willingness to compromise by subscribing to democratic rules, but with a greater emphasis on groups as collective bodies or on elites leading the groups than on a collection of individual attitudes (Rustow 1973). In Rustow's model, a prolonged and inconclusive struggle between groups ends when neither genocide nor expulsion (nor, presumably, secession) is possible. Decisions are thus taken to come to terms with the situation by agreeing to peaceful competition for power. This requires the adoption of democratic rules, including the appropriate checks and balances, and the protection of rights. Once such a framework is in place, it may be consolidated by subsequent generations of politicians, elites, and voters and may be adapted to bring previously excluded groups, such as poorer classes, into the political process. One could presumably adapt this model to include the middle and working classes as combatants in the "long and inconclusive struggle," as well as older elites and ethnic and religious groups, in attempting to trace the democratic compromise. Valenzuela suggests that neither the prevailing political culture nor social structure was especially conducive to democracy in nineteenth-century Chile, yet the willingness of elites of different persuasions to work together helped to create a framework for democratic politics (Valenzuela 1999: 191–247).

Although no one would dispute that democracy is likely to work more smoothly if key groups are willing to compromise rather than fight, we are left with a model that may prove too narrow to offer general explanations of democracy. There may be cases, as in the American Revolution, where one group takes control of the political system from another, rather than compromising, and then absorbs other groups into the democratic process, or, as in much of Scandinavia, where incremental concessions are made without the need for prolonged conflict. Even where Rustow's model, broadly interpreted, does apply, we are still left with questions about cause and effect. If rival groups acknowledge the need to live together within the boundaries of one nation, what brings about this desire? External threat might be a significant factor, as in the Low Countries, or economic factors may increase the inducement to moderate conflict. Businesspeople, and possibly state bureaucrats, had strong interest in resisting the fragmentation of Nigeria after 1966, and this required a search for a means of accommodating diverse groups. Democracy itself might even be a cause rather than an effect of reconciliation between groups. Perhaps democracy is established for reasons other than group reconciliation, such as the insistence of a departing colonial power or military government, and rival groups then work within the democratic framework.

There is also the converse problem of explaining why group conflict is not resolved through democratic accommodation in many parts of the world, even when this would seem to be the rational course to follow. In Cyprus and Northern Ireland, external pressures may help to keep conflicts on the boil and, especially in the latter case, elites have only limited control over the behavior of their followers. The relatively lowly social position of the followers may be such that they have much less to lose from continued conflict than the elites.

For the third world countries seeking elite compromise as a recipe for democracy in recent years, the experience of the West may be of limited value. It is more difficult to envisage a democratic settlement at the elite level for at least two reasons. First, the masses already have the vote, and even if this asset is frequently devalued by rigged or noncompetitive elections, it gives them a degree of autonomy from the elites that the masses did not enjoy in most of Europe until well into the nineteenth century. Second, indigenous elites in the third world are frequently enmeshed in alliances with groups or governments abroad, which may provide them with additional resources and thus enable them to win or retain power without the need for compromise with their adversaries. Yet the Chilean example might suggest that the elite compromises of the nineteenth century continue to exert a benign influence on democracy, which would explain why democracy has fared better in Chile than in Brazil.

A final problem with Rustow's model, like that of Almond and Verba, is that of ascertaining what people's attitudes really are. Whereas Lipset's social and economic variables can be quantified, can we really be sure that particular democratic outcomes occurred because certain groups favored a particular course of action? Did elites in England after the seventeenth-century civil war, or Spain after the death of Franco, make a conscious effort to resolve their differences in order to enjoy newfound prosperity? Or were they merely abandoning a form of conflict that was no longer appropriate to the new political, economic, or ideological order (the abandonment of the doctrine of the divine right of kings, the demise of the republican threat, the defeat of fascism in Europe)? If that were the case, any democratic settlement would depend less on reconciliation between old warhorses and more on the constitutional adjustment made by members of more narrowly political institutions. These might include the constitutional monarch or leaders of parties with effective power bases rather than royalist absolutists and republicans, or communists and fascists who had moved away from the center of the stage.

Social Structures and Interactions
Between Social Groups

Moore, like Rustow, focuses on the interaction between groups in society but with greater emphasis on whole social groups rather than elites (Moore 1967: 413–470). While Rustow sees democracy evolving out of reconciliation, Moore sees it as emerging out of revolution, with the victories of the Puritans in England, the Jacobins in France, and the antislavery states in the United States paving the way for democratic development. He offers an elaborate model in which democracy is facilitated by the emergence of a strong bourgeoisie or an aristocracy going into commerce and shorn of feudal tendencies by the counterweight of the monarchy. This is in contrast to the communist model, where the aristocracy remained indifferent to commerce, and a large peasant mass survived, thus facilitating revolution in the absence of the safety value of bourgeois democracy. It is also in contrast to the fascist model, where the upper class used political and social levers to keep the labor force on the land and make the transition to commercial farming in this non-market-oriented way. This, together with industrial growth, which was presumably controlled by the levers of state power rather than market forces, again left limited room for an autonomous bourgeoisie (Moore 1967: 413–422).

Moore's approach, with his emphasis on the interaction between social classes, is perhaps the closest we get to a Marxist explanation of democracy, although Marxists have not, until recently, shown any great interest in pluralist democracy in the West. Such democracy is (or was) seen as a necessary staging post on the road to revolution—and as something preferable to bourgeois rule without political competition—but not as something to be remarked upon or admired for its own sake. While liberals celebrated the benefits that political competition and participation brought to the citizen, Marxists dwelt on the limited scope for political choice while the ruling class controlled the means of production (see especially Miliband 1973).

Moore's model obviously ignores the fact that communism and fascism spread to many countries through conquest or contagion. Nevertheless, even if we focus on the countries where these systems were homegrown, we are asked to make lengthy teleological links between past and present. Did the social structures of nineteenth-century Germany and Russia make communism and fascism more likely outcomes than democracy? Or did the outcomes depend more on responses to such events as the 1919 Versailles settlement, which provoked a nationalist reaction in Germany, or the crippling effect of World War I on the political order in Russia? Even if one argued that the social histories of these countries made them less able than others to cope with such strains in a democratic way, the experience of West Germany in achieving democratic consent after 1945 might suggest that the pathways to democracy mapped out by Moore are too restrictive. A society with a tradition of order imposed through upper-class manipulation of state structures may find that this order helps to facilitate the moderation of political demands associated with democracy, once an authoritarian regime has been defeated. As Huntington observes, "Countries that have had relatively stable authoritarian rule (such as Spain and Portugal) are more likely to evolve into relatively stable democracies than countries which have regularly oscillated between despotism and democracy. . . . A broad consensus accepting authoritarian norms is displaced by a broad consensus on acceptance of democratic ones" (Huntington 1984: 210).

This is in contrast to the British model of order and democracy emerging out of elite competition within which the rules were gradually institutionalized. Democracy today, like communism and fascism in earlier times, has spread through conquest and contagion to many lands, including those that Moore would regard as fertile ground for authoritarianism. But the survival of democracy cannot be attributed to conquest and contagion alone. Each country will have elements in its history and culture that can be exploited as democratic assets, whether they be the tradition of pluralist competition in Britain, egalitarianism and participation in Scandinavia, or order in Germany.

Political Institutions

The question of the ability of the political system to channel and contain conflicts, without being driven to authoritarianism or chaos, leads us to consider the role of political institutions. Heper contrasts the success of Spain and Brazil in achieving relatively stable democracy with the more halting progress in the rest of Latin America and Turkey (Heper 1991). Spanish-speaking Latin America, he argues, evolved from nineteenth-century societies in which caudillos, or personal rulers, ruled over an "inchoate, inarticulate populace" in which there were few shared norms. Diffuse, vertical hierarchies of patron-client networks continued into the twentieth century with the object of gaining the benefits of distribution through direct access to the executive without the medium of political parties. If parties did not perform their textbook role of aggregating interests, governments could not moderate demands and attempted instead a strategy of "co-optive incorporation," which failed on account of their limited distributive capacity. In the absence of adequate institutionalization and therefore legitimacy, governments resorted to repression. Spain was different in that the nineteenth century saw the transformation of an oligarchic structure into one of bourgeois hegemony. This brought the idea of common (as opposed to individual) interests expressed in the form of ideologies and the development of coherent policies with legal-rational bureaucracies to implement them. Interest groups and parties linked to different sections of the economy evolved together with pragmatic political parties. All these institutions made democratic compromises easier after the end of Franco's authoritarian rule.

Brazil was closer to Spain than the rest of Latin America. In the absence of much European settlement, Lisbon had a free hand in transforming a hierarchical and authoritarian polity and the idea of "organic representation of the community" based on Lockean pre-democratic principles. Political institutions were thus strong and, when authoritarian rulers gave up power, they were able to exercise firm control over the transition to democracy. We are again led to the conclusion that democracy is more likely to endure if it stems from strong, rather than weak, authoritarianism, but with the emphasis this time on the underlying strength and adaptability of institutions rather than on the characteristics of political culture. Yet Heper concedes that overpowerful institutions can be as damaging to democracy as weak ones. In Turkey, the state was reconsolidated along bureaucratic lines and remained isolated from society (Heper 1991: 201–202). In functionalist language, the political subsystem remained stunted, and the sort of autonomous political activity accepted as healthy in most Western democracies could easily be interpreted as a threat to the public interest.

Heper (1991: 202) argues that one of the strengths of his approach is that democratic evolution is seen in a broad historical perspective, instead of being explored from the starting point of conflict within the previous authoritarian regime. There is also the advantage of focusing more directly on the political. Material wealth, democratic attitudes, and an interdependent relationship between social groups will be of little use in facilitating democracy unless institutions evolve that can translate political choices, demands, and decisions into actual outputs via institutions such as parties, pressure groups, legislatures, and bureaucracies, whose roles and existence are accepted by most of the population. Some critics may argue that such institutions will be merely a reflection of social and economic development, and Heper hints such a link when he describes the transformation of an oligarchic social structure into a bourgeois hegemony, though the precise nature of the link remains unclear. An institution such as the office of prime minister in Britain may come into existence by historical accident yet have a significant bearing on democratic development by making the head of government dependent on both the majority in the legislature and the wider electorate. In contrast, the decision of Latin American countries to adopt a directly elected presidency has left them with relatively weak political parties in systems where capturing the executive prize becomes more important than building winning coalitions in the legislature. In the absence of the checks and balances of the U.S. system, this can strengthen authoritarianism at the expense of democracy.

Stephens's study of Latin America offers a useful, detailed complement to some of the questions raised by Heper (Stephens 1989). While acknowledging that initially the economy and the class alliances it generated shaped the prospects for democracy, Stephens argues that the institutions shaped by these forces subsequently acquired a weight of their own and contributed decisively to regime outcomes (Stephens 1989: 331–333). Hence, the willingness of elites in the Southern Cone to accept working-class participation in the political process—in the belief that their own interests were secure—facilitated the development of durable institutions that could survive the rigors of economic depression and military intervention. In contrast, elites in Central America were unwilling to make comparable concessions, and the institutional basis for democracy remained fragile. Diamond et al. also put the emphasis on political institutions, together with the elite choices that shaped them, though they cite Brazil as a less successful case. It is bracketed with Mexico and Peru, where the presence of abundant mineral resources and large (presumably hostile) indigenous populations led to harsh colonial rule followed by independence won by armed force by European settlers. These settlers lacked legitimate authority among the wider population. These cases are contrasted with the more successful ones of Argentina, Chile, Costa Rica, and Uruguay, where the initial aristocracy broadened its base to accommodate lower social groups within democratic institutions (Diamond et al. 1999: 5). The contrast between Heper's analysis in 1991 and that of Diamond et al. in 1999 might raise a suspicion of evidence being weighed differently in the light of experience. Brazil might have been seen as a greater democratic success in 1991 than its neighbors to the south, but by the end of the decade the impeachment of President Fernando Collor, widespread corruption, and the inability to develop an effective party system might have suggested the need to explain the shallowness of Brazilian democracy.

We are still left with insufficient clues as to how far institutionalization can develop autonomously of social and economic development and of external pressure from foreign governments or global capitalism. And if it is wrong to seek an understanding of democratic development by taking strains within the pre-democratic regime as a starting point, is it not equally dangerous to go to the other extreme of implying that countries that followed the wrong sort of evolution in the nineteenth century are preordained to remain authoritarian or, at best, unstable democracies? No doubt the historical pedigree will help, but what are the prospects for countries that were not born with silver spoons in their mouths but have the will to build democratic institutions and have an extensive knowledge of the experience of democracy elsewhere?

Sequences in Development

Having considered what are said to be the basic ingredients of the democratic cake as well as the extent of disagreement as to the proportions in which they should be combined and the distinctive flavor that each contributes, we are left with the question of the sequence in which the ingredients should be added. Dahl explored this question in 1971 and concluded that "polyarchy" (his real-world approximation to the ideal of liberal democracy) fared best if political competition preceded "inclusiveness"

(Dahl 1971: 203). In other words, Western countries enjoyed the advantage of a long period of competition for power based on a narrow franchise, during which the main rules and conventions of political decisionmaking were able to evolve. When political rights were gradually extended to the rest of the adult population, they could be admitted to the club, to change the metaphor, on the understanding that they abided by the existing rules or only sought to change the rules in certain accepted ways, thus ensuring stability and continuity. Many third world countries, in contrast, began their independent existence with universal suffrage and an awareness on the part of party and pressure-group leaders of the ways in which participation through lobbying and the ballot box had advanced the claims of diverse groups in the West. Hence, there were high expectations and pressures on the political system at a time when the system had barely become institutionalized and when the resources available to meet mass demands were meager.

The contributors to the volume by Binder et al. look at a wider range of chronological orders of events (Binder et al. 1971). They suggest that a country may be confronted with a variety of crises in the process of political development—crises of identity, participation, penetration, legitimacy, and distribution. An ideal path on the road to democracy would, perhaps, be one along which the question of identity—which areas and groups belong within the boundaries of the nation-state—is resolved at an early stage, as in Rustow's model. And the question of legitimacy—who is entitled to rule and how they should obtain office—would also be resolved before the demands for increased participation, and a redistribution of resources to less privileged groups, put too much pressure on the system. The crisis of penetration—how adequately the writ of the state can run through society in collecting revenue and enforcing its authority—is also resolved better before the participative and redistributive pressures become too great.

The obvious inference from this model is that Western democracies have had built-in advantages in being confronted with these crises in the best chronological order and with ample time for consolidation between one crisis and the next. The question of legitimacy in Britain was largely resolved with the 1688 revolution, which settled most of the outstanding questions about the role of the monarchy in a parliamentary system. And, disregarding Ireland, the question of identity was largely resolved by the Act of Union with Scotland in 1707. State penetration increased steadily in the nineteenth century with the development of a professional civil service and a growing volume of social legislation, despite the facade of a laissez-faire economic policy. Only late in the day were there irresistible pressures for universal suffrage or a significant redistribution of wealth. Such developments can be contrasted with those in many third world countries where all the crises crowd in on one another. Newly established governments with limited penetrative powers tried to cope with the demands of newly enfranchised citizens (universal education, hospitals, piped water, and adequate roads for marketing their crops or even for sufficient foodstuffs in the shops) at a time when questions of the scope or desirability of one-party rule or the right of Ashantis, Biafrans, or the Baganda to autonomy or independence were still in dispute.

As with the Moore and Heper models, the approach by Binder et al. risks the charge of historical determinism or of giving advice of the "if I were going to Dublin I wouldn't start from here" variety to third world democrats. Are we to argue that prospects for democracy are irredeemably poor because the crises of legitimacy or participation occurred at the wrong time? Or can countries arrive at the right destination in spite of themselves, especially after their experience of nondemocratic alternatives? A determination to establish democratic norms, aided by knowledge of the experiences of long-standing democracies, might compensate for some of the inherent weaknesses.

For analytical purists the words "crisis" and "development" leave the Binder et al. approach open to further criticism. It is not clear how one recognizes the beginning or end of a crisis, or even its existence. Did the crisis of participation in Britain begin with the pressures leading to the 1832 Reform Act, or that of 1867, or with the later demands for trade union recognition? Was it resolved with the completion of universal suffrage in 1928, or did it resurface in the 1960s with the rise of "direct action" pressure groups that rejected the underlying consensus? Was the crisis of legitimacy resolved with the acceptance of parliamentary democracy by the eighteenth century? Or did it resurface in the 1980s when people questioned the right of a government to pursue extreme policies under an electoral system that gave it 60 percent of the seats in Parliament in return for 42 percent of the votes? As for identity, the question of whether Northern Ireland should belong to the United Kingdom or to Ireland has become a more prominent matter of dispute since the early 1970s, after a long period of apparent calm. And the right of a ruling party that held barely 12 percent of the seats in Scotland to rule that part of the kingdom contributed to pressures for greater Scottish autonomy.

The propensity of apparently resolved crises in the West to recur calls into question the concept of development, as does the inability of many third world countries to resolve any of the crises outlined by Binder et al. The concept is, perhaps, discredited because of its association with the modernization theorists of the 1950s and 1960s who envisaged third world countries treading the same paths that Western countries had trodden in earlier centuries, without making sufficient allowance for indigenous culture, social structure, and economic dependence on the West. What the critics of the modernization school would put in its place in assessing the prospects for democracy is less clear. Some, such as Huntington, argued the case for

order and strong institutions as preconditions for democracy, whose immi-
nence had now receded beyond the distant horizon (Huntington 1968:
244–245), whereas others insisted on a more self-sufficient economy to end
the undemocratic process of Western exploitation and/or the development
of working-class participatory structures to ensure equality of wealth and
resources as well as political rights (Amin 1987; Jonas 1990).

By the late 1980s, the language of class was being replaced increasingly
by that of "civil society" and "indigenous culture." The concept of development was criticized as implying following in the footsteps of the West. Ake
saw democracy in terms of the devolution of power to local and functional
groups, with ethnic diversity as something to be celebrated rather than a
problem in the way of modernization (Ake 1996: 132). The contributors to
the Glickman volume on democratization in Africa also see ethnicity as a
building block that can contribute to democratization. They suggest that the
insecurity that may drive minorities to rebellion can be ameliorated by such
devices as proportional representation, federalism, bicameralism, and constitutional checks and balances on the powers of rulers (Glickman 1995).

The practicability of these departures is another matter. If rulers are
strong enough to impose order in the way advocated by Huntington—
though many clearly lack this strength on account of limited resources and
dubious legitimacy—why should they subsequently want to share their
power with anyone else? The self-sufficiency argument has been abandoned
by some of its strongest advocates (see especially Frank 1991) in the face
of the reality of global interdependence and in the absence of much economic or democratic development in the countries where it has been
attempted. The mass participatory argument fails to explain how elites are
going to be persuaded to enter a bargain that gives all the benefits to their
adversaries, in contrast to the more subtle democratic transitions in the real
world where both authoritarians and democrats have been willing to concede on some points if their interests could be guaranteed on others.

The advocates of economic autonomy or participatory democracy, like
the developmentalists they criticize, are open to the charge of operating
from too high a level of generality. Even if we can separate their political
analysis from their ideological preferences, we may find that what they
offer is a useful impressionistic picture of processes that may help or hin-
der democratic development, but upon closer inspection the actual objects
in the picture become blurred. Achieving national identity with a legitimate
center of government, building up effective state structures, and responding
to (or articulating) pressures for participation, distribution, and economic
autonomy are clearly tests that many political systems and political institutions have to undergo. The ability to achieve sufficient consensus in sur-
mounting them will augur well for democracy, though the actual processes
are often difficult to recognize until they have receded into history, and

sometimes not even then. Do we know, for example, whether the Nigerian civil war finally resolved the crises of identity or merely ushered in a truce? Does the attempt to impose Shari'a law in some northern states suggest that new questions of identity are emerging? Has the ending of apartheid resolved the crisis of participation in South Africa, or does it raise new questions about the rights of the European (or even Zulu) minorities? Those who are doubtful about the value of such broad concepts as have been examined above may prefer to take refuge in narrower studies of transitions to democracy in individual countries.

External Influences

Few authors have offered external influences as a primary explanation of democracy. But it is clear from what has been said already that democracy would not have taken root when it did in many countries without the impact of external forces. These forces may be direct, as with the Allied occupation of the former fascist countries after 1945, or may involve sanctions against nondemocratic governments in the form of trade boycotts and the withholding of aid and investments, actual or threatened, as in Chile and South Africa, or merely the influence of ideas and political practices. Just as many African states succumbed, one after another, to one-party or military government, so many subsequently followed each other in restoring multiparty politics. While their own experience of authoritarian rule may be a major reason for this, the success of neighboring countries is also likely to have an influence. Authoritarians who had previously been able to praise the achievements of authoritarian rulers in more developed countries ("Mussolini made the trains run on time," "the Russians were the first to put a man in space," "Franco resisted decadence and social permissiveness in Spain") were left with fewer models to emulate as these regimes collapsed, their achievements appearing more modest, and the levels of both repression and incompetence laid bare.

In the West, friends of third world authoritarian rulers became fewer and less reliable. President Jimmy Carter had more scruples in his dealings with these rulers than had his predecessors, and even the more conservative U.S. presidents have had to face a more critical lobby opposed to "aiding the dictators." Additionally, the ending of the Cold War has raised questions as to whether there are any good practical reasons for supporting foreign despots who were once seen as a bulwark against communism. Most academic literature is skeptical about external influences as a major element in democratization, but Green argues that the liberal aspirations of powerful Western countries and international bodies (including the European Union, the United Nations, and the Organization of American States) have had an important impact (Green 1999: 1–41).

This is not to argue that Western pressure has been entirely on the side of the democrats. U.S. support for the Contra terrorists who opposed the elected government in Nicaragua had much to do with the electorate's eventual decision to remove the Sandinista government, in the hope of ending terrorism and the economic deprivation that went with fighting the terrorists. And one could argue that U.S. support for the ruling elites in Guatemala and El Salvador provided them with a lifeline and enabled them to use repression rather than reconciliation in dealing with the opposition, which in turn continued to resort to violence in the belief that it would not be allowed to compete in free and fair elections. Similarly in Africa, European powers sustained General Mobutu Sese Seko in power until 1996 in the hope of maintaining stability and protecting foreign investments.

Global businesses may have no specific ideological preferences between democracy and authoritarianism, and may even prefer a sustainable democratic regime to an authoritarian one that is losing its capacity to rule in the face of popular resistance or internal intrigue. However, businesses want a return on their investment, low prices for their raw materials, and a minimum of competition from countries building up competing industries. This may lead them, and the Western governments over which they have influence, to support the suppression of democracy if there is a prospect of people electing a government that threatens their interests. External pressures can quite easily topple a democracy through economic sanctions, support for subversion, or even invasion, but their ability to create a democracy is more limited. By its nature, democracy cannot be imposed in the way that authoritarianism can. External influence can only add a helping hand if some of the preconditions we have mentioned are already there. Foreign influence has fluctuated over the years, but with modern communications and a realization of the impact of pressure group politics, there must be few countries under authoritarian rule today in which opposition groups do not have allies in the West to speak for them who can, at the very least, embarrass Western governments that are on friendly terms with the authoritarians.

Lessons for the Third World

Many of the lessons for the third world arising out of the literature reviewed appear to be negative. Most third world countries have not enjoyed the economic development cited by Lipset or the civic cultural attitudes cited by Almond and Verba. The sequences in development conducive to democracy in the West have not generally occurred in the third world, and the developmental crises have frequently crowded in on one another over a short period of time. Institutional developments have generally been limited. We have seen that most Latin American states, despite their long period of independence, have built only rudimentary links between government and governed, whereas the more recently independent states of Africa and Asia have had little time to develop institutions. The structures bequeathed by the colonial powers were more concerned with sound administration than democracy, and most political parties appeared only in the decade or two before independence. The long history of the Congress Party in building a base of support in India is very much an exception to the general rule. The pressures on, and willingness of, elites and social groups to achieve reconciliation are limited, if only because the benefits derived from membership of the nation-state are limited if the nation is poor and the state's administrative capacity is restricted. Many third world countries, however, may begin with the advantage that the initial animosity between rival groups is less than that between groups such as the Protestants and Catholics in much of Europe or even between the working and middle classes in some instances. Informal coalitions do clearly emerge between different ethnic and religious groups, and the government of larger countries such as India and Nigeria would be impossible without such coalitions.

We need to remind ourselves that third world countries are not just poorer versions of those in the first world or imitations of those countries as they existed a century ago. Countries in Europe did not have their economic systems transformed to meet the requirements of wealthier nations on another continent, for none existed, and although their frontiers were sometimes drawn arbitrarily, a sense of nationhood based on language, culture, and history was probably more recognizable in nineteenth-century France, Germany, or Spain than in twentieth-century Sudan or Nigeria. Whether these differences are ones of quality or quantity is a matter of debate. The dependency school, as exemplified by Wallerstein, argues that the advancement of Western countries necessitates the continued impoverishment of the third world (Wallerstein 1974). Critics have argued that this view is overdeterministic and that governments and their citizens can, within limits, make their own political choices, which may either stimulate development or preserve dependence (Chazan et al. 1988: 21–25). Similarly, with regard to the question of artificial frontiers, one could argue that ethnic conflicts in Nigeria and the Sudan are different only in quantity from disputes about the positions of Northern Ireland or Quebec in relation to Britain or Canada. Yet in the case of both dependency and national identity, there is surely a difference between countries where such problems exist (and are not necessarily the most serious problems) and countries where survival depends on fluctuations in the price of a single primary product or on preventing a major ethnic group from seceding or massacring its adversaries, and where there is not much conception of the well-being of the nation. This is not to argue that all third world countries are equally at the mercy of global capitalism or that all are artificial shells with no focal points of national unity, but merely to note that the closer they are to such conditions, the greater will be the difficulty in establishing democracy.

Although the national frontiers drawn by the colonial powers make little sense in terms of ethnic homogeneity, the fact that the international community guarantees these frontiers in a way that it did not when the nation-states of Europe were emerging imposes a certain discipline on rival groups. Irrespective of the economic damage that national disintegration might cause, this option is seldom available, except in the case of secession from loose federations by countries such as Bangladesh, Singapore, and the West Indian islands, where the facts of geography made for little national unity in the first place. Secessionist struggles continue to be waged by minority groups within countries such as India, Indonesia, Morocco, and Sri Lanka, but most rival groups have accepted the need for some form of accommodation in the absence of any realistic alternative. One question mark over the preservation of existing frontiers is, of course, the impact of the breakup of the USSR and Yugoslavia. The emergence of an independent Croatia or Ukraine might create a precedent for Tamils, Ibos, or Sudanese Christians to demand their own territories, but the viability of such territories might depend heavily on the willingness of the West to provide sufficient aid.

Whether the need to live within most of the existing frontiers will provide a basis for democratic competition in the way described by Rustow is another matter. Group leaders might merely share the spoils of office and allow some trickle-down of wealth and patronage to their followers without necessarily permitting free elections. A major challenge might emerge if some followers were dissatisfied with their share of the spoils and demanded greater control over their leaders, but whether this would lead to democratic concessions or greater repression would presumably depend on the relative resources of leaders and followers.

As for Moore's thesis about democracy depending on the evolution of an autonomous bourgeoisie, the prospects again appear unpromising. Many third world countries have achieved little of the industrialization that is concomitant with the emergence of a large middle class. Where industrialization has occurred, it has often been dependent on the goodwill of the state rather than the efforts of an autonomous middle class. Whereas entrepreneurs in nineteenth-century Britain could build factories, seek their own raw materials and markets, and promote legislation to provide an infrastructure of railways, ports, and urban developments, and ultimately use their independently earned wealth to enter politics and shape society, their third world counterparts are more dependent on the state. Much of the state interventionism that was fashionable in the heyday of economic planning has now gone. Under external pressure to follow free market policies, few states now attempt to impose import licenses, control foreign exchange, or run extensive public enterprises, all of which were once useful sources of patronage. The entrepreneur who fell afoul of the government would not enjoy the fruits of such patronage. But other forms of state manipulation still flourish and may even be expanding. The privatization of state assets provides a useful means of rewarding government supporters, and government contracts remain a lucrative source of income. It is significant that those who have done most to sustain opposition to authoritarian governments in Africa have come from professions such as the law and academia (and in Latin America the church), which enjoy the greatest insulation from government. If they have contacts with popular opposition leaders in exile or power bases in local communities led by sympathetic chiefs, they may then be able to offer a government in waiting.

The extent to which the state does actually constrain autonomous behavior has been questioned by writers using the concept of civil society to indicate the presence of increasingly autonomous groups, whether they be the grassroots social movements that have arisen in response to repression in Latin America, or the more staid autonomous groups that have grown in stature in much of Africa as the state has become increasingly incapable of performing its basic functions. We shall look at these developments in more detail in subsequent chapters. Although the state may have lost much of its effectiveness, it would be stretching Moore's model unduly to argue that the conditions that he pronounced as conducive to democracy exist in much of the third world today.

In the end, it may be the external factors that will do most to provide a democratic opening, though this is not because all the external powers are anxious to promote democracy or because indigenous populations are hostile to it. At first sight, the external forces seem to be on the side of repression both directly and indirectly. Where democratic elections have produced governments that were hostile to Western interests, as in Guatemala and Iran in the 1950s and Chile in the 1970s, Western powers were quick to subvert them and sustain their authoritarian successors. The nature of economic dependence on the West is said to maintain societies where ruling elites collaborate with global capitalism while the majority of the population remains in poverty—a situation not conducive to democratic consensus. Yet one can find examples to illustrate a less one-sided set of relationships. Entrepreneurs in Kenya and Zambia have pursued interests that have reflected their needs much more than those of global capitalism, and Western powers have failed to subvert many rulers hostile to their interests. These rulers have often been dictators, such as Ayatollah Khomeini, General Idi Amin, and Colonel Mu'ammar Gadhafi, rather than democrats, but their longevity might also give hope to democrats standing on platforms that are not entirely subservient to Western interests.

At least as important as the policies of foreign democratic governments is the experience they can offer. Democracy emerged only slowly in the West and was not generally an outcome for which political actors actually strove. If we go back to the developments that were said to have helped the evolution of democracy, there is no reason to believe that this was the outcome sought by entrepreneurs promoting economic development, rival groups seeking to bargain with their adversaries, or political actors building institutions to strengthen their own positions or attempting to resolve developmental crises. Even the cultural conditions cited by Almond and Verba as conducive to democracy are as likely to be a response to a democratic environment as a precondition for its emergence. Yet when democracy did emerge, it became valued in its own right as a more equitable and efficient means of resolving competing interests.

When the colonies of the Western democracies began to demand independence, neither they nor their colonial masters demanded anything other than a constitution that embodied democratic values. (The case of the Latin American colonies, which gained independence from nondemocratic Spain and Portugal in the nineteenth century, was somewhat different: There was no immediate expectation of democracy, but authoritarian rulers did not enjoy the traditional institutions and power bases of their metropolitan counterparts, and eventually they had to seek forms of legitimacy that owed something to public support.) For reasons that will be examined in later chapters, the democratic expectations were frequently not realized, but the ideal was never completely extinguished. While many Western rulers had retained nondemocratic bases for their legitimacy until well into the nineteenth century, including divine right, custom, or the moral superiority of the upper class, the legitimate credentials of twentieth- and twenty-first-century third world rulers have usually had some connection with democracy. If they cannot claim a popular mandate, they will at least claim to have removed a nondemocratic regime, to be devising ways of establishing a democratic one, or to be offering democratic choice through intraparty competition. The pre-twentieth-century claims to legitimacy based on divine right, custom, or social superiority might carry some weight at a purely local level, but they would make little sense in a larger nation-state composed of communities with varied cultures and traditions.

Even if there is not the drama of a prolonged intergroup conflict followed by a democratic reconciliation, as in Rustow's model, there may at least be a realization that democratic choice, if necessary buttressed by checks and balances to protect weaker groups, offers one of the few means of reconciliation. Group conflicts in the third world have tended to be less prolonged and are more likely to consist of a series of fluid, shorter-term alliances that may eventually encompass the majority of the population. The restoration of democracy in Ghana in 1969 was thus helped by the mending of fences between Ashantis and other Akans, first at a military and then at a civilian level, while almost every permutation of alliance between

North, East, and West has been attempted in Nigeria. Such alliances do not guarantee democracy, but compromise between powerful rival groups will make the achievement of democracy easier.

Concentrating now on the practical rather than the philosophical plane, we have already noted people's experience and knowledge of authoritarianism at home and abroad. Authoritarian governments have generally done little to improve people's material well-being and have therefore done little to win the allegiance of the masses. Simultaneously, they have frequently executed, tortured, imprisoned, or exiled the more articulate members of the population who have attempted to resist them. In pre-nineteenth-century Europe, people suffering such deprivations might have conceived of no alternative other than a more efficient or more benevolent form of authoritarianism. In the third world today, they—or at least their leaders—are aware of the democratic alternative and may strive positively to achieve and maintain it.

We arrive at a precarious vantage point for observing democracy in the third world and one to which we shall return in subsequent chapters as we try to understand specific features of the landscape. Where democracy exists, it does not appear to have sprung from the same roots as in the West, although some of the roots have an affinity with their Western counterparts. Relations between interdependent elites and social groups are important, though not necessarily in the ways outlined by Rustow and Moore. Public attitudes are more important, but less in Almond and Verba's sense of tolerant attitudes toward everyday political life and more in a belief that democracy must prevail because of recent experience of the alternatives. The luxuries of extensive economic development to make politics less of a life-and-death struggle, and steady consolidation of the polity as political crises are resolved one by one over a long period, are not generally available. However, the lessons learned from other countries' experiences and the willingness, in some cases, of wealthier countries to offer assistance at crucial moments (as in the eventual rejection of the Latin American military juntas) may give a boost to democracy that Western countries in their formative years did not enjoy.

Even these somewhat shallow democratic roots are by no means universal in the third world. One does not have to look far to find their opposites in group intransigence (as in Lebanon or Sri Lanka), antipathy toward democracy as a compromise between good and evil (as in much of the Middle East), or Western actions that aid authoritarianism rather than democracy (as in Central America). But where the soil is less barren and the commitment of political actors is substantial, who is to say that institutions will not eventually develop to make the aspiring democracies more secure, despite their different origins from those in the West?

3

Democracy and the End of Empire

Experience of colonial rule is a factor common to the vast majority of third world states, although it is not exclusive to them. Western and old Commonwealth countries, such as the United States, Belgium, Norway, and Australia, also emerged from the tutelage of foreign powers, but the gap between the foreign masters and the elites in these dependent countries was generally much narrower in terms of ethnicity, culture, and economic position than was the gap between European colonial masters and aspiring elites in Africa, Asia, and Latin America. And below the elites were societies that were radically different from the metropolitan societies over which Europeans ruled.

Decolonization in the third world was therefore much more a leap into the unknown than it had been in Norway or Australia, where institutions modeled largely on those of the departing masters might be expected to serve the needs of the new nation without undue strain. Transferring the letter and spirit of the "Westminster model" to Australia—where the level of economic development was relatively high, education was almost universal, and most people shared a common language and culture—was a very different matter from transferring such a model to Nigeria, with its economic underdevelopment, mass illiteracy, and cultural heterogeneity. The more gradual pace of decolonization also gave the older colonies an advantage. They were able to experiment with metropolitan institutions (such as elections and legislatures) long before independence and introduce their own adaptations (such as federalism or appointed ceremonial heads of state) as part of an evolutionary process, instead of unwrapping them after independence with little notion of how they would work.

The timing of the transfer of power was also significant. Supporters of Dahl's thesis, that democracy will be built on firmer foundations if contestation precedes participation, will note that the West and old Commonwealth countries became self-governing for all practical purposes before

43

World War I, when demands on the state were fewer than today. The crises of identity and penetration, to move to Binder et al.'s terminology, had largely been resolved, whereas the crisis of distribution in meeting mass demands was still on the distant horizon. Most African and Asian states, in contrast, gained independence after World War II when expectations of social welfare and economic intervention were more widespread as nationalist politicians and their followers sought to emulate the all-embracing role of the state now common in the West. However, the basic problem of establishing effective legitimate authority throughout the land was not yet resolved. Indeed, the colonial powers often raised people's expectations further by promoting welfare and development in the terminal years of colonialism in the belief that this would make for more viable postindependence governments. The establishment and survival of democracy in the third world thus required the rapid adaptation of institutions alien to indigenous society (or the rapid discovery of alternative institutions for those bold enough to make such a search) and the establishment of legitimate bases of authority in culturally heterogeneous societies. It also required the ability of political structures with limited administrative experience and expertise to cope with a range of public demands in societies with very limited economic resources.

Our concern in this chapter is with the relationship between the extent to which democracy was or was not established and the nature of colonial rule, the processes of decolonization, and the legacies these left. This leads us to a two-part set of questions: (1) In what ways did colonial rule itself encourage or discourage democratic development directly or indirectly? and (2) What was the process of the transfer of power? Was there a preparation for independence, or did independence result from irresistible nationalist pressures or the collapse of the metropolitan power? If there was preparation, how comprehensive was it, and what were the objectives and priorities? Was democracy high on the lists of priorities of either the colonists or the nationalist heirs apparent, or were there greater concerns with a swift, peaceful transfer of power to any group that appeared capable of sustaining stable administration?

The Impact of Colonial Rule

The impact of colonial rule varied according to its timing, the nature of the societies being colonized, and the policy choices of the colonial powers. Some of these variables, the cases approximating to them, and implications for democracy are shown in Table 3.1. The variables of the timing of colonization, the depth of colonial penetration, the nature of the center of power, and relations between colonizers and indigenous peoples are to some extent interdependent.

Table 3.1   Variations in Colonial Rule

Variable	Spanish Latin America	Brazil	India	British East and West Africa	British Southern Africa	French Africa	Possible Implications for Democracy
Timing of colonization							
Pre-democracy	+	+					No democratic foundations
Democratic era			+	+	+	+	Democracy seen as ultimate destination
Depth of colonial penetration							
Shallow			+				Outcomes depend on strength and norms of indigenous indigenous
Deep				+	+	+	Society weak in relation to state, therefore possible authoritarianism
Destructive	+	+					Society weak, democratic legitimacy difficult to establish
Main center of power							
Metropolitan rule		+	+	+		+	Consensus between colonial and indigenous elites may facilitate peaceful transfer of power
Settler rule	+				+		Settlers may resist majority rule
Relations between colonizers and indigenous populations							
Attempted assimilation						+	Nationalism blunted; opportunities for consensus
Racial exclusiveness			+	+	+		Conflict between nationalists and collaborators
Racial laissez-faire	+	+					Conflict between a variety of ethnic groups

+ Indicates the presence of the variable.

Pre-democratic colonization, that is, colonization that took place at a time when the colonial powers themselves had no pretensions to internal democracy, occurred in the sixteenth and seventeenth centuries when limited administrative and technical knowledge made deep colonial penetration of societies difficult. In contrast, the scramble for Africa occurred in the nineteenth century, when material advancement had facilitated both political pluralism in Europe and technological opportunities for deeper control over the colonies through such means as the railway, the telegraph, the steamship, and the Maxim gun.

He stood upon a little mound,
Cast his lethargic eyes around.
And said beneath his breath:
"Whatever happens we have got
The Maxim Gun and they have not. . . ."

We shot and hanged a few and then
The rest became devoted men. (Belloc 1970: 184)

Questions of racial assimilation versus exclusiveness also became more clear-cut when improvements in communications and health enabled more Europeans to bring their wives and families to the colonies, where previously the absence of European women had made for more interbreeding. By the nineteenth century, a choice was available between the British policy of an arm's-length relationship with the indigenous populations and the French policy based on the belief that there could be no higher social goal than to bring Africans and Asians within the ambit of French culture. Yet despite the interdependence of some of the variables, Table 3.1 indicates enough permutations to suggest that each group of countries had distinctive features that had some bearing on their ultimate prospects for democratic development. Some tentative hypotheses about the implications of the variables for democracy are suggested in the right-hand column of Table 3.1.

The Timing of Colonization

The colonization and subsequent liberalization of a territory by a pre-democratic country, as in Latin America in the sixteenth and seventeenth centuries, would suggest poor prospects for democracy. There were few democratic examples for nationalist politicians to emulate, yet there was no aristocracy comparable with that in Europe with legitimacy based on heredity. Heper sees a link between the origins of the Spanish Latin American states, in which neither democratic norms nor deference sustained governments, and their continued problems in searching for democracy in the twentieth century. In the absence of shared norms on which to build effective institutions, power passed to caudillos building support through patron-client networks. The continued absence of effective institutions to filter public demands as new social groups emerged made repression more common than democratic accommodation (Heper 1991: 199–203). Such generalizations obviously cannot explain all the varied political outcomes in Spanish Latin America, from the relative democratic stability of Uruguay to the prolonged violence of Guatemala and El Salvador. Stephens illuminates some of the subtler light and shade by looking at such postindependence

variables as the relative significance of labor-intensive agriculture, economies based on mineral extraction, and the behavior of such institutions as
were established (Stephens 1989).

Brazil was different again in that, although it gained independence
from a nondemocratic power, its tropical location precluded extensive
European settlement. Portugal was therefore able to transfer a hierarchical
and authoritarian model of government that was the antithesis of democracy
but was at least more conducive to the development of stable institutions
than was the disorder of Spanish Latin America. As Huntington has suggested, stable authoritarianism may evolve into stable democracy more easily than unstable authoritarianism, as democrats use the institutions they
have inherited to pursue new ends (Huntington 1984: 210). A contrast could
be made between the relatively orderly and controlled, if prolonged, transition from military government to democracy in Brazil in the 1970s and
1980s and the more confrontational relationship between military rulers and
civilian politicians in Argentina and Chile. Whether one believes that these
differences will ultimately make for a superior form of democracy in Brazil
depends largely on how far one supports Huntington's emphasis on stability as a precondition for democracy, as opposed to those who take the more
populist view that democracy depends on the masses capturing and transforming the political structure to achieve greater participation and social
equality.

Where colonization was embarked upon by metropolitan powers with
democratic political systems, albeit on a restricted franchise, the contribution
of the colonial powers was more ambiguous. The political structures they set
up in Africa, Asia, and the Caribbean were certainly not democratic, at least
until concessions were made on the eve of independence, yet they could not
hide their domestic democratic politics completely from their colonial subjects. Indigenous education, which economic development required, could
not easily avoid some exposure to the culture of the metropolitan society, and
higher education often required residence in the metropolitan country where
democracy could, for good or ill, be observed firsthand. The educated elites
were bound to contrast the ability of the British and French to choose their
own governments with their own inability to do so, and in many cases they
sought to build power bases at home to bring about the desired changes. They
were also able to seek allies in the metropolitan countries in the open political systems that prevailed there, in a way that would have been unthinkable
for any eighteenth-century Latin American visitor to Lisbon or Madrid. While
official governmental acknowledgment of the goal of democratic self-
government might have been slow in coming, nationalism built on knowledge
of, and contacts with, democratic institutions and individuals in Europe had a
longer history. The colonial powers were also unable to envisage handing
power over to any form of government other than a democratically elected

one, once the case for independence had been conceded. None of this guaranteed that democracy would be sustained after independence, but it did make it likely that democracy would remain a point of reference—and at least an ultimate ideal to which people aspired—in a way that it was not in postindependence Latin America.

The Depth of Colonial Penetration

Young brings out some of the significant variations in the depth of colonial penetration (Young 1988: 37–40). Spanish and Portuguese colonizers destroyed many indigenous civilizations, although administrative and technical knowledge in the sixteenth century did not allow them to build elaborate power structures. The societies that eventually revolted were dominated by Creole elites who had little concept of democracy or of a reversion to earlier values. In Asia, in contrast, the colonial state was superimposed on existing structures, and its imprint was less dislocative and comprehensive than in Latin America or subsequently in Africa (see especially Manor 1990: 20–38). Africa was the most extreme example of deep colonization. The scramble for Africa in the nineteenth century coincided with the developments of the industrial revolution. The colonial powers were able to provide professional bureaucracies, greater resources, and permanent military forces to maintain their authority. At the same time, they had articulated a clearer racialist ideology, with a strong belief in European and Christian superiority.

It is tempting to draw inferences for democracy from these different levels of colonial penetration. The elites who replaced Spanish rulers in Latin America ruled with an intolerance of dissent and of democratic participation, which is common to settler communities, and indigenous civilizations had been too shattered to resist them, whereas the fate of democracy in Asia depended more on the fertility of the indigenous social soil, which the British had left relatively undisturbed. Hindu India, with its traditions of dispersed power and compromise between elites, was able to sustain a pluralist system after independence, whereas the more authoritarian culture of Pakistan was less conducive to democracy. Africans, like the Latin Americans, had had their traditional political structures largely uprooted (even though the colonial presence was much briefer and memories of an earlier culture were fresher), and they had little practical alternative but to build an independent state that was modeled on metropolitan power. By the second half of the twentieth century, that meant democracy based on universal suffrage. Such a simplified analysis runs the risk of treating the depth of the colonial penetration as merely an independent variable. The relative shallowness of penetration in eighteenth-century India was due not only to a technical inability to adopt the solutions favored in nineteenth-century Africa but also to a recognition of a culture that Europeans treated with some deference, in contrast to their general attitude toward African civilization. One could argue that history had given India a substantial start over Africa in building political institutions. The relationship between the depth of penetration and democracy is already an ambiguous one. Colonial penetration ensured that the formal postindependence political structure was modeled on Europe, if only because clearly defined national frontiers cut across the boundaries of the earlier political kingdoms, but the incongruence between the formal democratic structures and political reality soon became apparent. This could be attributed, in part, to practical inexperience in democracy under colonial rule; however, it also reflected an imbalance between state and society, compared with Europe. Whereas in Europe, and especially Britain, the state had evolved to meet the needs of dominant social groups and its power was constrained by them, in Africa the state had been imposed to ensure the subordination of indigenous groups. The authoritarian governments that discarded nominally democratic constitutions soon after independence were not merely imitating their colonial predecessors but were filling a vacuum that would have been filled in Europe by political parties, pressure groups, and a variety of other autonomous bodies.

The strength of the state in relation to society in Latin America following the destruction of precolonial structures has facilitated similar authoritarian tendencies. But postindependence history has been much longer, and the variety of democratic and authoritarian outcomes at different times and places should caution against attributing too much to events occurring more than 200 years ago. There may be the common factor of the difficulty in establishing a legitimate center of authority once the old structures had been swept away, but time has allowed new social, economic, and political structures to evolve in a way that has not yet been possible in Africa. Depending on circumstances, these can facilitate outcomes as varied as the long-standing ritual of two-party competition in Uruguay and the crude authoritarianism of General Augusto Pinochet in Chile.

Centers of Power

When the colonies were ruled by men who served on brief tours of duty but who regarded the metropolitan country as home, the granting of independence was largely a matter of negotiation between two parties—the nationalist movement and the colonial power—though the situation was sometimes complicated if there were ethnic or religious minorities that the nationalist movement could not or would not embrace. Negotiations for independence might involve lengthy disputes over the protection of minority rights, but there was no question of minorities demanding the right to rule over the majority. When control of the colonies was largely in the hands of settler populations whose ancestors had migrated from Europe, as in Spanish Latin America and British Southern Africa, the situation was more complicated. Minorities might insist on the right to rule over majorities on the grounds of administrative experience, wealth, superior education, or racial superiority. In Spanish Latin America and South Africa this right was conceded, and the struggle for democracy based on equal citizenship has been a prolonged and often violent one, as it was in Zimbabwe, where the settler minority took power despite the opposition of the metropolitan country. Even if the principle of "one adult, one vote" has been conceded, conflict may continue as the minority races strive to defend their economic advantages, as in Central America.

Countries without settler populations from the metropolitan power would appear to have an easier road to democracy. Yet the absence of European settlers may also indicate a relative absence of wealth available for exploitation, and we have seen that poverty generally militates against democracy. At best, the absence of settler colonial rule, or of settler rule after independence, relieves a country of a major liability in the building of democracy, but more positive influences will have to be present for democracy to thrive.

Relations Between Colonizers and Indigenous Populations

As previously noted, a contrast existed between the British practice of retaining a sharp distinction between colonists and indigenous populations and the French attempts at assimilation. The latter practice was applied to every level of society, from giving African primary school children an education similar to that of their French counterparts, to allowing the colonies to elect deputies to the French Parliament. Munslow has argued that the French system made for less of a split between older urban elites and the petty bourgeoisie and that political parties in French Africa were able to develop one-party regimes with more extensive popular support than their counterparts in English-speaking Africa (Munslow 1983: 226). In theory, then, nationalism might be blunted and a consensual atmosphere conducive to democracy might develop if all citizens see themselves as part of a wider French Community, in contrast to the conflict between nationalists and alleged collaborators in English-speaking Africa, though former French colonies have not been noted for their democratic achievements. Algeria and the states of Indochina gained independence only after bloody conflicts, and many French-speaking states in tropical Africa have been wracked by military coups. It may be that attempted assimilation, like deep colonial penetration, weakens or destroys autonomous centers of power. Such centers can be troublesome and destabilizing, as the Ghanaians found in Ashanti and the Nigerians in the north, but they may also contribute to a pluralist system that eventually becomes institutionalized, whereas the French system makes for a more authoritarian conformity or for violent reactions against such conformity.

The Latin American system is best described as one of neither assimilation nor exclusiveness but of "racial laissez-faire." The number of female European immigrants was much less than that of their male counterparts, so there was inevitably much interbreeding. While the distinction between ethnic groups was less clear-cut than within the British Empire, a pecking order developed within which those with the lightest-colored skins were generally the most socially privileged. In countries that lacked many of the other preconditions for democracy, these distinctions made the search for consensus in society even more elusive.

The Transfer of Power

The conditions most favorable to democracy suggest a number of hypotheses about the kinds of transfer of power that are most likely to achieve that end. These hypotheses are set out in Table 3.2. Most of the hypotheses are not mutually exclusive, but they do reflect the different analytical perspectives from which third world politics are viewed.

Hypothesis 1, on the need for adequate preparation for independence, could be linked to the modernization school fashionable in the 1960s, which saw democratic development largely in terms of following in the footsteps of the West, and which therefore required a rigorous tutelage from the colonial masters. Hypothesis 2, on the need for consensus between colonial rulers and nationalist politicians, places the emphasis on actual political behavior and the choice arrived at, and is closer to the more recent public policymaking approach (see especially Philip 1990). Hypothesis 3, on the need for politicians and parties with mass bases, implies, as does hypothesis 1, an expectation that third world countries could tread a similar path to the West in their formative years. Hypothesis 4, on maintaining stability and containing mass participation that will otherwise lead to the system being unable to cope with unsatisfiable demands, is closer to Huntington's emphasis on order as a precondition of democracy (Huntington 1968). Hypothesis 5, on the need for consensus between the main groups in a political system, or at least their leaders, takes us back to Rustow's thesis that democracy is not necessarily sought as an end in itself but emerges

Table 3.2 The Transfer of Power and Democracy: Some Hypotheses

Hypothesis	Latin America	Old Common- wealth	India	West Indies	British and French Tropical Africa	Portuguese Africa	Congo
1. Democracy requires careful, long-term preparations involving colonial rulers and nationalists.		+	+	+			
2. Democracy is helped by consensus between the colonial power and nationalist politicians over the transfer of power.		+	+	+	+		
3. Democracy requires politicians with effective power bases.	+	+	+	+			
4. Democracy requires the transfer of power to politicians who can contain mass demands.		+					
5. Democracy is helped by consensus between groups (or their leaders) within a colony.		+	+	+			
6. Democracy is helped by a high level of social and economic development.		+					
7. Democracy is helped by economic autonomy.							

+ Indicates the presence of the condition.

because rival groups that have an interest in preserving the existing nation-state find that there is no alternative but to reach an accommodation (Rustow 1973). Finally, there are those who seek democratic salvation through economic success, though in different ways. Hypothesis 6, on the need for a high level of achievement on such indicators as per capita income, industrialization, literacy and longevity, harks back to Lipset's work in 1959, which belongs to the modernization school.

Hypothesis 7, on the need for economic autonomy and on the incompatibility of democracy with economic dependence on the West, belongs to the economic dependency school, as espoused by such writers as Frank (1984) and Amin (1987). With the growth of a global economy, the goal of economic autonomy now has very few supporters.

The task in this chapter is not to go over the merits of these different perspectives on democracy again but to discuss the extent to which the political actors involved in the transfer of power were willing or able to move the incipient independent nations closer to the conditions in which democracy was said to be more likely to prevail.

The Preparation for Independence

The countries that made little preparation for the independence of their colonies are easy to identify. The Spanish and Portuguese Empires in Latin America collapsed as the strength of the metropolitan powers ebbed, with little attempt at any orderly transfer of power. Portugal was equally unwilling to yield its African empire in the twentieth century, until a combination of guerrilla warfare in the colonies and the collapse of the authoritarian regime in Lisbon left it with little alternative. Power in Indonesia and the Congo was abandoned rather than transferred, as the maintenance of a Dutch or Belgian Empire became too expensive, and the French departed from Guinea in haste after a referendum had rejected continued membership in the French Community. In none of these countries has democracy emerged, at least until several generations after independence.

Where attempts at preparation have been made, the results have been more varied, as indeed have been the attempts. It is often difficult to establish whether particular policies were adopted with specific objectives of preparing a country for independence, or whether they were means to other ends, such as facilitating economic exploitation through building an economic infrastructure or expanding education or alleviating the suffering of the poor through improved welfare provision. The pronouncements of metropolitan politicians did not always clarify the situation. Some, such as Malcolm Macdonald, as early as the 1930s saw self-government as the ultimate destination but with little notion of any timescale within which specific preparations would have to be made (Hargreaves 1979: 3). Others, such as Winston Churchill, vowed not to preside over the liquidation of the empire yet allowed the forces of dissolution to occur under their noses, as concessions were made step by step.

The French were late in conceding the principle of complete independence, having clung to the myth that the colonies were an extension of metropolitan France until the late 1950s, by which time they had learned lessons from costly wars against nationalists in Indochina and Algeria who did not regard themselves as extra-metropolitan Frenchmen. The interval between conceding the principle of independence and the formal transfer of power was very brief, but earlier attempts to socialize citizens into the French way of life may have done something to enhance the prospects for democracy by providing educated cadres and stimulating at least some economic development.

The extent to which there was any real preparation for dismantling the largest empire of all is a matter of dispute. Hargreaves (1979), Flint (1983), and Low (1988) all insist that such preparation to dismantle the British Empire did take place. According to Flint, new attitudes were emerging in the Colonial Office by the eve of World War II, influenced by the rise of Nazism, the riots in the West Indies in 1938, the appointment of Malcolm Macdonald as Colonial Secretary, and the publication of Lord Hailey's *African Survey*. The riots and the *Survey* suggested a need for immediate social and economic solutions—hence the 1940 Colonial Development and Welfare Act, which allocated £120 million to the colonies over the next ten years. However, the rise of Nazism and Macdonald's ideological preferences implied the need for a democratic Britain to offer the long-term prospects of democratic self-government abroad, and not merely material development. The need to persuade the anticolonial Americans to join in the war and to dispel notions about a Japanese "liberation" of Asia no doubt helped to strengthen the arguments of decolonizers within the government and the Colonial Service.

What sort of democratic blueprint was available? Britain did not seriously consider the idea of restoring power to traditional authorities, which would have been of doubtful practicability, given the incongruence between the boundaries of the traditional territories and the existing colonies and the fact that many traditional functions had been compromised by their incorporation into colonial administration. Yet the Westminster model was seen as unsuitable in a radically different setting, and colonial peoples were expected to work out their own form of democracy (Flint 1983: 400–401). If the world had moved at a rate that suited British politicians and administrators, social and economic development might have proceeded apace to produce strong educated elites and articulate but moderate citizens, while nationalist demands for independence would have remained muted until most of Africa and Asia had achieved a level of development comparable with that of the old Commonwealth. In any event, the pace of nationalist demands outstripped the pace of development.

The case of India has been largely ignored so far, though it has been noted that Britain treated Indian civilization with greater deference than was accorded to Africa. India was never humiliated with the title "colony," and it was administered separately from the Colonial Office. The question of its independence remained controversial among British politicians until the 1940s, but the logistics of maintaining control over such a vast subcontinent after the war—against the wishes of a deep-rooted and well-organized nationalist movement, quite apart from any moral arguments—made continued British rule untenable. And once the Indians had succeeded in achieving independence, it became increasingly difficult to contain nationalist demands, whether by force of arguments or force of arms, in other parts of the empire.

The riots led by ex-servicemen in Accra in 1948, in what had previously been regarded as a model colony, gave an early warning that Africa might offer resistance similar to India's. The nationalist upsurge in Africa hastened the transfer of power and rendered arguments about the social or economic readiness for independence increasingly academic. Indeed, some skeptics question whether there ever had been any real plan for decolonization. Davidson argues that it was merely a matter of European powers reacting to events, such as the Suez Crisis and the Mau Mau uprising in Kenya, and that there was little contact between colonial administrators and nationalist politicians (Davidson 1988). Pearce, too, sees no clear plan for decolonization, only judicious but limited land reform, with a Colonial Office "strategy for nation building" drawn up in 1947 largely as a public relations exercise. Like Davidson, he sees the growing strength of nationalism as the driving force behind decolonization (Pearce 1984: 83–86).

Much depends on what one means by words such as "plan" or "policy." Governments can hardly plan a decolonization program in the way that they might plan an expansion of nursery education, given all the imponderables involved. But it is indisputable that the attempts at social and economic development were seen, at least partly, as preparations for self-government, if not full independence, and that there was concern with the possible distribution of political power after independence, however inadequate the assessment. This could be contrasted with the virtual absence of such preparations and concerns in the Congo and the Portuguese colonies and the disastrous results that followed. Although the postwar rise of nationalism may have taken British governments unawares, as the contrasting French, Belgian, and Portuguese policies show, meeting nationalist demands at an early stage was only one policy option, not an inevitable outcome.

Britain's relative speed in shedding its colonies could be explained in both political and economic terms. Politically, Flint suggests that Britain already had plans for decolonization by the late 1930s, when nationalist movements were still insignificant, and that the only differences with the nationalists were over questions of timing and strategy (Flint 1983: 390). Fieldhouse argues that colonies were no longer necessary to secure the position of metropolitan capital as economic conditions improved in the 1950s, so that Britain was able to decolonize before the other (poorer) European powers, with the advantage of being able to handle nationalist demands before they became unmanageable and to enjoy good relations with the new governments (Fieldhouse 1988: 137–140). One may infer from such arguments that there are virtues in avoiding overly long preparations for independence, just as there are virtues in avoiding undue haste. To suggest that Britain achieved something close to an optimum transitional period would be pretentious, but the undemocratic effects of surrendering power to an unrepresentative minority by withdrawing too soon, as in South Africa, or of surrendering it to revolutionary forces by going too late, as in Portuguese Africa, were generally avoided by Britain.

Consensus Between Colonial Powers
and Nationalist Politicians

It may seem fanciful to suggest that there is ever much common ground between colonial rulers and nationalists. Where was the consensus between Churchill and Jomo Kenyatta, or Harold Macmillan and Archbishop Mikhail Makarios? I will attempt to demonstrate the importance of relative consensus by noting the converse cases of its absence. If, as in the examples in the previous section, the colonial power can see no moral reason for conceding independence and will only do so under duress, or if it wishes to transfer power to an unrepresentative minority, postindependence politics are more likely to be characterized by armed struggle than democratic consensus. Flint's suggestion of common ground between Britain and nationalist politicians does not imply so much a general convergence of values as a rejection of notions of colonies being retained indefinitely because the people would never be fit to govern themselves, because the colonies were already integral parts of the metropolitan power, or simply because the metropolitan power could not afford to let them go. Such minimal agreement is clearly not a sufficient condition for democracy, but experience suggests that it may well be a necessary one.

Mass Power Bases and Mass Containment

Hypotheses 3 and 4 shown in Table 3.2 offer apparently conflicting recipes for democracy. The earliest decolonizations involved creating elitist political structures that offered very limited scope for mass participation, as in Latin America and, to a lesser extent, the old Commonwealth—if only because such participation had not yet been conceded within the metropolitan country.

The attitudes of post-1945 decolonizers were more ambivalent and subject to varied interpretations. On the one hand, there was the popular image of the man in the bush, simple and uneducated but deserving of protection from the upstart nationalist politician, for whom a little learning was a dangerous thing, and who did not represent the real aspirations of the people. Colonial Secretary Oliver Stanley expressed concern about the gulf between politically minded Africans and "the vast bulk of African cultivators living under tribal conditions," while his successor, Arthur Creech Jones, denied that any African political party could bridge the gap between the aspirations of the rural masses and the political rituals of Accra (Hargreaves 1979: 34, 450). On the other hand, there was the practical consideration of to whom power should be transferred, since traditional rulers could not command the allegiance of the people throughout the modern nation-state, and there were

no obvious leaders to represent the people in the bush other than nationalist politicians. The colonial ideal might have been the emergence of a relatively conservative party that was able to win power by appealing to the
moderate sentiments and limited political horizons of the illiterate peasants
and then exercise power using similar moderation. But parties and politicians of this sort were in short supply, except possibly in northern Nigeria.
Votes were not won easily by self-effacing politicians who offered only
minor departures from the colonial status quo. Where such politicians
existed, they were generally outflanked by those who demanded "self-
government now" and promised material benefits to alleviate poverty. If
these radical politicians could boast of a spell of imprisonment or exile for
their beliefs, that enhanced their reputations still further.

The academic debate between modernizers like Almond (who saw
democracy in the West sustained by political parties with mass bases to
channel participation and who thought that they saw the beginnings of similar developments in the third world) and institutionalists like Huntington
(who emphasized the need for strong institutions that would moderate mass
demands to prevent the disorder that would result from unfulfilled expectations) came too late to have much influence on actual colonial policy.
Instead we find politicians and administrators attempting to smooth the transition to independence in a pragmatic way, without always appreciating the
dynamics of politics in the territories they ruled. Flint suggests that Britain
deliberately sought political leaders with mass bases, in preference to more
traditional leaders (Flint 1983: 400–401). Moreover, one could argue that the
French practice of allowing colonies to elect deputies to Parliament in Paris
encouraged many parties to model themselves on France, but one needs to
be careful in using terms like "mass bases" and "participation."

The parties that led the colonies to independence were highly visible
throughout the land and often appealed to people across social divides that
had rarely been bridged before. Austin, for example, refers to the "primary
school teachers, clerks of government and commercial offices, petty
traders, storekeepers, local contractors [and] not very successful business-
men with a one-man, one-lorry transport enterprise or a small import-export
trade" who formed the backbone of the early Convention People's Party
(CPP) in Ghana (Austin 1964: 16). This party attracted mass support at
election time and provided upward social mobility for some of its members
and their immediate followers, and it might have raised voters' hopes as to
how they would prosper once the party had won power. However, the
notion that the CPP and other nationalist parties stimulated mass participation
beyond the ritual of electioneering is more difficult to sustain (see especially
Pinkney 1988: 38). In most of Africa and Asia outside India, the time interval
between the creation of nationalist parties and the accession to power of their
leaders was so short that any mass organization was weakened almost as

soon as it had been created, as party leaders were able to use the machinery of state—with all the resources that this implied—rather than the party, to decide who got what, when, and how. If there were participatory pressures on politicians, it was not so much in the sense of mass bases channeling demands upward (by the time of independence, the party structures were often too ramshackle to channel such demands) but in a more general sense of people seeing a gap between their initial expectations and their actual condition and having no wish to keep politicians in power who had failed to meet their expectations. Since opposition parties had generally been proscribed or bought off, ruling parties were faced at best with growing public unrest and disorder, and at worst with displacement by the military.

It was generally the parties that had enjoyed a much longer life before independence, as in India and the West Indies, and had therefore generated a greater degree of support and legitimacy for both themselves and the pluralist systems over which they ultimately presided that proved most resilient. In tropical Africa, in contrast, the party structures were more fragile, and many sank as they reached the rougher waters of postindependence politics and were unable to maintain public support as they tried to cope with growing austerity.

Was the general failure of democracy in tropical Africa the result of Britain's insistence on politicians building mass bases that led to "the politics of ethnic reality," as Flint (1983: 411) asserts, or was it the result of the shallowness of the power bases in reality? The equation of competitive party politics in Africa with tribalism—and thus with a zero-sum game in which one set of constituents only gain material benefits because others are losing them—has frequently been asserted by leaders of one-party states and military governments. But the reality has often been more complicated. Parties need to build coalitions of diverse groups in order to win a majority. The shallowness of the power bases was probably more serious than the alleged tribalism, and it revealed itself as ruling parties were brushed aside by the military. While nationalist and international pressures may have left the colonial powers with little alternative but to concede independence more hastily than they would have wished, a major effect of this was to leave new nations with fragile political structures that made the survival of democracy difficult. A country with a more developed party structure, such as India, was able to fare better, despite its greater poverty.

Huntington's emphasis on containing participation in order to achieve stability, which is seen as a precondition for democracy, leaves room for argument about cause and effect. Democracies such as India and Jamaica have survived challenges to authority that might well have destroyed more authoritarian governments showing less willingness to compromise or conciliate. Participative pressures that demand more from governments than economic or administrative circumstances enable them to deliver, whether in Salvador Allende's Chile or Kwame Nkrumah's Ghana, are clearly a threat to democratic stability. Yet whether any transfer of power in a world aware of the ideal of universal suffrage, in an age of mass communications, can explicitly limit participation is another matter. More important than the volume of participation may be the need to provide and maintain channels through which it can flow with minimal disruption. This has been attempted within the framework of some one-party states, but the safety value of allowing people to vote their rulers out, no matter how inadequate the alternative, may in the end offer a better recipe for stability than greater authoritarianism. Ultimately, the system that is best able to help the articulation of mass demands may also be the system that is best able to prevent such demands from threatening stability.

Democracy and Consensus Between Groups

The consequences of not having consensus among major groups in society are clear enough. Britain's attempt to set up a Central African Federation (from what are now Malawi, Zambia, and Zimbabwe) in the 1950s failed because Europeans and Africans could not agree on their respective rights, and attempts to include Chinese-dominated Singapore in a Malaysian federation met with a similar fate. Authoritarian governments may be able to maintain their rule over large dissident groups; democratic ones could not do so without ceasing to be democratic. For the colonial power or nationalist successors seeking to build democracy, the challenge is to establish means of reconciling the aspirations of different groups within a given territory or to decide when and whether democracy can be saved by conceding the secession of parts of the territory (as in the partition of Ireland and India, and the eventual abandonment of the Central African Federation).

There are few instruction manuals to help the would-be democratic decolonizer, but with hindsight one can note the relative success of countries where government depends on the support of a multiplicity of small groups, in contrast to the failure where two major groups confront each other, as with Protestants and Catholics in Northern Ireland, Greeks and Turks in Cyprus, Christians and Muslims in the Sudan, and Chinese and Malays in the enlarged Malaysia. In less polarized countries, there is at least scope for constitutional engineering to minimize confrontation. The relative success of federalism and checks and balances in India could be contrasted with the failure in the first republic of Nigeria, where the creation of three large states rather than several small ones heightened confrontation between north and south.

The Economics of Democracy

The desirability of stimulating social and economic development in the years before independence was hardly disputed, at least by those colonial powers that envisaged independence as the ultimate goal. Whether such development was seen as merely a means of improving people's material and spiritual well-being, as a means of ensuring the establishment of a viable nation-state, or as a means of enhancing the prospects for democracy is less clear. The 1940 Colonial Development and Welfare Act led to increased investment in the British colonies over the next decade. Forty percent of the revenue was spent on education, health, housing, and water, and in the West Indies the state surpassed the churches in the provision of social welfare (Edie 1991: 30–33). In the Gold Coast (Ghana), there was a tenfold increase in state welfare expenditure in the decade before independence, compared with a mere doubling in the previous thirty-five years, and even in the Congo there was a rapid expansion of health care and primary education (Young 1988: 55–56). If one puts the least charitable interpretations on such expenditure, it could still hardly be seen as an attempt at maintaining economic exploitation, though such exploitation obviously continued independently of welfare programs.

Flint dismisses the notion that the British were planning the "development of underdevelopment" by arguing that such a goal would have implied strengthening the indigenous bourgeoisie—rather than seeking political leaders with a legitimate mass base and emphasizing social and economic development to precede political advancement—in line with Lord Hailey's recommendations (Flint 1983: 401–409). Even the argument that increased welfare provision was an attempt to appease nationalist politicians is unconvincing because the nationalists offered little serious challenge outside India until the 1950s.

Trying to interpret what the colonial powers, and especially Britain, were trying to do is more difficult than interpreting what they were not doing. Increased welfare provision obviously existed alongside continued economic exploitation through unequal trading relationships and the eviction of colonial subjects from their own land so that they could be employed by expatriates and settlers for minimal wages (see especially Heavey 1991: 136–151). It may be that there was little consistency in colonial economic policy, with the compassionate missionary, the unscrupulous trader, and the well-meaning administrator all having an imprint. A vague notion of nation building made little attempt to anticipate any conflict between democracy and stability, and Low notes the paradox that economic development often implied more authoritarian than democratic measures, such as imposing better cropping patterns, cattle inoculation, and anti-erosion terracing (Low 1988: 45)

When the nationalist tide began to flow more strongly, especially after Indian independence and the Accra riots, political pressures became more important than social or economic ones. This did not mean any decline in economic or welfare provision, but it did mean the abandonment of any notion that independence would only come when the colonial powers judged that such provision was sufficient for the new nations to be launched. Given the acknowledged ability by this time of nationalists to undermine colonial authority, whether through civil disobedience in India or Mau Mau violence in Kenya, the growing disapproval of the principle of colonialism in the metropolitan countries and the wider world, and the high cost of maintaining the colonial military and administrative apparatus, the alternatives to an accelerated drive to independence were limited.

The prospect of the independent countries sustaining democratic political systems was not helped by the inheritance of social and economic structures that, despite the belated investment of the 1940s and 1950s, left the new nations with predominantly illiterate, rural populations and few opportunities for building centers of economic power independent of the state. If democracy was to thrive in such conditions, which became worse as the terms of trade deteriorated in the 1960s, such an outcome would have been contrary to the accepted wisdom of most political scientists on the conditions conducive to democracy.

Alongside the modernization theorists' view that economic development helps to promote democracy is the dependency theorists' view that such development is unlikely to occur because development in the West implies the exploitation and thus the "underdevelopment" of the third world. That such development and underdevelopment have frequently gone together is beyond dispute, as wealthy countries, which have had a head start in developing their industries, leave poorer ones with few opportunities for entering their markets, and this leaves the poorer countries as predominantly suppliers of primary produce to meet the needs of the rich. Yet there is room for argument about whether this is a universal tendency. The conclusion of dependency theorists, that democracy is impossible under such conditions of poverty and exploitation and that it can only be realized by achieving economic autonomy, is more difficult to accept, because the countries that have come closest to achieving such autonomy, such as Albania and Cuba, have not shown many democratic tendencies. While economic autonomy may be a desirable end, it is likely to require considerable authoritarianism to cope with the austerity that it implies, at least in the short term. If democracy was weakened, or rendered impossible, by a transfer of power that failed to promote economic autonomy, one could argue that such failure was not just the fault of the colonial powers and the economic interests they served. It might also have been a consequence of the pressing demands of nationalists and world opinion, which gave greater priority to immediate political independence than to any long-term considerations of the requirements of either democracy or material well-being.

Conclusion:
The Prospects for Democracy at Independence

To compile a retrospective independence day "balance sheet," listing the assets and liabilities that might contribute to the realization or nonattainment of democracy, would be a formidable task. To establish whether such assets were subsequently squandered by the profligacy of political actors, or whether the assets lost their value on account of circumstances beyond the control of indigenous politicians, would be an even more formidable task. In this section, I will merely summarize some of the more obvious factors that might have contributed to democracy at the time of independence and then proceed to look at subsequent changes in the balance sheet in the next chapter. To pursue the analogy, independence day was perhaps treated more like payday, with the recipients wanting to celebrate with the apparently ample assets in hand rather than scrutinizing the overall balance sheet with a view to ensuring a secure future. My thinking here is not just of economic assets in the narrow sense, though many of these were squandered with gay abandon on projects that made little economic sense, but of the sort of assets and liabilities suggested in Table 3.2, which might either facilitate or undermine democracy.

In the early years of independence, the tendency of politicians and, to a lesser extent, political scientists was to focus on the apparent assets. Especially in the countries granted independence willingly after 1945, the apparent consensus between nationalist politicians and the colonial powers on the desirability of liberal democratic constitutions (hypothesis 2 in Table 3.2) seemed to augur well for the future. Why should Ghana, Nigeria, or Kenya not follow the same paths as New Zealand or Canada? Why should anyone have been expected to anticipate the descent into civil war in Nigeria or brutal authoritarian rule in Uganda? One could, perhaps, question the depth of democratic commitment on the part of some of the nationalists, who might give lower priority to democracy if it clashed with other objectives, such as order, socialist planning, or a paternalistic conception of what was good for society. But a more serious problem was the liabilities, which were easy to overlook in the postindependence euphoria.

Turning to the other hypotheses about the conditions conducive to democracy, four of the conditions appear to have been generally inadequate, and one appeared only fitfully on the assets side. The preparation for independence (hypothesis 1) involved varying degrees of planning, but in few cases, if any, was a level of socioeconomic development achieved (hypothesis 6) that could facilitate substantial elite or mass autonomy from the state, and thus greater political pluralism. There were cases, such as the Congo, where events went to the opposite extreme, and state structures disintegrated to the extent that there was no structured means of regulating political competition.

The inadequate social and economic foundations might have been overcome if sufficient consensus had existed between groups in society as to how to distribute the limited resources available (hypothesis 5). There is no intrinsic reason why even the poorest communities should not maintain such consensus. But the culturally heterogeneous territories that existed within the new nations were more likely to produce irresolvable conflicts or conflicts that could only be resolved by authoritarian means. In India, the fact that each group was a small fish in a big pond may have helped to ensure a willingness, if not a necessity, to compromise; otherwise, it has generally been in the smallest states, such as Botswana, Mauritius, and the West Indian islands, that consensus has been relatively easy to achieve. Elsewhere, uneasy power sharing in times of relative prosperity has frequently collapsed under the strain of greater austerity. In much of Africa and Asia, the cleavages have been along ethnic or religious lines, though mass resentment at elite privileges may fuel the flames once elite wealth fails to trickle down sufficiently from patrons to clients. In the long-standing independent Latin American states, the conflicts are more along class lines, with elites frequently unwilling to redistribute enough of their wealth to satisfy the poor in a way that is possible, or at least easier, in Western countries where the volume of wealth available for redistribution is much greater and the plight of the poor less severe. To these problems can be added an economic dependence on the outside world that is different in quantity, and some would say quality, from that found in Western democracies, which means that governments may have to follow the dictates of powerful interests abroad rather than democratic pressures at home.

Finally, there are the problems of politicians building democratic power bases that help ensure their responsiveness to the popular will, while at the same time giving them the legitimacy to make unpopular decisions at times of crisis, without too wide a disparity between the demands of the governed and the willingness or perceived ability of the government to meet these demands (hypotheses 3 and 4). Authoritarian governments may deal with such problems in a variety of ways, but in a democratic system political parties are usually seen as the means of both channeling demands and moderating them. In countries such as India, Jamaica, and Trinidad, parties with strong, deep bases developed well before independence and appear to have performed such functions, however imperfectly, after independence. But in most of Africa, Asia, and Latin America, this has not been the case. In Latin America, parties emerged long after independence and often became little more than appendages of the state rather than independent centers for power, whereas in Africa and Asia outside India, parties emerged only on the eve of independence. Opposition parties had little traditional or ideological loyalty to sustain them, and therefore little raison d'être if their supporters were deprived of government patronage or even basic amenities in their constituencies. Ruling parties, no longer faced with competition, could easily wither as control of the machinery of state became a more important asset than control of, or participation in, the party apparatus. If the military intervened—in the absence of any other means of changing the government—control of the presidential palace, the broadcasting stations, and the main airport were sufficient to give them power. The erstwhile ruling party, without popular support or the resources of the state, would offer little resistance.

In retrospect, we can see that there was little basis for any expectation of the triumph of democracy once the countries of the third world became nominally independent. Even if our balance sheet had remained constant, there would have been only limited democratic assets on which to draw. In any event, the liabilities, both in the narrow economic and in the broader political sense, became greater. It is to the dynamics of this deterioration that we shall now turn.

4

The Eclipse
of Democracy

Some False Dawns

There was never a total eclipse of democracy. There have been third world countries with a record of continuous pluralist democracy, as we shall see in Chapter 6, but they are the exception. What is remarkable is that almost all third world countries have had at least nominally pluralist political systems at some time in their history, yet the majority did not (or could not) build on these to establish durable forms of democracy. The eclipses were, in other words, preceded by false dawns, but these dawns differed in character between the various countries and regions. Moreover, the subsequent failure of democracy may require different explanations, depending on the bases on which democracy had been established.

At the outset, there is a distinction between pluralist systems that "evolved" as a result of the interaction between forces in society, as in much of Latin America and the Middle East, and those that were "planted" as part of the colonial transfer of power, as in much of tropical Africa and Asia. In both groups of countries, one can suggest similar broad influences to explain the eclipse of democracy: economic, social, institutional, behavioral, military, and external. But these influences generally worked differently in the countries where pluralism had evolved from those where it had been planted. Before we look at the dynamics of this, I will briefly identify the processes by which the false dawns broke.

In Latin America, colonial rule was abandoned long before the development of the concept of liberal democracy; there were therefore no democratic constitutions planted at the time of independence. Political systems fluctuated between authoritarianism and general disorder until social changes, resulting mainly from economic development, led to new groups demanding participation in the political system. This is a process familiar to people in Western Europe, but in these new nations, unlike the countries of

Western Europe, there were no old established aristocracies enjoying some "traditional" claim to legitimacy and a degree of deference from lower social classes. In the absence of these assets, ruling elites had to rely more heavily on force to defend their positions, and groups challenging them had to rely more on violence to advance theirs.

Even today we can see legacies of this conflict in some Central American republics, where members of elites resort to rigged elections and the employment of armies to defend their positions, while the masses resort to guerrilla warfare. But further south, uneasy accommodations were arrived at in many countries by the interwar years or earlier, as elites began to feel secure enough to concede demands for universal suffrage and free elections. The story is a complex one, with many variations between countries, and is analyzed succinctly by Stephens (1989). She draws particular attention to the broader, more stable democracies established in Argentina and Uruguay—where industrialization was achieved relatively early and the export economy was based on non-labor-intensive agriculture—and the less stable initial democracies of Chile and Peru, where industrialization came later and the export economy was based on minerals. The economic structure of the latter countries made for a greater polarization between elites and the working classes, which organized into "radical mass" parties. Brazil offered yet another variation, with exports based on labor-intensive agriculture, and the state—rather than "clientistic" or "radical mass" parties—shaped "the political articulation of the subordinate classes" (Stephens 1989: 287). Here, the initial democracy was restricted but relatively durable. ("Restricted democracy" can be taken to mean that even if most of the formal trappings of democracy exist, such as universal suffrage and competitive elections, elites will veto attempts to challenge their privileges beyond a certain point, whether by harassing or banning radical parties or by calling on the military to intervene if such parties wield power in an unacceptable way.)

Although the detailed histories varied between individual countries, there were common problems of the absence of widespread consensus on what constituted a legitimate basis of government. Any democratic arrangements therefore depended heavily on ad hoc truces between contending groups, which might be broken with any change in the relative strength of each group or by shifts in policy, such as moves toward greater egalitarianism or state control, which other groups might find unacceptable. Authoritarian rule, whether civil or military, might thus return. Until the 1964 coup in Brazil, this alternation between authoritarianism and democracy, whether full or restricted, was a common feature of South American political life. Democrats might have preferred to do without the authoritarian phases, but there was always the hope that, as in the West, social and economic development would eventually make democracy secure. What happened subsequently in Brazil, Argentina, Chile, and Uruguay shattered such illusions, as much more brutal and more comprehensive forms of authoritarianism engulfed these countries.

The Middle East also produced various forms of evolved democracy. Generalization is, again, difficult, with differences between states under direct Western colonial rule, such as Algeria, Libya, and Tunisia, where the existence of an alien regime helped to polarize conflicts between nationalists and colonial rulers, and states that had emerged from the disintegrating Ottoman Empire and had come under varying degrees of European control of influence. Such control was, however, different from that in colonies in tropical Africa, in that these states were regarded from the outset as candidates for independence—lodgers in the imperial household rather than long-term subordinates below stairs. In these states, as in Latin America, many traditional structures of authority had been weakened or destroyed, and means had to be found of accommodating new groups that emerged as a result of social and economic changes.

> The irrigation engineer and the local government official stood juxtaposed to the prominent local landowners. The village primary school teacher threatened the values, status (and indeed financial position) of the traditional village teacher of the Koran. The salience of agriculture in the economy, the limited industrialisation and lack of absorptive capacity of the economy tied the graduates of the educational institutions to a career with the state apparatus, either the army or bureaucracy. (Cammack, Pool, and Tordoff 1988: 38)

In such a fluid situation, traditional elites were unable to rule on their own, and by the mid-twentieth century many Middle Eastern countries had established what Pool (1991) calls quasi-democracies. Elected parliaments played a significant role in decisionmaking, but they were built on a narrow social base, and elections were frequently rigged by kings and prime ministers. Elite privileges were preserved by such processes and underwritten by foreign policies that invoked close collaboration with the West and the establishment of foreign military bases. This quasi-democracy had few attractions for the new middle strata of teachers, bureaucrats, technicians, and engineers produced by the expansion of education or for the reformist army officers who shared many of the values and backgrounds of these groups (Pool 1991: 11–14). Although democracy in countries under more direct colonial tutelage was often seen as desirable in itself, apart from the political outcomes it might have produced, democracy in the Middle East, as a result of the socialization processes noted in the previous chapter, was more easily equated with the sustaining of privileges and the surrender of Arab interests.

Social changes had not produced the working-class movements demanding mass participation found in much of Latin America but a "modernizing" middle class that saw salvation in terms of land reform, nationalization, social welfare, and closer links with the Eastern bloc. Perceptions of democracy were not, as in tropical Africa, based on ideals learned at English-speaking educational institutions or on the experience of living in Europe or North America but rather on the culture of the West, which was seen as the source of many of the people's ills. The limited social and economic development experienced in the Middle East thus led not to an expansion of the embryonic democratic forms but to the seizure of power by young army officers who then presided over authoritarian, if frequently left-wing, governments that did not feel the need to make the customary promise to return to democratic norms in the foreseeable future.

The emergence of planted democracy requires less explanation. We have seen that any mutually agreed transfer of power between colonial rulers and nationalists after 1945 could hardly have taken place on any basis other than the acceptance of a liberal democratic constitution. For the colonial powers, readiness for independence implied a belief that people were capable of operating a democratic polity, in addition to enjoying the social and economic assets that the postcolonial afterlife was deemed to require. Hence, there was a reluctance to grant independence to Kenya, Malaysia, or Zimbabwe until political conflict based on violence had largely subsided. For their part, the nationalist heirs apparent generally accepted the democratic ideal and had everything to gain from the legitimacy that success in a free election would confer on them, especially if the result of such an election was in little doubt.

Virtually all the colonies that achieved independence by negotiation after 1945, as opposed to those that took it by default or by revolutionary wars, started life as democracies to the extent that they enjoyed universal suffrage and had had at least one free competitive election, often supervised by the departing colonial power. But, unlike the democracy achieved in the false dawns in Latin America and the Middle East, democracy in these former colonies owed little to the configuration of forces that normally leads to an ability and a willingness, if not a necessity, to make the compromises that a plural system, however fragile, requires. Levels of social and economic development were generally low, and there were few strong social groups able to mount a serious challenge to the incumbent elites. Mass movements could hardly have been expected to emerge in such a setting, and there were few political institutions with sufficient historical depth or current strength to ensure that political conflicts flowed through the regularized channels that democracy requires, given the late emergence of political parties, electoral processes, and legislatures. If the democratic "balance sheet" described in the previous chapter had remained constant, or even improved on the credit side as a result of economic growth or prudent political judgment, it is conceivable that planted democracy might have flourished despite its shallow roots, as indeed it did in a few countries. But for the most part, worsening economic conditions, the indifference of politicians and their constituents to democratic values and procedures, and the growing confidence of armies in their ability to topple governments (whether out of moral indignation or a lust for the fruits of office) ensured that the eclipse of democracy was witnessed in most of Africa and Asia.

The Undermining of Democracy

Table 4.1 presents some hypotheses on the reasons why the initial, and sometimes the second and third, attempts at democracy failed. Many of the variables involved can be seen as the mirror image of those that were suggested in earlier chapters to be conducive to democracy. For example, economic development can lubricate the wheels of democracy while economic decline can intensify a crude struggle for power; consensus between dominant groups and the construction of effective institutions can contribute toward effective democracy, while irreconcilable conflicts and the absence of effective channels for mediating conflict can contribute to a praetorian state in which there is no effective center of authority. But the forces that make for the rise and decline of democracy are not completely symmetrical.

Table 4.1 The Undermining of Democratic Forms: Evolved and Planted

Variable	Undermining in Evolved Democracies	Undermining in Planted Democracies
Economic	Greater class conflict with economic development	Economic decline
Social	Conflict over the extent of inclusion or exclusion	Lack of social cohesion
Institutional	Institutions lacked autonomy from the state	Institutions failed to function effectively
Behavioral	Fear of mass pressure led to undemocratic behavior by elected politicians	Mass indifference facilitated undemocratic behavior by elected politicians
Military	Widening ideological divide between the military and ruling politicians, actual or potential	Military realization of their ability to exploit their position
External	External responses to ideologically unacceptable rulers	Limited efforts by external powers to defend democracy

The creation of democracy, by its nature, requires a process of steady building rather than a big bang, whereas its destruction can come much more suddenly through an economic crisis, a careless decision by political actors, or a military coup. The root causes of these events may, of course, have been festering for some time, but their actual occurrence still depends largely on human choices.

Table 4.1 suggests that although similar variables—economic, social, institutional, behavioral, military, and external—can be used to explain the eclipse of democracy in both evolved and planted democracies, their similarity masks wide differences in the aspects of the variables that are important. We shall examine the arguments for the eclipse of democracy in more detail presently, but for the moment let us look at them in broad terms.

Economics is important in the evolved democracies because economic developments such as industrialization, the exploitation of mineral resources, or changed relationships with trading partners may give rise to changes in the relative resources and demands of different social classes, which come into sharp conflict with one another. In the planted democracies, in contrast, it is more likely to be economic decline, possibly following a deterioration in the terms of trade or the failure of attempts at industrialization, that undermines both the ability of politicians to satisfy their constituents and the already limited commitment of the population to the existing order, once the material benefits dry up.

Social changes may undermine evolved democracies on account of the unacceptability of new political demands being voiced. Universal suffrage may be acceptable to the elite but not the inclusion of trade unions or peasant cooperatives in the political process with their demands for greater equality or social welfare. And attempts to advance or resist such causes may prove impossible within democratic channels. In the planted democracies, the social problem is less one of confrontation between distinctive classes than lack of social cohesion to provide either a solid base on which ruling coalitions can build or a society that provides democratic counterweight against attempts at authoritarianism.

Institutional weakness is a problem in the evolved democracies in that institutions frequently lack autonomy from the state and are thus easily captured, with little resistance, by opponents of democracy. The problem in many planted democracies is that institutions have failed to function at all, even after attempts to sustain them through state resources, and there are thus inadequate links between formal state structures and the population as a whole.

Political behavior in the evolved democracies has frequently taken the form of elected politicians short-circuiting the democratic process out of fear that mass pressure will sweep away their offices and privileges, whereas in the planted democracies it is often the passivity or indifference of the masses that makes undemocratic elite behavior possible.

The military may destabilize the evolved democracies because of a widening ideological divide between army officers on the one hand and elected politicians, actual or potential, with more populist power bases, on the other. In the planted democracies, the military threat is less the result of an ideological divide (social cleavages are less clear-cut) than the consequence of soldiers recognizing their ability to intervene in politics to their own advantage as fewer and fewer people have the will to defend what is left of the democratic structure.

Finally, the *external* response in the evolved democracies is largely positive, in that outside governments or institutions may take steps to subvert elected but ideologically unacceptable rulers, whereas in the planted democracies the problem is less often that of subversion than of inability or unwillingness to come to the aid of elected politicians, as in Nigeria in 1966 and Ghana in 1972. Having asserted that the variables described above are the most important ones in explaining the eclipse of democracy, we can now look at the arguments in greater detail.

Economic Explanations

The eclipse in the evolved democracies in the 1960s and 1970s was qualitatively different from what had gone before. Previously there had been alternations between precarious democratic governments and army-led governments that intervened partly out of self-interest and partly to restore order but that were generally modest in their objectives and narrowly selective in their persecution of political opponents. In contrast, the military regimes that overturned pluralist systems in much of South America and South Korea in the 1960s and 1970s favored a more radical break with the past in terms of economic policy and a more brutal suppression of a larger number of political opponents. Explanations of this phenomenon have been offered by both functionalists and Marxists. Both agreed that the transition from a predominantly rural, primary producing economy to the beginnings of an industrial economy imposes social and political strains.

Huntington and Nelson (1976: 168) draw attention to the conflict between the goals of economic growth and participation in the later stages of modernization. In nineteenth-century Europe, participation was contained because the expectations of the masses were lower in the absence of more developed economies to emulate and the absence of structures, such as mass parties, popular pressure groups, and welfare-minded bureaucracies that might be expected to deliver material benefits. In contrast, Weiner pointed out the way in which elites in late-developing countries have created an institutional framework in imitation of the existing developed countries, only to find that such institutions become strained as economic change produces a growing, articulate working class. Because the institutions were created as imitations rather than in response to indigenous demands, they lack durability and are liable to be removed by military coups (Weiner 1971: 176).

From a different ideological standpoint, radical Latin American scholars have developed the "bureaucratic authoritarian model" to explain both military intervention and what follows it. The political system is seen to pass from a populist phase in which multiclass coalitions of urban and industrial interests, including the working class, use the state to promote industrialization around consumer goods, to a bureaucratic authoritarian phase in which the coalition consists of high-level military and civilian technocrats working with foreign capital. Electoral competition and popular participation are now suppressed, and public policy is concerned with promoting advanced industrialization. Such a process is said to come about because the market for simple manufactured goods has been satisfied, and the market dictates a deepening of industrialization through the domestic manufacture of intermediate and capital goods by highly capitalized enterprises, often affiliated with multinational corporations. Brazil after 1964, Argentina after 1976, Chile after 1973, and Uruguay after 1975 are all examples (see especially Collier 1990: 19–32; O'Donnell 1990; Cammack 1985; and Im 1987: 239–241). The political implication of such a process is that because a mass electorate is unlikely to vote for policies that will reduce living standards in the immediate future, only an authoritarian government will be able to impose them. And in the absence of traditional elites enjoying any legitimacy or coercive power, only a military takeover can ensure that capitalist development takes precedence over popular demands.

The bureaucratic authoritarian model has been criticized on the grounds that (1) it is difficult to fit the facts of individual countries to the processes described, and (2) the policies of the governments concerned have varied from the extremes of free-market economies and political suppression in Chile to the more interventionist and pluralist polices in Brazil. In other cases, such as Colombia and Venezuela, democratic regimes have achieved economic restructuring without bureaucratic authoritarianism, presumably because elites were able to obtain popular consent (see O'Donnell 1986: 9).

Both the functionalist and bureaucratic authoritarian schools clearly have a point. The growth of an entrepreneurial class, and an urban labor force wrought by economic development, is likely to make for new political pressures with which formal political structures may find it difficult to cope. Cammack offers a more modest perspective in referring to "the political economy of delayed and dependent capitalist development" in South

America, in which military governments in Argentina, Chile, and Uruguay have (or had) a common desire for the transformation of "the dynamic of the state apparatus of class relations" (Cammack 1985: 28). If the rise of populist, participatory politics was not to the army's liking, it needed to seek alternative arrangements and civilian allies to help it pursue new directions. No doubt some of the earlier reasons for military intervention, such as dissatisfaction with the incompetence of civilian politicians, continued to play a part in the downfall of democratic systems. But whatever titles one gives to the new nondemocratic regimes, their severity had implications for subsequent political developments. If future polities failed to settle their conflicts within the democratic arena, they would be aware of the bleak alternative that might lie in store.

In the planted democracies, the general pattern was one of economic decline in countries where governments were already fragile and ruled over citizens who had limited attachment to democratic governments only as long as they continued to provide material benefits. However, many governments were left stranded as these benefits began to dry up. The case of Ghana might be regarded as typical of much of tropical Africa. Between 1955 and 1960, under favorable world economic conditions, Ghanaian gross domestic product rose by 5.1 percent per year. In the 1960s it grew at a lower rate than the growth of population, and in the 1970s it fell by 3.2 percent a year (Bequele 1983: 223; Kraus 1985: 165). Ghana's dependence on world economic forces, and especially on the prices of exported cocoa and imported oil, might lend support to Bretton's view: "Political institutions [in Africa] are facades to retain the loyalty of the masses, while the socio-economic substance—money, financial wealth and economic opportunities—serve as the infrastructure for the effective government" (Bretton 1973: 94).

Planted democracy did not necessarily give way to brutal authoritarianism in the way that evolved democracy often did. Military governments frequently emerged as low levels of performance and legitimacy left civilian governments vulnerable to even the most ill-organized and inarticulate soldiers. But in societies of limited economic development and limited class polarization, they seldom offered radically different ideologies or policies. Some of these military governments degenerated into arbitrary personal dictatorship, as in the Central African Republic, Equatorial Guinea, and Uganda. But for people other than the most politically aware, the differences compared with civilian governments were barely visible. In other cases, notably in Côte d'Ivoire, Cameroon, and much of East Africa, ruling parties ended any nominal liberal democracy by snuffing out such opposition as existed and establishing one-party states. Some of these continued to permit intraparty elections to the legislature and thus claimed to be upholding democracy. Yet if most of the power was concentrated in the hands of a nonelected president, and the raising of major national issues was not permitted in parliamentary elections, it was a very limited form of democracy. In still other cases, the partial disintegration of political authority described by Chazan (1988) was a significant development. At the same time, it is difficult to envisage communities detaching themselves too far from the state where there are long-standing expectations of state provision of not only law and order but also of an elaborate economic infrastructure to facilitate the marketing of crops and the importation of essential supplies. Generations of economic dependence cannot be wished away.

The main hope for a second bite at the democratic cherry in countries that began as planted democracies was not so much a revolt against authoritarian excesses, though such excesses undoubtedly existed, but a realization that authoritarianism did not offer any better solution to problems of everyday hardship than democracy. (The other alternative of detachment from the state was more of a reaction to events than a consciously pursued policy.) If a majority of intellectuals or thwarted opposition politicians found authoritarianism positively distasteful, and not merely another form of failed politics, there was the possibility of a nucleus around which pressure for democratic restoration might develop.

Social Explanations

Many of the social changes that led to the eclipse of democracy are implicit in what has been said about economic change, such as the emergence of new groups with new demands that placed strains on political systems in Latin America. In some cases, though, the course of economic change was severely constrained by the prevailing social structures, and in others it was social structures that remained relatively constant but provided rocks on which attempts at establishing democracy might founder. The evolved, limited democracies of the Middle East belong to the first category and the planted democracies of much of tropical Africa and Asia to the second.

The rise of the new groups in the Middle East, such as teachers, bureaucrats, engineers, and modernizing soldiers, reflects not so much a result of market forces but a consequence of government policies. At other times or places, the growth of such groups might have augured well for democracy, but in the Middle East, unlike the countries that had imbibed some Western values under close colonial tutelage, liberal democracy was seen as a more alien concept, especially if it failed to achieve the desired ends. In this case, the end was a more egalitarian, nationalist, state-directed society, and the existing elitist, exclusionary pluralism stood in its way. If radical groups could not gain entry into politics by persuading existing elites to broaden the basis of participation, and elites were just as hostile to Western notions of democracy as their challengers, then political change required the intervention of the military and the demolition of the limited democratic edifice. As in Latin America, though in different circumstances, the main social factor that undermined initial attempts at democracy was conflict over which groups should be included in the political process and on what terms.

In the planted democracies, the problem was less one of the inclusion or exclusion of distinctive social groups than of a general lack of social cohesion. Political structures had changed rapidly in the brief run-up to independence, because of the largely uncritical acceptance of the need for liberal democratic constitutions, yet social structures could hardly be expected to change at the same rate. At least three arguments can be put forward.

First, Low refers to "the plethora of localised agitational propensities" in tropical Africa, which the colonial powers always had sufficient coercive power to crush in the last resort, though they had become increasingly assertive with the rise of nationalism, which itself implied confronting those in authority. The events that led Nigeria into civil war might be seen as an extreme version of such confrontation. But lesser challenges, such as those from Ashanti and Ga groups in Ghana and the north-south conflicts in Benin, were more troublesome to governments attempting to operate relatively open systems than they would have been for colonial governments for whom the maintenance of order was the first priority. Low thus argues that the emergence of authoritarianism in Africa was partly due to a desire to "hold the lid on" these conflicts (Low 1988: 47–48).

Second, Munslow notes that extra-constitutional checks and balances found in the West in the form of powerful economic institutions, newspapers, and educated citizens organized into pressure groups are not found in tropical Africa. It was therefore difficult to follow the spirit of a "Westminster constitution," especially when people's main experience of politics had been under undemocratic colonial rule (Munslow 1983: 223). One could argue that in some cases it was the strength rather than the weakness of economic institutions, especially expatriate ones, that threatened democracy. But experience does suggest that when initially democratic governments tried to strengthen their positions, whether out of a genuine fear of threats to order or a desire to monopolize the fruits of office by imposing preventive detention, rigging elections, or buying support through corrupt dealings, there were few articulate or effective groups to stand in their way.

Third, there was no obvious reason why the bulk of the citizenry, any more than in the Middle East, should have rushed to defend liberal democratic values once they were under threat. Although many precolonial communities had organized their affairs in largely democratic ways (though many had not), there is a wide gulf between such local democracy within a relatively homogeneous face-to-face community and attachment to a form of democracy with such refinements as freedom of expression and association, secret ballots, or independent judiciaries, all of which had been imported recently. Chazan argues that, even in the 1980s, the upholders of democracy in Ghana came largely from the middle class, while commoners continued to voice populist concerns and propound statist ideas. The advocates of democracy had propounded liberty but were not concerned with equality (Chazan 1988: 119). There is a dilemma for democracy in the masses taking an instrumental view of it. It may survive as long as it contributes to material well-being, yet it is hardly worth going to the wall to defend if it does not. This is certainly not a purely third world dilemma, as witness much of Europe in the 1930s, but it can be a more acute dilemma if there are few other elements in society to help tide democracy over lean times. In these planted democracies, the initial demise of democracy was not the result of dramatic changes in society, as in much of Latin America and the Middle East, but more a coming to terms with reality. In retrospect, the prospects for democracy at independence were not as good as many people had viewed them at the time. Society offered little respite if material conditions deteriorated or if politicians tested democratic structures to destruction.

Institutional Explanations

Political structures are easily recognizable. A legislature, a political party, or a pressure group either exists and has its own organization or it does not. Institutions are more elusive, and Huntington's definition of "stable recurring patterns of behaviour" (Huntington 1968: 196) points us in the right direction. Although a parliament may exist as a structure, if it meets infrequently and then only to approve what the government tells it to approve, or if it flits unpredictably between different activities such as raising peasants' grievances or voting to condemn dissidents to death, it is hardly an institution. For it, or for a party of a bureaucracy, to be an institution, it would have to perform a distinctive role that has an important effect on the working of the political system. In the third world, structures can be created that have the same names as their Western counterparts, such as parties or bureaucracies, but their institutional roles, if any, are often different and unpredictable.

The "crises and sequences in development" approach, adopted by Binder et al. (1971), suggests that structures created as particular stages of socioeconomic development may, instead of performing the institutional roles expected of their counterparts in the West, precipitate crises in which violent unconstitutional change is likely. In simple terms, the thesis is that non-Western countries adopted structures such as elections by universal suffrage, mass parties, pressure groups, and the development of welfare-oriented bureaucracies at a relatively early stage in economic development, and in an environment in which (in contrast to the early years of industrialization in the West) internal and international communications facilitated a rapid transmission of information and demands. This information made for an awareness of living standards and political rights in more developed countries and thus fed into growing public demands on authority.

The structures came into being for a variety of reasons. They were badges of nationhood and symbols of legitimacy in largely new nations that could not resort to traditional aristocratic bases of legitimacy, yet they reflected neither the reality of elite power nor the achievements of the masses in extracting democratic concessions. They were a baby, as it were, for whom no one acknowledged parentage and who might grow into a wayward adolescent in the absence of parental affection. Economic development would not by itself precipitate a political crisis, it is argued. But if this development is accompanied by the opportunity for pressure via the ballot box, mass movements, or the bureaucracy for a redistribution of resources that is not to the liking of ruling elites or the army, then the subsequent crisis can be explained by both the fact that the existence of the political structure has facilitated such pressures and that the base of the structures is too insecure (insufficiently institutionalized) for them to resist counterattack from elites wanting to protect their own interests. Thus, in South Korea in 1972, "The popular sector was politically excluded: competitive elections were abolished; strikes were prohibited; the organisation of labour unions was severely restricted; and the basic human rights were violated arbitrarily" (Im 1987: 239). The need for such repression can be gauged from the threat that a pluralist political structure had posed in the previous year:

> The opposition party candidate, Dae Jung Kim, included popular democratic demands in the New Democratic Party's platform. His campaign theme was the realisation of the populist era based on a populist economy. According to Kim, popular democracy would be in opposition to the developmental dictatorship of the Park regime, and a populist economy would be based on popular welfare, fair distribution of the fruits of economic growth, an employee share-owning system, agrarian revolution and new taxes on the rich. (Im 1987: 254)

Similarly in Argentina, and more especially in Chile, political structures that had facilitated popular participation, in a way that would not have been possible during the early stages of industrialization in Europe, proved too much of a threat to elites and seemed too brittle to facilitate any compromise between elites and populist demands.

If there is a general argument that the importation of Western political structures can precipitate conditions conducive to military intervention, there is also a particular argument that the similarity of the imported product to the Western equivalent is only superficial. In Brazil, Cohen argued, military autocracy was not due mainly to economic forces but to a democracy "imposed from above," which discouraged stable political competition. This was apparently the result of a more positive state role in economic development than was common in the earlier industrializing countries, which could afford to adopt a more laissez-faire approach. Parties and pressure groups developed from the top down in response to state activities rather than from the bottom up in response to popular demands, and this left the opposition weak and discouraged stable political competition (Cohen 1987). In functionalist language, the problem was one of a weak political subsystem—the area of voluntary participatory bodies such as mass parties and pressure groups, which normally reinforce a democratic system. Modern analysts would probably speak of an insufficiently vibrant civil society. Without it, a largely passive population is left at the mercy of elite manipulation.

In the planted democracies, the institutional problem is not presented as much in terms of the shadow of a strong state or of elites reacting to what they saw as mass threats to their survival. There may have been threats to order and stability but not generally the threat of lower social groups usurping power. The literature more frequently presents the problem as one of weak institutions that failed to provide adequate channels through which political demands could flow and political decisions be executed. Parties and bureaucracies are particularly singled out for their inadequacy, though legislatures could also be cited as playing generally marginal roles compared with their Western counterparts. Pressure groups are often presented as being of two diametrically opposed types. First, there are groups of little significance, which lack such sanctions as withdrawing electoral support or organizing effective campaigns of noncooperation, on account of the people's limited commitment to secondary groups. Trade unions may thus lack the discipline and organization for mounting effective strikes. Second, there are the groups that act less as channels of communication than as dangerous tidal waves that can leave a chain of devastation in their wake, as with multinational corporations that seek to subvert governments or set their own terms for dealing with them. In neither case do groups contribute much in terms of institutionalization.

Political parties have been criticized for their failure to adapt from being nationalist movements to parties of government (Alam 1986: 56). They have also been criticized for failing to realize the need for force to back up rhetoric in their early years in power, only to go to the other extreme later, with the result that the military stood out dangerously as one of the few groups that had not been cowed and that now provided virtually the only alternative government in the absence of any loyal opposition (Liebenow 1985: 129, 134–135). Governments lacking a strong party base might have turned to bureaucracies, but these were seen to be equally inadequate in adapting to the postcolonial order. There was the perennial problem in poor countries that bureaucracies could not easily be depoliticized because, under colonial rule, bureaucracy and government had been virtually synonymous and administrative decisions, such as the location of a new school or the allocation of an import license between competing firms, took on greater political significance (Munslow 1983: 225). Moreover, many bureaucracies could not even retain the role and effectiveness that they had previously enjoyed once the colonial power had departed. Rothchild and Chazan speak of a more formal hierarchy, with greater bureaucratic regulation and abstract administrative norms under colonial rule, in contrast to the more personalized and patrimonial arrangements after independence, with a need for more personal incentives and sanctions from the ruling class (Rothchild and Chazan 1988: 57).

Perhaps the contrast is overdrawn, but the different basis of bureaucratic power after independence is inescapable. Not only did the new bureaucracies lack the ultimate coercive power of the metropolitan nation and the experience and expertise of its officials, but the new structures might well have been viewed differently by the populace. The new bureaucrats were people from the same political culture as their clients and therefore more susceptible to indigenous political pressures or even to what some people would call corruption rather than to abstract administrative norms (see especially Price 1975: 160, on Ghana). As political parties atrophied, politicians came to lean more heavily on bureaucracies in formulating and propagating policies, and bureaucracies consequently lost much of their distinctive institutional role. If, as Liebenow (1985: 134–135) argues, the new nationalist governments were less evenhanded than the colonial bureaucracies in dealing with conflicts between groups and individuals, this partiality was likely to permeate the bureaucracy as well.

Two potentially important groups of institutions for mediating conflict, parties and bureaucracies, were thus reduced to (or perhaps confined to) a relatively subordinate status. And if conflict could not be meditated adequately through such institutions, it was more likely to manifest itself in a rawer, less democratic form, with a power struggle involving ruling politicians relying on patronage rather than consent, groups in society relying on bribery and intimidation rather than votes, and the army stepping in as the final arbiter. It is not, of course, argued that political structures ought to have functioned in the same way as their Western counterparts. There are myriad ways in which political pressures and decisions can be channeled and processed, but the problem in many of the planted democracies was that the traditional and colonial institutions had been left behind with no adequate alternatives yet in place.

Behavioral Explanations

If political outcomes depend on an element of human choice rather than more impersonal forces, there is again a distinction between the processes at work in the evolved and the planted democracies, though both may have the ultimate effect of aborting democracy. In the evolved democracies, the growth of mass demands for greater participation and equality (whether actual or perceived) associated with social and economic development created a dilemma for both the advocates of change and elected politicians. Excessive public demands or shows of militancy might provoke a repressive reaction. Ruling politicians, whether initially committed to democracy out of conviction or expediency, might make decisions that not merely maintained order or responded to pressure but also brought an end to democracy itself.

Chalmers argues boldly that the imposition of military-dominated regimes in Latin America has been the product not of the general characteristic of the state, society, and culture but of particular historical crises and the choices people made during those crises (Chalmers 1977: 38). Valenzuela argues that in Chile a political crisis preceded (and presumably contributed to) the socioeconomic crisis, with naïve democrats preferring to allow the military to destabilize the system rather than working for compromise within traditional mediating institutions (Valenzuela 1978). Without being as explicit, other literature also stresses the failure of political actors to reach consensus rather than the adequacy or otherwise of the political structure for doing so. Loveman emphasizes the variety of groups in Chile that were willing to destroy the whole political structure if that was the price to be paid for destroying President Salvador Allende's regime (Loveman 1988: 261–262). Sunar and Sayari note the incompatible courses pursued by the main parties in Turkey, with the ruling Democratic Party determined to exploit the authoritarian structure it had inherited and the opposition Republican People's Party determined to politicize the army as a means of challenging authority (Sunar and Sayari 1986).

In the planted democracies, the problem has been explained less as one of a mass threat to order than of mass indifference. At best, democracy was a distant ideal.

> In 1969—and very possibly still today—the legitimacy of the Ghanaian state in the eyes of its ordinary rural citizens appeared to depend on its long-term conformity to the model of representative democracy. But it was also clear that the prudential and moral requirement of obedience to whatever was currently the government was a much more definite and salient precept for all but the most politically engaged than any vague conception of how the polity ought legitimately to be organised. (Dunn and Robertson 1973: 314)

Young suggests that because the colonial claim to legitimacy in Africa had been based on conquest rather than election, there was limited resistance to authoritarianism after independence. Single-party and military governments echoed the colonial approach by claiming legitimacy on the basis of trusteeship and good government, weaving together radical and populist language and exclusionary political institutions (Young 1988: 27). This might suggest an exceptionally docile or gullible population. There was certainly little attachment to abstract notions of liberal democracy, for the bulk of the population had had no experience of such a phenomenon, and this made the piecemeal dismantling of democratic institutions—through rigging elections, harassing the opposition, or muzzling the media—easier than it would have been in other countries. But ignorance of the works of John Stuart Mill did not make people any more docile when they faced hyperinflation and shortage while they witnessed the opulent lives of politicians and their favorites. It was the failure of democratically elected governments to deliver the expected benefits that provoked greater public discontent. Yet when governments responded to this discontent by resorting to greater authoritarianism, as in the crushing of the 1961 rail strike in Ghana or the urban discontent in Western Nigeria after the removal of the Action Group from power, public resistance was relatively weak. Although this phenomenon can be explained partly in terms of the nature of predominantly rural, illiterate societies in which the organization of resistance was difficult, the absence of deeply held democratic values made life easier for politicians choosing to adopt authoritarian methods to crush democracy. Economic crises should not, of course, be accepted as the only reason for the resort of politicians to undemocratic methods. Many might have found accountability to the electorate irksome anyway and could thus have modified the political system to enhance their own wealth and prestige (the relatively prosperous Côte d'Ivoire was no more democratic than the economically declining Ghana by the late 1960s), but a combination of economic decline and mass indifference to liberal democracy was generally a lethal combination.

Military Explanations

The military are often portrayed as victims of circumstance when (initially) democratic governments are toppled. Governments have relied on them increasingly to suppress dissent because government by consent has broken down, it is said, and the military have thus become politicized. Alternatively, governments have failed to deploy sufficient force to crush illegal protest, and the military have little option but to intervene to restore order. To blame the army for the eclipse of democracy would be like associating fires with the presence of the fire brigade.

The fragile condition of many third world governments was undoubtedly conducive to military intervention, but there was no inevitability about this process. Some poor countries, such as Cameroon, Kenya, and Malawi, managed to extinguish pluralist politics with little explicit help from the military, while wealthier countries, such as Greece and Uruguay, where democracy appeared to have been institutionalized, succumbed to military government. Much clearly depended on the choice made by both soldiers and politicians, but certain general trends can be discerned.

In the evolved democracies, there was often a clear divergence of ideology and perceived corporate interests between army officers and elected politicians. In much of the Middle East we have seen how young army officers, who belonged to the modernizing professional classes, overthrew the narrowly based elected governments. These governments had been subservient to the West and hostile to social developments that would have threatened the dominance. In Latin America the situation was more complex, with a wealth of variations between individual countries, but certain features of civil-military relations stand out (for a more detailed discussion, see Pinkney 1990: 28–34). First, armies had a long history in countries that had been independent for more than a century and therefore had time to develop a sense of corporate identity and a notion of which political actions advanced or threatened their corporate interests. Second, the position of army officers as relatively privileged men in a well-established institution—used more for defending elite interests than fighting foreign foes—made them natural defenders of the status quo, unlike their radical counterparts in the Middle East. This does not imply unquestioning subservience to civilian elites, and there were cases of officers declining to support conservative causes, as in Peru in 1968, but the trend was nonetheless a right-wing one. Third, training in, or under the influence of, the United States during the Cold War helped officers to equate radical popular movements with communism, which was seen as an alien threat to Latin America especially after the Cuban Revolution. As political conflicts became more polarized, with left-wing governments perceived as a threat to established interests in Brazil and Chile, and guerrilla movements challenging authority in Uruguay and Central America, the ideologies and interests of army officers pointed not to attempts to arbitrate between competing groups or to remain aloof from politics but to attempts to intervene in such a way as to crush democracy where it produced, or seemed likely to produce, reforming governments.

Of the planted democracies, the South Korean Army shared its Latin American counterparts' fear of communism and equated most popular movements with communism, largely as a result of the way in which the army had been built up with U.S. support to contain the threat from North Korea and China. The army terminated South Korea's brief experience of pluralism in the early 1960s, but in most of Africa and Asia, armies occupied more free-floating social and ideological positions in societies where social and ideological divisions were less tightly drawn. The political alternatives in these countries were not generally those of diametrically opposed radical and conservative governments but of rival elite groups. Armies had not had a century in which to develop a distinctive subculture that might give them notions as to how society should be ordered or what their role should be within it, but they had had enough time to develop a sense of corporate interest. Thus, a budget that reduced the amenities enjoyed by Ghanaian officers in 1972 led to swift military retaliation and the suspension of democracy for eight years. And an attempt by a populist government in Bangladesh in 1975 to pare down an overly large army, find an economically more productive role for it, and place it under the control of provincial governors in a decentralized structure also led to a coup (Rizvi 1985: 224).

In evolved democracies, military intervention was a cause of the eclipse of democracy in the sense that, in the polarized situation produced by social and economic forces, army officers intervened largely because of the ideological gulf between themselves and elected politicians, or politicians likely to be elected—whereas in the planted democracies, military intervention was generally part of an intraelite squabble. The timing of intervention had less to do with a critical point in ideological or social conflict than with a growing realization on the part of officers that they could exploit their positions. The retirement of expatriate officers and the ending of agreements, formal or informal, that the former colonial powers would defend civilian governments enhanced the prospects of a successful coup, and every success in neighboring countries helped to build up an army's self-confidence and sense of anticipation. Many of the coups were, of course, directed against governments that had long since abandoned democracy. But in Nigeria in 1966, Ghana in 1972, Sierra Leone in 1968, and Pakistan in 1977 and 1999, it was democratic systems, however imperfect, that were overthrown. The unpopularity and ineffectiveness of the elected governments made the task of the military easier. In the end, though, it was the perceived interests of military men, together with the elements of chance that invariably accompany such conspiracies, that brought democracy to a halt.

External Influences

It is in the evolved democracies that the clash between the wishes of elected governments and their supporters and the interests of external powers (especially the United States) has been most marked. Muller produced evidence showing that the breakdown of democracy in Latin America owed more to U.S. subversion than to dependent development. Thus, U.S. aid to pro-coup armies in Brazil, Chile, and much of Central America brought about the breakdown of democracy, whereas other countries, such as Jamaica, Trinidad and Tobago, Costa Rica, and Venezuela, also experienced economic development and the emergence of import-substituting industries without such a breakdown (Muller 1985). This raises questions as to why the United States should choose to subvert some governments rather than others. The strategic position of the country may be one factor, as in Nicaragua, where there was a fear of Cuban influence gaining a foothold on the Central American mainland. It might also be the case that social and economic development in Brazil, Chile, and Central America produced a polarization conducive to the rise of strong left-wing groups that was not found in the other countries. If that were so, we would have to see external intervention as an added threat to democracy rather than the primary cause. The curtailment of democracy in Argentina and Uruguay without any apparent foreign assistance suggests that many of the necessary antidemo-cratic ingredients, including a right-wing army, were already present. In the Middle East, it was more often the Eastern bloc that had an interest in over-throwing the elected yet elitist and pro-Western governments in the 1950s and 1960s. However, beyond moral support for the conspirators and indi-cations that they might be treated favorably in the event of successful coups, the external influence was marginal.

In the planted democracies, there is little evidence of external powers from either East or West wishing them ill, though the countries acquired more enemies when their politicians became more authoritarian, or were replaced by authoritarians. Foreign exploitation or lack of adequate aid may, of course, have made democracy more fragile, but these were not new problems. In some cases Western powers favored military leaders over civilian rulers who had abandoned democracy, as in Ghana in 1969 and Uganda in 1971. But with the exception of some Francophone African countries, these preferences were not generally a primary reason for suc-cessful coups.

At worst, external powers contributed by default to the demise of democracy. It is possible that aid to build a more solid infrastructure, or even "first aid" to avert immediate crises, might have saved the elected governments of Balewa, Bhutto, and Busia. However, the short time inter-vals between independence and the ending of democracy suggest that there were more fundamental weaknesses that could not easily have been reme-died from the outside. Indeed, Kofi Busia led a country (Ghana) in which democracy had already been given a second chance after an authoritarian interregnum, and attempts to build second and third republics in Nigeria were no more successful than was the first attempt under Prime Minister Abubakar Tafawa Balewa. To lose one democratic constitution may be a misfortune. To lose two or more might suggest not so much carelessness as defeat in the face of impossible odds.

Conclusion

The six variables that have contributed to the eclipse of democracy can be seen partly as independent variables and partly as different perspectives from which to view the same phenomena. If, for example, one examines the transformation of Ghana from a pluralist system in 1957 to a one-party state based on uncontested elections by 1965, or the more sudden move from multiparty competition to military dictatorship in Chile in 1973, any one of the variables (except perhaps the military in Ghana) could be taken as a vantage point from which to view democratic disintegration. There would be room for argument about which variable was the most important or whether attempts to assign importance are even useful, as the variables might be regarded as part of an integrated whole. There are certainly close links between the economic, social, behavioral, and external factors in the evolved democracies. Observers with a preference for economic determinism might see sharpened social conflict as a natural outcome of particular stages of development as a more articulate disadvantaged group challenges elite privileges. Behavioralists might focus on current rulers abandoning such democratic norms as exist, and military specialists might note that the military intervene if they have no confidence in the ability of civilian politicians to achieve the desired outcomes. At the same time, external powers take a greater interest in these affairs as the political and economic stakes become higher. Similarly, in the planted democracies, there is nothing particularly remarkable about a juxtaposition of economic decline, the crumbling of already fragile institutions when they fail to deliver material benefits, political behavior (characterized by arbitrary rule on the one hand and mass indifference on the other), and soldiers waiting like vultures to swoop on the decaying political system.

If that were the whole story, not only would democracy have been eclipsed in all countries with the social and economic characteristics outlined, but the eclipse would have occurred in similar ways, in broadly similar countries, and over a similar time span. Yet this is clearly not the case. Some countries retained pluralism through two-party alternation, as in the West Indies, some through one-party domination by consent, as in India and Botswana, some though intraparty competition, as in East Africa, and at least one (Papua New Guinea) through a loose multiparty system. Where democracy was eclipsed, it was sometimes through military intervention, which itself took varied forms. In Uruguay the eclipse was total but brief, in Brazil partial but long, in Chile total and long, and in Ghana and Nigeria intermittent with democratic interludes.

Those who reject determinism might place more emphasis on the decision of individual actors, but these are always constrained by economic, cultural, and institutional factors; a poor government cannot easily expand social welfare; a government dependent on the support of a narrowly defined social group cannot easily make concessions to that group's adversaries; and a presidential constitution cannot easily facilitate power sharing. The unique history of each country, set against certain common historical developments in the region in which it is situated, will again help to ensure a diversity of outcomes. Thus, the relative subordination of political institutions to the strong state that antedated them in Latin America, or the problems of social cohesion in the African states where the boundaries of traditional kingdoms had been replaced by arbitrary European-imposed frontiers, weakened attempts at democratic developments. Moreover, the extent of these handicaps and the skills with which political actors overcame them were not the same in any two countries. Uruguay's party system was much more resilient than Brazil's in relation to attempts at state domination, and the Gambia made light of its (possibly less serious) artificial boundaries compared with Nigeria.

Any of the variables described in this chapter could be singled out and shown to be different in nature and impact in any one third world country, as compared with all others. But taken together, the variables placed considerable impediments in the way of democratic development. Attempting to explain why such impediments were eventually removed in many countries, or in a few cases brushed aside so that democracy was never extinguished, opens up another large area of inquiry.

5

State, Civil Society, and Democracy

The relationship between the state and the population over which it rules has been implicit in much of the previous discussion. Do citizens accept the legitimate authority of their rulers? Are the elites who control the state tolerant of potential challengers? Do institutions exist that facilitate communication between government and governed? How much autonomy does the state permit for groups in society? To what extent are the demands that groups make upon the state advanced by peaceful and lawful means, and to what extent does the state respond nonviolently and within the law?

There is nothing new in the notion that politics consists of something more than formal structures, such as constitutions, parliaments, cabinets, presidents, electoral systems, bureaucracies, and local government. Academic literature has for a century recognized the importance of public opinion as well as the ability of ordinary individuals to wield influence through voting and by joining political parties and pressure groups. For several decades the concept of political culture has been invoked to assess broad public attitudes. Liberal democracy has always prided itself on allowing a large sphere in society for activities that have nothing to do with politics. People can worship, socialize, or enjoy hobbies, entertainment, sport, or the arts without these activities necessarily having any impact on the political process. Hence, there is culture that extends beyond political culture.

A newer development in political science has been to distinguish between the wider society and the "civil" society, which forms a part of it. Harbeson distinguishes civil society from society in general by asserting that civil society "is confined to associations to the extent that they take part in rule setting activities" (Harbeson and Rothchild 1994: 4). This may provide a useful starting point, though the word "convention" rather than "rule" would allow for less formal ways in which the political process is often conducted. One might also quibble with the word "associations" unless these are taken to include loose groupings such as villagers demanding better water supplies or bus passengers challenging state monopoly services, as well as groups with a more formal existence. For this study, let us take civil society to mean those aspects of society, and behavior within it, that have a direct or indirect bearing on the political process. Such a definition is unavoidably imprecise, because the boundary between the political and the nonpolitical is not always clear. Can we be sure that workers are on strike simply to pursue wage demands, or are they trying to destabilize the government? Is a bishop's sermon on human brotherhood purely theological, or is it an implicit attack on the government's treatment of ethnic minorities? Is a lawyer defending a client against wrongful arrest merely carrying out a professional duty or challenging a government that sees the client as a subversive influence? Are Kenyan Asians who celebrate an Indian cricket victory over Kenya showing their disloyalty to the Kenyan state?

The boundaries between civil society and the wider nonpolitical society are unclear and constantly shifting, yet the concept of civil society may be invaluable in helping us to map the relations between government and governed and the extent to which these are conducive to democracy. In this chapter we shall look at a possible ideal liberal democratic relationship between state and civil society and then examine the changing fortunes of states and society in the third world since the 1980s. We shall examine the interaction between them and the extent to which this has created democratic openings or consolidated elite domination.

State and Civil Society:
The Liberal Democratic Model and Third World Reality

As noted above, the liberal democratic model implies freedom for a range of activities that have no political purpose and that may indeed detract from earnest political activity. The politician may envy the footballer or pop singer who can attract adulation from a mass audience, or the birdwatching club that absorbs its members' attention in a way that a debate on the merits of the taxation of land values will not. But the liberal democratic model also assigns a wide role to *civil* society by allowing a range of groups and individuals to articulate political demands and by encouraging them to contribute their time, expertise, and money to the maintenance of institutions that the state supports but does not necessarily wish to monopolize. Those who form part of this network include magistrates, school governors, supporters of charities, and representatives of farmers, doctors, businesses, and trade unions. The assumption is that a strong state and a strong civil society, each with a clear notion of its own role and limitations, are mutually reinforcing. Take away the strong civil society, and the state cannot be sure that a more atomized collection of individual citizens will respond to its rule or respect its authority. Take away the strong state, and the conflicting demands from civil society cannot be mediated, and mutually agreed decisions cannot be implemented.

How close are state-society relations to the liberal democratic model in third world countries? Variations in the depth and timing of colonial rule made for a variety of possibilities, but the fact that countries were colonized at all meant that the state was likely to be seen as an alien imposition rather than something that belonged to, or represented, civil society.

> [Under colonial rule] everything began and ended with the government, as demonstrated by the ludicrous practice of officials commissioning pit-latrines in villages. In effect local creativities and initiatives were blunted, and any sense of personal responsibility was detrimentally skewed. Many commonly refer to public property as *"aban"*—"it belongs to the aban"— with the implication that it can be stolen, abused or destroyed with no direct consequences. *The government is still considered to be a foreign entity,* and too many people feel no compunction or obligation to protect its property or services. Those officials who enriched themselves by corruption were not stigmatised in the eyes of society. *The entrenched and pervasive system of government, after all, had no effective means of making public servants accountable for their misdeeds.* Their lack of accountability, therefore, promoted social vices like embezzlement and corruption. Post-colonial leaders have generally not sought to redress the social contradictions bequeathed by colonialism. (Agyeman-Duah 1987: 614–615. Emphasis added.)

This description of the state in Ghana may not apply to the whole of the third world. In tropical Africa colonial penetration was deep, in contrast to Asia and most of Latin America, with colonial rulers utilizing such nineteenth-century technology as the steamship, the railway, the telegraph, and the Maxim gun, and imposing European administrative structures on what they saw as "backward" societies (Young 1994: 43–76). But the indigenous perception of the state as something alien has a wider application. The people of England might have taken a similar view after the Norman Conquest, but the state in 1066 was less highly visible, neglecting not only the provision of pit latrines but also most aspects of health, education, transport, commerce, and social welfare. Over the subsequent 900 years, the state became more attuned to indigenous needs and values, and its legitimacy came to be disputed only by insignificant minorities. In contrast, even many of the third world countries with the longest postcolonial histories, such as those in Latin America, are still ruled by states whose roots in society are uncertain. Independence in much of Latin America had been gained before liberal democracy had become a creed for nationalists to follow, and the power of newly independent governments rested more on force than democratic consent. This did not prevent the eventual evolution of democracy, but states remained suspicious of challenges to their authority from within society and have frequently tried either to co-opt or suppress the challengers (see especially Peeler 1998: 159). In contrast to our ideal liberal democratic model, civil society remains weak and democratic checks on authority can be tenuous.

In Africa, Agyeman-Duah highlights the public contempt for the state and its nonaccountability to society. One might have expected the same model as in Latin America—a strong state oppressing a weak society—but such a state has not generally emerged. This might be explained in terms of a time lag, with African politicians controlling an independent state created in the 1950s and 1960s not enjoying such a powerful machine as the more mature Latin American states created in the eighteenth and nineteenth centuries, yet the story is more complicated than that. The African states are not only newer, but they were immediately expected to shoulder the burden of a range of economic and welfare functions and to satisfy a range of popular aspirations that would have been unknown a century earlier. There may have been a lack of accountability in the narrow sense of inadequate public scrutiny of particular activities, but citizens did demand such amenities as adequate roads, schools, health centers, and safe water as well as economic policies that would sustain minimal living standards. In terms of their limited ability to satisfy these aspirations, most African states might be regarded as weak, and their ability to coerce sections of society that revolt against the inadequate provision remains tenuous. Although rioters can be shot and dissidents imprisoned, governments in such poor countries lack the resources for full-scale repression found in totalitarian systems, just as they lack economic resources to deliver adequate material benefits. The weaknesses of states may also be attributed to the behavior of politicians who have sought to survive through neopatrimonial styles of government that involve building power bases by using public resources to reward friends, relations, and supporters, rather than seeking a broader mandate from the population. But this style can itself be attributed partly to the inability to deliver benefits to the wider society.

We are left with weak states over most of tropical Africa, but civil society does little to provide an alternative basis for democracy, except at the most parochial level. The deep colonial penetration in Africa left little room for society to develop its own political institutions. National boundaries had been drawn in an arbitrary manner by the European powers, often cutting across ethnic communities, so that there was little sense of belonging to entities called Kenya, Nigeria, or Uganda. Where the institution of chieftaincy survived, it was often adapted to suit the needs of the colonial administration, and low levels of literacy and poor communications made it difficult to build new social structures alongside the traditional ones. When independence arrived, there was therefore no strong civil society to act as a check on overly mighty rulers or to provide alternative means of decisionmaking when the state began to disintegrate.

As noted above, colonial penetration in Asia was generally less deep. This was partly because (1) the early European colonizers did not have the technological resources for centralized government that they were later to enjoy in Africa, and they therefore left more of the indigenous power structures intact; and (2) they regarded indigenous Asian culture as belonging to a higher plane than that of Africa (Young 1994: 43). While Africans were considered pagans in need of conversion to Christianity and the civilizing effects of European education, Asians following the Buddhist, Hindu, or Muslim religions were subject to less interference, even if some specific religious practices were prohibited. When independence arrived, the state had to pay due regard to the strength of civil society. This did not always point in a democratic direction, as politicians with local power bases, religious fundamentalists, and people of high social status pursued demands that were not always susceptible to democratic compromise. But it did show that the political direction of each country depended on much more than the ability of a nationalist leader or a military dictator to gain control of the machinery of state. Our focus here does not allow for a detailed discussion of the survival of democracy in India, the frequency of military intervention in Pakistan, or the ability of the Malay and Chinese elites to preserve a largely authoritarian system in Malaysia. But it is worth noting that the different civil societies in each country play a larger role in shaping political destiny than they do in Africa or Latin America.

Although the previous discussion has emphasized the diversity of state-society relations between different parts of the third world, we can still pursue some *common* threads that are relevant to the fortunes of democracy over most of Africa, Asia, and Latin America. Some of the elements of continuity include: (1) limited democracy beyond elections; (2) elite domination; (3) ethnic and religious conflict and threats of conflict (especially Africa and Asia); and continued (and possibly increased) dependence of state and society on the West (Pinkney 2001: 99).

While different governments have come and gone, even the relatively developed regimes have left only limited room for democratic participation beyond the act of voting. This can be attributed largely to the thinness of civil society in Africa and Latin America, while in Asia the institutions of civil society are often hierarchical rather than democratic.

Elites, whether political, economic, social, or religious, have been able to dominate to a much greater extent than in the West, with interludes of popular mobilization in Chile and Argentina very much the exception to the general rule. In some Latin American countries, political conflict along class lines had developed in a way comparable with Western Europe, though often with fewer devices for achieving peaceful compromise. However, over much of the third world, conflict has run along ethnic or religious lines from the bloody conflict between Hindus and Muslims on the morrow of Indian independence to the genocide against the Tutsis in Rwanda. Such conflicts are generally more difficult to manage than those based on social class, with each group having an exclusive identity that sets it apart from its adversaries. Finally there is the constant factor of dependence on the West, in contrast to the Western countries' lack of dependence on any more developed nations when they began to democratize. In economic terms this dependence means that society may be shattered by a slump in the world price of a product such as tea, coffee, or cocoa that provides the society's main source of income; in political terms it means that aid is frequently dependent on conforming to whatever happens to be the West's current notion of good government. In the 1960s this meant economic planning and attempts to build a strong state. Today it means a slimmer state and competitive elections. Either way, the democratic will of the indigenous population, or even of indigenous elites, may be subordinated to the wishes of foreign donors and creditors.

The Retreating State

Although elements of continuity have ensured that the third world still looks very different from the West, there is also a significant contrast between the third world of the 1960s and the third world of today, as suggested in Table 5.1.

    I constructed Table 5.1 initially with reference to the countries of East Africa, yet many of the generalizations have a much wider application. The features under the heading "Postindependence Model" apply to the countries of Africa and Asia in the decades immediately after independence, mainly in the 1950s and 1960s, but they would also fit much of Latin America during the same period, even though the countries there had been independent for much longer. This was the era in which there was still substantial faith in big government and state-controlled development, and in which institutions in both state and society were more monolithic than they subsequently became. While few people openly prescribed authoritarianism

Table 5.1 State and Society: Postindependence and Post–Cold War

Postindependence Model	Post–Cold War Model
Centralized government	Governance
Authoritarianism	Greater pluralism
Bureaucratic domination	Elements of new public management
Clientelism	External tutelage
Military influence or military domination	Increased armed insurgency
Materialist values in collectivist environment	Entrepreneurship, self-help, and imported post–material values (Pinkney 2001: 99)

as preferable to democracy, there was frequently an assumption that the state and its agents were the driving force for development and that they should not be obstructed by groups in society that were ignorant, tribalistic, or "pre-modern." Tanzanian bureaucrats and party officials apparently knew that it was in the interests of the peasants that they be moved from family homes to new villages, and the Ghana government knew that higher priority should be given to establishing a national airline than to self-sufficiency in food. There was even enthusiasm for military involvement in government, especially in the Middle East and Latin America, because the military belonged to the "modern" sector of society and were capable of disciplined, rational decisionmaking

Although democracy was not entirely absent, it was seldom seen as a major ingredient in economic development. There was little external pressure on countries to maintain or restore democracy, yet there was often external pressure to undermine democracies where these obstructed the Cold War objectives of East or West, notably in Latin America. The United States supported military intervention in Brazil and Chile, and Britain did little to prevent it in Ghana, Nigeria, or Pakistan. Regarding the ultimate ends of political activity, the desirability of development, in the sense of increasing the material wealth of nations, was accepted largely uncritically and with little concern for its impact on the environment or the quality of life. In the vast majority of cases, the desired development did not materialize, and this failure was a major reason for the collapse, or partial collapse, of the postindependence democracy we have described.

The reasons for the failure of third world countries to achieve the desired development are largely outside the scope of this study. Dependency theorists attribute it to the unequal relationship between "core" and "peripheral" countries, in which the already developed condition of the former leaves the latter in a subordinate role as suppliers of food and raw materials (see especially Amin 1987 and Frank 1984). Others argue that state structures in the third world were inadequate for the tasks they had been set, which takes us back to the explanations of weak states (see especially Chazan et al. 1999); still others put the emphasis on the choices made by political actors (see especially Philip 1990: 485–501).

These explanations are not mutually exclusive and may even reinforce each other. Politicians may find that both the global economy and the states over which they preside are not conducive to development and that they cannot therefore win popular acclaim for transforming their countries in a way similar to the rulers of Japan or Singapore. As a result, they may try to survive by ensuring that the greatest rewards are given to those whose support they most need, whether it is contractors who contribute to party funds, chiefs who can deliver votes at election time, or soldiers who might otherwise turn their guns on the presidential palace. Clientelism, in the sense of targeting rewards at specific individuals or groups rather than carrying out an electoral mandate, became the general rule. This could only be effective as long as the state coffers were adequate to meet the clients' needs. With economic decline brought about partly by world events and partly by the dissipation of internal resources, the rewards dried up and with them the residual support that authoritarian rulers had enjoyed. Some survived through greater reliance on coercion, but many faced growing demands for democratization from groups that had been largely excluded from state patronage or had recently been deprived of it.

The initial pressures for democratization coincided with the scaling down and ultimate ending of the Cold War. We shall look at the post–Cold War attitude of the West to democratization in detail in Chapter 7, but here let us note that the demise of communism meant that there was less inspiration and support for left-wing governments and political parties. Consequently, this meant that Western governments could support the restoration of democratic elections with less fear of the "wrong" side winning. Even authoritarian governments that had been relatively successful in promoting economic growth, as in Brazil and Chile, were under pressure to democratize if they wanted Western aid, while economically unsuccessful authoritarians were squeezed between dissatisfied constituents and Western donors.

The post–Cold War model represented not just a shift from authoritarianism to democracy. Indeed, one could argue that the extension of democratization was in many cases less than dramatic but that the relationship between state and society changed significantly to introduce a more pluralist order. This order is important for understanding the dynamics of such democracy as now exists, and indeed for understanding the scope for authoritarian rulers to resist democratization.

Most of the contrasting variables presented in Table 5.1 imply a shift from relatively monolithic structures and values to a more pluralist, if not fragmented, order. There are now few countries that do not at least pay lip service to permitting competitive elections and allowing a range of opinions to be voiced. Government is generally less authoritarian, and it is also less hierarchical and centralized. The concept of governance has not been embraced as wholeheartedly as in the West, but there have been moves away from a more centralized executive in which few major decisions had escaped the control of the president and his courtiers. Areas of decision-making have often passed to decentralized structures and to technocrats working under the watchful eye of foreign donors. Where the state has not abandoned public services and public enterprise altogether through privatization, it has frequently delegated the provision of services to nongovernmental organizations (NGOs). These bodies, like their cousins in the West, come in various shapes and sizes. Some are indigenous, having been created to meet immediate local needs, such as the care of abandoned children, while others are part of international agencies such as Oxfam and religious charities. Some, such as the educational trusts in Tanzania, even have tax-raising powers. If governance is perceived as a process in which decision-making is in the hands of a multiplicity of largely autonomous agencies, new public management (NPM) has been the favored device for sustaining such a process.

> Donors agree that what most developing countries must do to improve public sector management is to sweep away the traditional public admin-istration paradigm that underpins their bureaucracies and introduce the . . . NPM. For development agencies and international consultants . . . effi-ciency units, performance measurement, contracting out, market testing, agency status, commonly called the NPM, are a blueprint. (Turner and Hulme 1997: 230)

Such a blueprint has offered a formidable challenge to creaking third world bureaucracies, many of which had changed little since colonial times. One may question whether the limited resources available, the prevailing values, and the resistance of politicians to attempts to insulate areas of administration from patronage are not insuperable obstacles to any com-prehensive NPM. Attempts to contract out the health service in Ghana and refuse disposal in Dar es Salaam both provide cautionary tales of what can happen when the letter of NPM is followed but not the spirit (Larbi 1998: 377–386; Menda 1999: 9). But sporadic attempts at NPM, together with privatization, retrenchment, and the transfer of much service provision to NGOs, have all helped to chip away at the previously monolithic state bureaucracy and disperse decisionmaking more widely.

The contrast posited in Table 5.1 between clientelism and external tute-lage is again a matter of degree rather than polar opposites. Until the 1980s, foreign donors were anxious not to offend actual or potential Cold War allies by asking too many questions about how third world governments were dispensing patronage, and the extensive state intervention of the period gave ample scope to politicians to reward friends and relations with employment, contracts, import licenses, and soft bank loans. The ending of the Cold War, the retrenchment necessitated by economic decline, and the loss of donor patience with corrupt politicians all reduced the scope for these activities and thus the power of those who controlled the machinery of state. As an increasing number of impoverished governments turned to the International Monetary Fund (IMF) for assistance, the Fund introduced structural adjustment programs (SAPs) that imposed policy guidelines on the recipients. These usually included privatization and reduced public expenditure and employment. Neither the IMF nor the third world govern-ments (even if they had wanted to) had the resources to ensure that every detail of every SAP was implemented, and much of the earlier clientelism continued in the absence of adequate scrutiny. In some cases the new economic order actually increased the scope for patronage as governments sold privatized enterprises to favored clients at minimal prices. But the total effect was nonetheless to reduce the role of the third world state to that of one of several actors rather than the predominant force that it had previously been.

The role of the military was another area in which there was a significant change of emphasis, though not a complete turnaround. Third world armies have seldom been simply the obedient servants of elected governments, confining their role to fighting or deterring foreign enemies, which the liberal democratic model assumes. In most of Latin America and most of North, West, and Central Africa, together with Turkey, Myanmar (Burma), Pakistan, Bangladesh, Indochina, Indonesia, Thailand, and South Korea, soldiers have at some time since the 1950s deposed civilian governments. Even when soldiers have not been in power, their influence on the size of military budgets, senior military appointments, and the purposes for which troops should be deployed have often been much greater than in Western countries. This is (or was) another manifestation of the power of an organ of the state, and one that was not generally conducive to democracy. In some cases, especially in Pakistan, Turkey, and the relatively developed countries of South America, armies were close to the textbook model of hierarchies, with unquestioning discipline and distinctive internal values (see especially Finer 1962: 9). In others, there was a greater risk of ethnic fragmentation, internal infighting, or junior officers usurping their superiors, but most military governments required a degree of cohesion within the army. (Exceptions to this are cases like those in Uganda and the Central African Republic where Generals Idi Amin and Jean-Bédel Bokassa became personal rulers who happened to be soldiers, rather than officers ruling through a coherent military command.)

The post–Cold War model provides a different picture. The surviving military governments can be counted on the fingers of one hand, the majority having fallen as a result of their inability to deliver the promised national salvation and the resistance that their violations of human rights provoked at home and abroad. Military influence behind the scenes continues (see especially Luckham 1995: 49–61; and Luckham 1996: 119–177). But armies, like civil bureaucrats, have fallen victims of retrenchment as well as public opprobrium. Even in the post–Cold War era, Western distaste for authoritarianism does not guarantee that military governments will be ostracized or destroyed, as the coups in the Gambia and Pakistan in the 1990s show, yet it makes military intervention less likely.

Just as state power has become widely dispersed, so too has armed force. Standing armies survive, but the major threat to governments is often from nonstate armed groups, some of which scarcely merit the title of "army." They include: (1) groups with distinctive objectives, such as the

Marxist guerrillas in Peru and the Christian Sudan People's Liberation Army; (2) groups whose proclaimed objectives make little sense to outsiders, such as the Lord's Resistance Army in Uganda; (3) groups that want to capture the state to enjoy the spoils of office with little pretense at any ideological mission, as in Liberia and Sierra Leone; and (4) nonpolitical groups using arms in the pursuit of crimes, such as cattle rustling, drug dealing, and diamond smuggling.

There are also cases where "national" armies, nominally under the control of the state, develop an entrepreneurial role of their own, as has been alleged with the Ugandan Army using its occupation of the Congo to indulge in illicit trade in gold, diamonds, and cobalt (Kivumbi 1999: 7). How do we explain these developments? The demise of military government, on account of its brutality and political ineffectiveness, may make a career in the regular army a less attractive prospect than in the days when the army occupied the center stage. What is more, it may increase the attractiveness of joining a nonstate armed group for the young man who is ambitious, adventurous, or unemployed. As retrenchment reduces the number of regular soldiers and policemen, some of those discharged take their weapons with them, and these are augmented by the more readily available supplies from postcommunist Eastern Europe.

Some armed groups may be regarded as rebels without a cause who merely treat the gun as a useful tool for extracting resources that would otherwise be beyond their reach (and growing poverty and inequality probably increase the inducement for such behavior). Other groups promote causes that have become more prominent in the post–Cold War environment. While ethnic and religious tensions have simmered in many countries ever since independence, the relative effectiveness of states, national armies, and foreign backers in the past had often provided a restraining hand. With the ending of the Cold War, maintaining stability in third world countries became a less urgent Western priority, and the challenge to stability often became greater as groups asserted their identities more confidently, whether in Indonesia, Somalia, or Rwanda. Violence based on ethnic or religious identity was obviously not condoned in the West, but there was a temptation to see the problem as insuperable, especially in light of the U.S. failure in Somalia and the French and Belgian failure in Rwanda. Or if it was not insuperable, it reflected a powerful worldwide trend as people sought alternatives to the discredited ideologies of socialism and communism—and even the capitalism that had promised much but delivered little. Such resources as were available to douse the fire were more likely to be used in the Balkans than in less strategically important third world countries.

Our final factor in the weakening of the state overlaps with the previous one. The greater assertion of ethnic and religious identity is one aspect of a greater diversity of values and interests. This does not imply some era of consensus and conformity in the past, and there were clearly cases of violent religious, ethnic, and class polarization in countries such as the Sudan, Nigeria, and Chile during the Cold War years, but it is arguable that the conflicts have become increasingly multipolar. In the postindependence model, different groups might vie with each other to control or influence the state, but at least the state was able to dispense a degree of rough justice in deciding how to resolve rival claims. As states have retreated in the face of retrenchment, privatization, the delegation of functions to NGOs, and demands for greater respect for civil liberties, this may be seen as both cause and effect of the promotion of more diverse interests and values. In some cases the state can do little but acknowledge that long-standing dissidents should be free to propagate their opinions or that entrepreneurs operating in the black economy should be given freedom to ply their trades openly. But such political and economic freedom gathered a momentum of its own, and power bases could be built that were increasingly independent of the state. The rapid expansion in the number and roles of NGOs added to the diversity. While many still consider themselves as nonpolitical, and are concerned with meeting immediate needs that the state is unable to meet, the mere fact that people participate in these nonstate institutions means that participation has an alternative channel, with more decisions taken independently of politicians or bureaucrats. In the case of foreign or foreign-supported NGOs, the impact may be more striking. Although the West has no monopoly of such causes as environmental conservation or the rights of women, children, or animals—to say nothing of basic human rights in the face of state persecution—the presence of foreign NGOs may advance these postmaterial causes partly through advocacy and partly through example. At the very least, they will give a more powerful voice to indigenous groups that previously had little impact. Yet jostling alongside these postmaterial values (for a discussion of the concept, see Inglehart 1977) has been a rise of entrepreneurial values, often without the moderating impact of a Protestant ethic to set limits to acquisitiveness. Writers in Kenya and Tanzania have noted the growth of a more acquisitive society in which people who have the necessary resources have few scruples about exploiting or appropriating public property where there had once been a greater sense of communal obligation (Githongo 1997: 41–45; Mung'ong'o and Loiske 1995: 176–179), and in Latin America O'Donnell paints an even more stark picture.

> The increase in crime, the unlawful interventions of the police in poor neighbourhoods, the widespread practice of torture and even summary execution of crime suspects from poor or otherwise stigmatised sectors, the actual denial of rights to women and various minorities, the impunity of the drug trade, and great numbers of abandoned children in the streets (all of which mark scant progress in relation to the preceding authoritarian period) reflect not only a severe process of urban decay. *They also express*

the increasing inability of the state to implement its own regulations. . . . To be sure these and other ills are not new, and some of them are more acute in a [sic] given country than another. But not only in Latin America, *they have become worse with the super imposition of huge cuts upon a feeble process of democratisation.* (O'Donnell 1993: 1358–1359. Emphasis added.)

The trail left behind by the retreating state is, then, a complex one that has produced a variety of winners and losers. The centers of power are now more numerous and diverse, voices are heard that were previously silenced, and significant political and civil rights have been won. But on the debit side, the ability of the state to serve has been attenuated, as well as its ability to exploit. Citizens may be less protected from crime and terrorism, and a more liberal attitude toward the rights of disadvantaged groups, and of the planet itself, is not necessarily matched by the resources to advance these rights. As greater poverty drives more people into crime and violence, the state or its personnel may react more violently. Where does all this leave the prospects for democracy? Does the greater disorder and instability condemn countries to a Hobbesian state of nature where life is nasty, brutish, and short, as well as undemocratic? Or does the greater pluralism and diversity bring conflicting interests more into the open so that means will eventually be sought to institutionalize conflict through representative institutions? Answers are elusive, but examination of the society side of the state-society equation may shed more light on the subject.

The Rise of Civil Society

That civil society has grown in almost all third world countries since the 1980s is hardly in dispute. Wherever we look, activities beyond the state and business sectors are on the march: Self-help groups care for the sick and disseminate new farming methods; churches campaign for human rights; action groups resist the construction of dams; journalists campaign against censorship; social movements press for minority rights; mass protests against value added tax are organized; and voters queue up to vote in multiparty elections. Foreign aid is disbursed increasingly via NGOs, from 0.2 percent of all aid in 1970 to between 10 and 13 percent by 1994 (Weiss and Gordenker 1996: 32), so that a large proportion of resources are beyond the control of the state. But do these diverse activities and institutions really add up to an entity called "civil society"? And while they are interesting in themselves, why should we expect them to contribute to the establishment or enhancement of democracy? What of groups that may have the opposite effects, even though they too are filling the vacuum left by the retreating state? Do we say that religious fundamentalists who want to keep women in subordination, activists who incite racial hatred, groups that advance their interests by violent means, or NGOs that follow the instructions of foreign paymasters rather than local communities are not part of civil society if we disapprove of what they are doing? On the latter point, one could use the semantic argument that violence and incitement are not "civil" activities, but for the purpose of political analysis it seems more sensible to take the totality of groups that influence the political process as we find them, whether their influence is benign or not. On the contribution of these groups to democracy, we can look at the subject from global, national, and subnational levels.

Global Influences on Civil Society

At the global level there have been pressures to increase the extent and scope of civil society as well as to limit its effectiveness. In addition to the explicit pressures for greater pluralism and a reduced role for the state, there have been pressures that result from the changing nature of global communications as television and the Internet give people access to information and opinions that their rulers might previously have been able to suppress. By the 1990s the prevailing ideology among Western donors was one of limiting the state to a largely enabling role while the private and voluntary sectors expanded. "The message of experience is that the state is central to economic and social development, not as a direct provider of growth but as a partner, catalyst and facilitator" (World Bank 1998: 14).

Civil society, and especially NGOs within it, was expected to do more. Yet did this imply greater democracy, whether in the sense of more people participating in decisions or in the sense of institutions becoming more representative and accountable? Few NGOs can operate without involving at least some citizens who would otherwise remain outside the polity, but most of this has been on the output side of politics, in such activities as building schools, helping discharged AIDS patients, or caring for homeless children. This is participation at the mobilization or therapy end rather than the citizen-control end of the spectrum (see Arnstein 1969: 216–224 on typologies of participation). It is possible, as Putnam and Etzioni suggest, that working together in nonpolitical activities may strengthen a sense of community that can then be carried over into the political sphere (Putnam 2000; Etzioni 1996: 301–302), but that may depend on whether the immediate environment is conducive to such participation—a point to which we shall return. A more skeptical view is that the empowerment of groups in civil society really means that people are required to pull their weight, make development projects more cost-effective, and thus shift responsibility for development to unpaid labor (Abrahamsen 2000: 143). Genuine participation, in this view, is precluded because the West is imposing a minimalist version of democracy by insisting on economic retrenchment and adherence to free market policies made in Washington and Brussels, rather than policies that reflect the wishes of third world citizens.

Abrahamsen argues that "the good governance agenda . . . is an intrinsic part of the technologies of power employed in international politics and one of the ways in which the North maintains and legitimises its continued power and hegemony in the South" (Abrahamsen 2000: 1). Hearn, too, pursues the argument about legitimization:

> Civil society . . . is seen as potentially playing a key role in fostering societal consensus around what is otherwise a divisive reform process. . . . Donors are bringing in "representatives of civil society" into the economic policy-making process in an attempt to widen support for it. It is an interesting observation on the political nature of civil society in African countries that donors have calculated that bringing civil society into the reform process will not undermine it but strengthen it. Donors apparently see civil society as a potential ally in their "free marketeering," which suggests that civil society is not a very deeply rooted locus of opposition to the free market. (Hearn 2000: 19)

Although these global pressures are mediated largely through Western governments and international financial institutions (IFIs), the more direct pressure of the global economy has also had an impact on civil society, especially in South America. In the days when large-scale indigenous manufacturing could compete more easily with foreign businesses, there was an economic base on which mass political parties, trade unions, and corporate business interests could be built. All these were manifestations of a civil society with substantial political leverage. In the 1970s and 1980s much of the manufacturing base was destroyed by global competition, often with the help of right-wing military governments that were persuaded to dismantle import restrictions. The subsequent restoration of democracy could put the constitutional clock back, but not the economic clock. Boron suggests that the bourgeoisie and the marginal masses now belong to different universes, with the latter not even able to become part of the exploitable labor force. Where previously the factory had provided common ground for the bourgeoisie and the worker, today that shared space has almost vanished. Governments have to deal with large masses of marginal people unable to be incorporated into the capitalist economy (Boron 1998: 58–59). The political implications of this are pursued further by Hagopian. Military governments had launched a two-pronged attack that destroyed democratic institutions through repression and helped in the destruction of economic institutions through encouraging global competition. The repression facilitated the growth of informal civil society organizations, for it was more difficult to control groups with no formal membership or officers than it was to ban a political party or trade union. These informal groups are inadequate by themselves as links between civil society and government once democracy is restored, yet the changed social and economic structures inhibit the restoration of parties and pressure groups to their former glory. Hagopian argues that Latin America is left with groups that can mobilize public opinion but cannot represent it adequately. There can be no permanent channels of access to the state if groups are merely organized around transitory demands, and citizens may be left unrepresented in such major areas as monetary and trade policy, social security reform, and consumer protection (Hagopian 1998: 99–143).

In most of Africa and Asia, outside the "tiger" economies, there was not enough industrialization in the first place for Latin American–style deindustrialization to occur. There has not therefore been a comparable process of demobilization of mass movements. But the global pressures mediated via the IFIs have been just as persistent, with similar demands for slimmer states and a similar assumption that economic efficiency requires a more pluralist political process. Hagopian's observations about inadequate access to the state appear to be just as pertinent, as attempts are made to build democracy without the elaborate subsystems linking society to the state, which are commonly found in the West. While global pressures diminish the power of states, the ability of civil society to forge new links with the state depends largely on the indigenous context. We therefore need to turn to politics within third world countries.

Internal Influences on Civil Society

The initial rise of civil society belonged to the authoritarian era of the 1970s and 1980s. Much of it had less to do with democracy than with personal survival in the face of falling living standards and the inadequacy of state services. Azarya and Chazan describe the way in which local groups in Ghana organized their own production and distribution, including widespread smuggling, independently of state-imposed price controls, marketing boards, and customs posts (Azarya and Chazan 1989: 121–123). In Tanzania, Tripp recorded the growth of new organizations and networks for self-reliance and cooperation in activities such as farming, fishing, and policing. Such groups pressed the government to relax the rules that had previously given the state a near-monopoly of control over production and social provision (Tripp 1997: 69, 73–74, 202). In Latin America, too, civil society took over much social provision (Kamrava and Mora 1998: 896), but here its role often extended to greater resistance to authoritarianism. We shall examine this in greater detail when discussing transitions to democracy, but what is important to note here is the impact of the more polarized nature of the more economically developed societies in terms of social class and ideology. This polarization meant that the poor sections of society, often supported by intellectuals and the Catholic Church, wanted to fight against the greater inequality and repression imposed by military governments— not merely to improvise in the face of greater poverty. This led to expectations that the social movements challenging the dictators might continue to have a major role once democracy was restored. As was noted previously, this did not happen, partly because the loose groupings suitable for resisting dictatorship are less suitable for the more mundane processes of sustaining democracy. Two other explanations are that many of the leaders of the social movements have been co-opted by governments and political parties (Peeler 1998: 159) or that perhaps there is no longer such a distinctive enemy to fight. If democracy has done little to tackle the poverty and social injustices of the authoritarian era, it is not clear where dissatisfied groups should now turn. Mass movements and Marxist alternatives belong to another era, and the limited alternatives offered by opposition parties may arouse little enthusiasm.

> Within this regime [i.e., Latin American regimes with electoral democracy] political parties can hardly be active components of civil society, articulating demands, channelling participation, influencing decisions; they become state instruments to legitimise the regime, socialising decisions in which they have had little influence, managing electoral processes as system-maintaining mechanisms. (Espindola 1997: 14)

In Africa the expectations raised by the rise of civil society were generally lower. Dicklitch's description of Uganda suggests a microcosm of a broader problem. The growth of civil society is hampered by a long history of ethnic conflict, a lack of democracy within many associations, and the co-option of many individuals and groups by the regime (Dicklitch 2000: 109–128). Although civil society has undoubtedly expanded, whether in terms of the number of NGOs or in terms of the growth of informal self-help activities, few African countries can escape the constraints of ethnic division, mass illiteracy, and governments that place their own limits on participation (see also the various contributions in Joseph 1999).

Three interconnected themes that emerge from much of the literature on third world politics all suggest that expectations of civil society playing a major role in the democratic process need to be handled with caution. First, a growing sector of civil society is occupied by groups with ethnic and religious bases; second, much of civil society remains (increasingly?) detached from concerns with democracy; and third, the connections between the state and civil society are often not conducive to the democratic process.

The rise of religion is common to many countries where the failure of politicians to deliver material benefits has led people to seek fulfillment elsewhere (Monga 1996: 127–143). In some cases, the consequence for the political system is little more than a loss of followers as congregations swell at the expense of party rallies. In others, religious groups may want to defend or advance their territory, especially when the return of democracy permits a more open articulation of demands. Even in a relatively peaceful country like Tanzania, the return of state schools to the churches has provoked opposition from Muslims, and Zanzibar's attempts to forge closer links with Islamic countries has provoked opposition from Christians (Ludwig 1996: 216–233). India has seen the rise to power of an explicitly Hindu party; growing evangelical sects in Latin America have links with populist right-wing politicians (Daudelin and Hewitt 1995: 221–236; Garrard-Burnett 1996: 96–116), and Muslims in northern Nigerian states are attempting to impose Shari'a law. Ethnic conflict, though seldom absent in the past, can also be fanned by democratization. In the absence of other obvious bases of support, political parties may appeal to ethnic loyalty, notably in Kenya, where opposition has fragmented along ethnic lines.

The close association of civil society with democracy may prove to have been a passing phase. Most groups in society obviously prefer a democratic system within which their rights are secure, but they have a range of other concerns that are more central to their existence, especially once a minimal form of democracy has been established. Tornquist warns against placing too much reliance on civil society for this reason (Tornquist 1999: 135–168). Once a major crisis is over, many NGOs go back to promoting development and welfare, priests return to their flock, and intellectuals to their professional careers.

This leads us on to the alleged inadequacy of the links between states and civil society. There is no reason for a democrat to object to ethnic or religious groups articulating their demands vigorously; democracies such as Belgium and Switzerland have thrived on cultural diversity. Neither is there necessarily any objection to many groups deciding that involvement in democratic politics is peripheral to their interests. The problem is rather that the points at which state and society do interact, and the processes by which they do so, are not always conducive to democratic outcomes, while the players who might have produced better results are absent from the game. The argument takes a different form on different continents, but the conclusions seem to point in a similar direction. In Latin America, the old mass movements and corporate structures cannot easily be resurrected in a postindustrial era, yet the newer groups with narrower and more transitory demands cannot easily gain a foothold in dealing with the state. In Africa there has always been the danger of seeing the combined activities of self-help groups and the pressures of intellectuals for democratization as constituting a potentially viable civil society (see Jeffries 1993: 32–33 for an early criticism of this view). In any event, the whole has often been less than the sum of the parts. The pressure for democratization and democratic consolidation may come from a small counterelite of religious leaders and urban intellectuals who have only tenuous links with the wider society, as in Harbeson's description of Kenya (Harbeson 1999: 37–55). Haugerud speaks of a separate informal civil society that may express dissent at funerals and football matches, and in bars and markets, but with few links with opposition parties (Haugerud 1997: 17). In such a situation, which has parallels in much of Africa (again, see the contributions in Joseph 1999), it is relatively easy for a government to call the bluff of the intellectuals and opposition politicians who lack a mass base, while paying little attention to mass demands that lack powerful advocates at the center.

In the case of India we draw direct links between the rise of groups with ethnic and religious bases and the ways in which civil society interacts with the state. Sharma speaks of the erosion of institutionalized forms of mediation that aggravates the "crisis of governability" and hinders national development, especially redistributive and reformist development. The emphasis is on paying off various groups rather than redistribution (Sharma 1999: 5–6). Jenkins speaks more explicitly about the power of ethnic/religious groups rather than modern interest groups. The ethnic/religious groups provide the basis for much of the subnational politics on which national politics depends. Because governmental accountability is mainly to these groups rather than to mass society, India is able to pursue free market reforms that might otherwise have been resisted (Jenkins 1999: 214–217).

Conclusion

There is a danger of condemning state-society relations either because they do not conform to a Western model or because they produce outcomes of which one disapproves. In most cases the outcomes appear to favor ruling politicians and bureaucrats who are subject to little accountability, scrutiny, or mass pressure; elites who find that pressure for a redistribution of resources is blunted; and favored ethnic or religious leaders (at least in Africa and Asia) who enjoy access and representation at the expense of modern groups. At the same time external powers, which channel a growing proportion of aid via NGOs, are able to determine many policies and priorities without the need for consent from either the indigenous population or its elected representatives.

It might be taking an overly prescriptive view of democracy to argue that it is incompatible with social inequality, sectarianism, patronage, and dependence on foreign tutelage, or even an element of elective dictatorship. But we do at least need to be able to make some assessment of what sort of democracy is feasible within the context of existing state-society relations.

The gains achieved for democracy since the early 1990s by a slimmer, less intrusive state and a freer, expanded civil society are certainly remarkable in much of the third world. The problem lies largely with the disparity between what many observers expected of civil society in the early 1990s and what has proved feasible when the resources of different groups within the state and society have become clearer. The Hobbesian nightmare of a raw state of nature, devoid of political order, has come true only in a few countries such as Liberia, Sierra Leone, Rwanda, and Somalia. What of the alternative of pluralism and diversity undergoing a journey toward institutionalization along democratic lines? Here the picture is more confused, but one can point to some limited successes.

The Indian state has largely kept the lid on communal conflict, although it has given religious and ethnic groups a wider role than many democrats might want. Nigeria's postauthoritarian election in 1999 involved substantial voting across ethnic divides. In South Africa, civil society was of fundamental importance to the demise of apartheid and might have been expected to gather a momentum that would overwhelm the new state, but it has so far been kept in check. But in many cases active participation in local and community groups has not led to more participatory political systems generally. It was the period of industrialization in the West that saw the most significant growth of civil society participation. Most third world countries have either undergone deindustrialization under authoritarian rule or are unlikely to achieve industrialization in the foreseeable future. This does not rule out the possibility of large numbers of societies establishing relations with states that involve greater representativeness, participation, and mutual cooperation, but the means by which this might be achieved remain unclear. If broader social and economic forces are hostile, much may depend on the perseverance of individual actors.

6

Some Cases of
Continuous Democracy

Explaining the transition to democracy has been a major concern of recent literature, and this can lead into a discussion of the ways in which the new democracies subsequently perform. But for a minority of countries the main question is not how democracy was established but how it has survived without interruption since independence. In this chapter, we look at India, a giant country with a population of nearly a billion, and seven smaller countries with populations between 1 million and 5 million. Of these seven "dwarfs" (with no disrespect to the countries or to people of short stature), Costa Rica has enjoyed uninterrupted democracy since the ending of civil war in 1948, and Trinidad and Tobago (hereafter Trinidad), Mauritius, Jamaica, Botswana, and Papua New Guinea have enjoyed uninterrupted democracy since independence. The Gambia, the weakest dwarf in terms of most indicators of development, was included in the first edition of this book, but it was slain by the military in 1994, after twenty-nine years of democracy since independence.

Below the dwarfs are "minnows," with populations of less than a million. Diamond observed that 75 percent of the states with populations of less than a million were democratic in 1988, compared with only 60 percent of larger states, and that five-sixths of the states with populations of less than half a million were democratic (Diamond 1999a: 117). It may be that the small populations facilitate something akin to the ancient Greek city-state style of democracy, though we should note that micro-states such as Kuwait, Equatorial Guinea, the Gambia since 1994, and Zanzibar (which enjoys substantial autonomy within Tanzania), have had their share of (often brutal) authoritarianism. Constraints of space, however, force us to concentrate on the countries with populations of over a million, so I shall relate the particular explanations of the existence of democracy in individual countries to the more theoretical literature and then give more attention to India as the only giant country in the third world that has sustained long-term democracy.

What is it that marks the continuous democracies off from the larger number of countries that have experienced authoritarian rule? Is it a matter of chance, with such factors as bungled military coups or the presence of the right leader at the right time enabling democracy to survive? Or do these countries possess distinctive features that mark them off from the others? Most of the literature focuses on explanations of democracy in individual countries, and little attempt has been made to develop a comparative framework for the continuous democracies as a whole. Table 6.1 brings the explanations together under a few broad headings to assist us in a search for common ground.

Table 6.1 can be related to the preliminary search for the conditions conducive to democracy set out in Table 2.1. The interrelations emphasized by Rustow and the interactions between social groups emphasized by Moore find little place in countries where social divisions are generally less clear-cut; and the sequences in development emphasized by Binder et al. receive little prominence, largely because we are looking at a more limited timescale compared with the evolution of Western countries from rural economies to modern industrial societies. But many of the other conditions for democracy explored in Table 2.1 emerge in the literature on continuous democracies. Economic development and political culture are important, though the distribution of economic benefits takes on a greater importance, and the behavior of political actors is often presented in the form of freely taken choices rather than a mere reflection of political culture. Political institutions are important, not just in the general sense of filtering public demands and facilitating compromise but also in the extent to which they facilitate or constrain freedom of expression and association, the rule of law, and political choices and participation.

In sum, the literature on continuous democracies is more concerned with micro than macro conditions. This may be partly a reflection of the more empirical concerns of the authors, as compared with grand theorists such as Lipset, Dahl, and Rustow, yet it may also reflect the dependence of third world democracy on precarious sets of delicate relationships rather than spectacular historical developments, such as industrialization or interactions between social forces. Value judgments will, as ever, color any assessment of what has happened, and students of continuous democracies are no more united than other political scientists in their perceptions of the democratic ideal. A minority, including Edie, see elite democracy, limited electoral choice, and limited participation as constraints to be overcome in the pursuit of a more participant, egalitarian democracy. The majority, whether directly or by implication, take a more Huntingtonian view of democracy as something that is primarily concerned with electoral competition and as more likely to degenerate into anarchy or authoritarianism than to become a democratic utopia if increased participation, populism, or the

Table 6.1 Conditions for the Survival of Democracy

Conditions	Arguments	Problems
Economic development and equitable distribution	• Greater wealth makes competition for resources less desperate (Lipset 1959). • Where pluralism depends on clientelism, adequate resources must be available (Edie 1991). • Social equality reduces social unrest (Crowder, 1988). • Spending on social welfare and economic infrastructure promotes social satisfaction (Booth 1999; Brautigam 1999; Close 1988; Crowder 1988; MacDonald 1986; Mitra 1992; Wiseman 1990).	• Little attention is paid to the extent, pace, and direction of economic growth. • Juxtaposition of clientelism and pluralism is exceptional. • Greater equality may lead to destabilizing pressures on the political system. • Egalitarianism and social welfare are often associated with authoritarianism.
Political culture	• Importance of tradition of free debate, consensus, elite continuity. • Importance of ethnically heterogeneous elite (MacDonald 1986). • Importance of cross-cutting cleavages (Gupta 2000; Payne 1988). • Importance of cultural diversity, with no single group able to dominate (Manor 1990; Mitra 1992).	• Pre-independence traditions are often difficult to carry over. • Cultural diversity may lead to compromise but not necessarily to democratic values.
Political behavior; political choices	Democracy is helped by: • A conciliatory style of individual leaders and the support they command (Brautigam 1999; Crowder 1988; Wiseman 1990). • Policies that produce widespread social benefits rather than prestige projects (Brautigam 1999; Crowder 1988). • Elite and mass support for moderation, especially when crises threaten the system (MacDonald 1986; Manor 1990; Payne 1988). • A will to preserve democracy on account of awareness of the alternatives (Wiseman 1990). • A realization that democracy makes for more competent, responsive governments (Wiseman 1990). • The projection of clear opposition alternatives.	• Moderation, social awareness, and conciliatory leadership may be a reflection of society rather than positive political choices. • Moderation may inhibit democratic choice. • Countries with experience of authoritarianism have often failed to restore or retain democracy. • Administrative efficiency may be a cause of democracy rather than a consequence. • Voters may not vote for distinctive party programs.

(continues)

Table 6.1 Cont.

Conditions	Arguments	Problems
Political institutions; pre-independence foundations	Democracy is helped by: • A long preparation for independence (Currie 1996; Manor 1990; Payne 1988). • Political institutions that are strong but subject to constraints (Brautigam 1999; Gupta 2000; Manor 1990; Mitra 1992), especially: • Competent, honest bureaucracy (Wiseman 1990). • Well-established, deep-rooted political parties (Manor 1990; Payne 1988).	• Some countries have maintained democracy without a long preparation for independence. • Are strong institutions a cause or consequence of democracy?
Individual freedom, rule of law	• Democracy is helped by freedom of association and expression and an independent judiciary (Crowder 1988; Edie 1991).	• Legal rights may be offset by extensive government or party patronage.
Extent of electoral choice and public participation	Democracy survives largely because it is limited by: • Limitations on the range of choices between parties and policies (Edie 1991; Payne 1988). • Limited public participation beyond electoral activity (Crowder 1988; Edie 1991). • The unlikelihood of power passing to the main opposition party or a radical third party (Crowder 1988; Edie 1991; Hewitt 1990; Payne 1988; Wiseman 1990).	• Controversy over whether the limitations enhance or restrict democracy.
Role of armed forces and external powers	Democracy is helped by: • Absence or weakness of armed forces, making military coups unlikely (Brautigam 1999; Wiseman 1990). • Socialization of armed forces into democratic values. • Indifference of foreign powers to political outcomes or their positive support for democracy (Currie 1996).	• Difficulty in proving such socialization. • Foreign indifference may reflect a country's economic weakness (or strategic unimportance), which may not augur well for democracy

pursuit of unrealistic demands for radical change is not kept in check. Bearing in mind the primary concerns and ideological standpoints of the authors, let us now consider their explanations of the survival of democracy. The headings below correspond with the headings in Table 6.1.

Economic Development and Equitable Distribution

The literature on continuous democracies does nothing to refute Lipset's assertion that, other things being equal, increased national wealth is likely to enhance democracy, as competition for resources becomes less desperate. Although they are by no means the wealthiest third world countries, Botswana, India, and Trinidad are all said to have found the preservation of democracy easier as a result of increased national wealth, or at least improvements in the physical quality of life (MacDonald 1986: 17–18; Crowder 1988: 456). We shall look at the quantitative data in Table 6.2 and then consider some of the academic explanations of the relationship between democracy and development.

Table 6.2 includes our eight continuous democracies, together with the United Kingdom as an example of a developed democracy, and Guatemala, Swaziland, and Pakistan as examples of third world countries that have not experienced continuous democracy. These three countries are not necessarily typical of the noncontinuous category, but their experiences suggest some interesting contrasts with the experiences of the continuous democracies. In the latter category, Costa Rica has the highest human development ranking, taking indicators of social and economic development into account, occupying 41st place among the nations of the world, with Norway 1st and Sierra Leone 162nd. The human development index is "a composite index based on three indicators: longevity, as measured by life expectancy at birth; educational attainment, as measured by a combination of adult literacy (two-thirds weight) and combined gross primary, secondary and tertiary enrollment ratio (one-third weight); and standard of living, as measured by GDP per capita" (UNDP 2000: 279).

The surviving continuous democracies occupy positions between 49th and 149th (or 49th and 122nd if we exclude the historical case of the Gambia). They therefore lie mainly outside the bottom 25 percent, suffering the greatest poverty and deprivation, and outside the top 25 percent that are in, or on the fringe of, the "developed" world. Are there any statistical clues as to why this small number of countries in the middle band are continuous democracies, when the vast majority are not? At first sight, there does not seem to be any magic formula for success. We cannot say that all the continuous democracies are more egalitarian, better educated, or more generous providers of health services, yet a comparison with the three noncontinuous democracies does yield a few clues.

Table 6.2 Indicators of Development in a Developed Democracy, Noncontinuous Democracies, and Continuous Democracies

Indicator	Developed Democracy	Noncontinuous Democracies			Continuous Democracies							
	UK	Guatemala	Swaziland	Pakistan	Costa Rica	Trinidad	Mauri-tius	Jamaica	Botswana	India	Papua New Guinea	Gambia
Human development rank 2001	14	108	113	127	41	49	63	78	114	115	122	149
Population (millions) 1999	59.3	11.1	0.9	137.6	3.9	1.3	1.2	2.6	1.5	992.7	4.7	1.3
% pop. urban 1999	89.4	39.4	26.1	36.5	47.3	73.6	41.1	55.6	49.7	28.1	17.1	31.8
GDP per capita 1999 (US$)	22,093	3,674	3,987	1,834	8,860	8,176	9,107	3,561	6,872	2,248	2,367	1,580
Av. growth of GDP per capita 1990–99	2.1	1.5	–0.2	1.3	3.0	2.0	3.9	–0.6	1.8	4.1	2.3	–0.6
GDP per capita minus HDI rank 2000	+5	–16	–24	–5	+6	+4	–19	+17	–55	0	–12	–23
% GDP from agriculture 1998	1.8	23.2	16.0	26.4	15.2	1.8	8.6	8.0	3.6	29.3	24.4	27.4
% GDP from industry 1998	31.5	20.0	38.7	24.7	24.3	47.5	33.1	33.7	46.1	24.3	42.3	13.7
% GDP from services 1998	66.7	56.8	45.3	48.9	60.5	50.7	58.4	58.4	50.4	45.9	33.3	59.8

(continues)

Table 6.2 Cont.

Indicator	Developed Democracy	Noncontinuous Democracies			Continuous Democracies							
	UK	Guatemala	Swaziland	Pakistan	Costa Rica	Trinidad	Mauritius	Jamaica	Botswana	India	Papua New Guinea	Gambia
Av. life expectancy (years) 1999	77.5	64.5	47.0	59.6	76.2	74.1	71.1	75.1	41.9	62.9	56.2	45.9
% adults literate 1999	100	68.1	78.9	45.0	95.5	93.5	84.2	86.4	76.4	56.5	63.9	35.7
% GDP spent on education 1995–97	5.3	1.7	5.7	2.7	5.4	4.4	4.6	7.5	8.6	3.2	No data	4.9
% GDP spent on health 1998	5.9	2.1	2.7	0.9	5.2	2.5	1.8	3.2	2.5	0.9 (1990)	2.5	1.9
% income going to poorest 20%	6.6	3.8	2.7	9.5	4.5 (1997)	5.5 (1992)	No data	7.0 (1996)	No data	8.1 (1997)	4.5 (1996)	4.4 (1992)
% income going to richest 20%	43.0	60.6	64.4	41.1	34.6 (1997)	45.9 (1992)	No data	43.9 (1996)	No data	46.1 (1997)	56.5 (1996)	52.8 (1992)
Political rights (1= most free, 7 = least free)	1	3	6	6	1	2	1	2	2	2	2	7
Civil liberties	2	4	5	5	2	2	2	2	2	3	3	5

Sources: UNDP (2000 and 2001), pp. 157–268 and 141–199; Freedom House (2001).
GDP = gross domestic product.

Costa Rica is relatively strong on economic growth, life expectancy, literacy, education, and health; Trinidad on life expectancy, literacy, and education; Mauritius on economic growth, life expectancy, education, health, and equality; Botswana on per capita income and education; and India on equality. Papua New Guinea has no obvious strengths. But, although it is poorer than Guatemala and Swaziland, it has a better record than Guatemala on economic growth, health, and equality and a better record than Swaziland on economic growth, life expectancy, and equality. The three noncontinuous democracies, in contrast, have generally poorer records on economic growth, education, health, and, except in the case of Pakistan, equality.

It does not seem to be the case, as I had believed in the first edition, that continuous democracies are overall better social providers relative to per capita income than other third world countries, but most of them do have particular strengths in individual areas of social provision. Most of them also have relatively buoyant records of economic growth. These strengths may help to reinforce democracy in a way that it would not be reinforced in a country like Guatemala, which has suffered economic decline, is a poor provider of health and education, and gives a meager percentage of GDP to the poorest 20 percent. Politicians presiding over such a performance might prefer to avoid the challenge of a free election if they can. The current record of Guatemala, to an even greater extent than Swaziland or Pakistan, when we look at their political rights in Table 6.1, points to the same conclusion. Their records are substantially worse than those of all the continuous democracies, excluding the historic case of the Gambia, suggesting that poor performers frequently need to resort to coercion.

While the figures do not suggest a magic social or economic formula for continuous democracy, they might suggest that some permutation of modest and rising levels of per capita income, buttressed by generous social provision and avoiding the worst extremes of inequality, will all help. Let us consider some of the arguments in the literature.

Much depends on the way in which the wealth is distributed and on the ways in which political actors channel it. Edie speaks of a "dual clientelism" in Jamaica, where two-party competition is preserved because both government and opposition are able to trade patronage for votes, and failure to dispense sufficient patronage can lead to electoral defeat (Edie 1991: 7, 17). While she deplores the narrowness of this clientelistic politics and looks forward to a more egalitarian society, she acknowledges that even the limited pluralism of Jamaica could give way to authoritarianism if the economy failed to provide an adequate resource base for dispensing patronage (Edie 1991: 7).

The egalitarian element in democracy comes out in much of the literature. Crowder noted the greater concentration of rural wealth in Botswana and the consequent dispossession of farmers who were forced to migrate to the towns, where many became shantytown dwellers and often remained unemployed (Crowder 1988: 472). This led to increased support for the (presumably antidemocratic) Marxist section of the opposition. But Crowder, like Wiseman, noted the counteracting egalitarian impact of government expenditure as a means of consolidating public support for the political system. There were few prestige projects (which are often associated with payoffs to narrow elites and foreign backers); there were improvements in communications, health, social services, and rural water supplies; and the foundations of a system of universal primary education had been laid. Such policies were made easier by Botswana's growing wealth from mineral resources after independence, which made it one of the richest countries in Africa (Crowder 1988: 456; Wiseman 1990: 33–73), but the consolidation of democracy owed more to the way in which the wealth was used than to its mere existence. Similarly in India, Mitra refers to steady and substantial improvements in the physical quality of life, with reduced infant mortality, increased life expectancy, expanded education, land reforms, and labor legislation (Mitra 1992: 10–11). In Costa Rica, too, Booth stresses the importance of relative equality (Booth 1999: 460), and Brautigam highlights the social democratic policies followed in Mauritius, including food subsidies, aid to small farmers, and curbing the power of landed elites (Brautigam 1999: 159).

How far can one generalize from these particular examples? The case of democracy in Jamaica being sustained by clientelism, which is in turn dependent on the economy generating sufficient resources, appears to be an exceptional one. Clientelistic systems, such as the notorious case of Bolivia, are more frequently authoritarian than democratic, with clients clinging to the coattails of ruling politicians and bureaucrats rather than threatening to vote for the opposition. Payne suggests that the unusual practice of allowing the loyal opposition to dispense a sizeable portion of state largesse provides financial insurance against the penetration of the political system by a radical third party, so that social discontent is channeled against the ruling party rather than the system as a whole (Payne 1988: 142–143). Such arrangements imply that the existence of a loyal opposition has been institutionalized. We have yet to explore the reasons for this, but such institutionalization is clearly not the general rule in the third world.

The relationship between democracy and the growth and distribution of wealth may offer more fruitful grounds for generalization. The wealthiest third world countries, including Singapore, Taiwan, the Middle Eastern oil producers, and even Nigeria during periods of oil boom, have not been the most democratic, and the wealth has often been used by elites to consolidate their authority. Yet poverty is even less conducive to democracy, as witness the fate of countries such as Afghanistan and Ethiopia, which have

struggled to maintain any coherent political structure. Given a modest degree
of economic growth in the continuous democracies, it is tempting to perceive
a link between welfare-minded political systems and democracy, as the
masses see something tangible in return for their votes and, in time, make
their votes conditional on such benefits. But the democratic achievements of
Botswana and India have to be set against the breakdown of pluralism in Sri
Lanka, which also had an egalitarian record, as well as the failure of democracy to emerge in Singapore. In each case, noneconomic factors upset the delicate balance between a state that is strong and confident enough to maintain
institutionalized political competition and a state that is either weakened by
ethnic conflict or is so strong that it can suppress competition.

The relationship between democracy (or its absence) and economic
dependency figures prominently in much of the literature on third world
politics, though it has a surprisingly small place in the literature on continuous democracies. Payne (1988: 142–143) writes of clientelistic politics
being shaped by the neocolonial Jamaican economy, but no theses appear to
have been advanced to the effect that global capitalism is more indifferent
to changes of government (or the reelection of existing governments) in
these countries than it has been in Chile, Guatemala, or Nicaragua. It may
be the case, however, that the continuous democracies have the advantage
of being insufficiently rich to be of major concern to the outside world.
And, perhaps partly for that reason, political conflict is less polarized than
in wealthier countries such as Chile and South Korea. The consequences of
a particular government being reelected or displaced are thus of less significance to the outside world, which will have little incentive to subvert
the democratic process.

Political Culture

The cultural features of the continuous democracies do not, at first sight, fit
any discernible pattern. The West Indian islands, the Gambia, Botswana, and
Mauritius are all states within which it might be more difficult to regard people from outside one's own ethnic group as alien in the way that groups from
the opposite ends of large countries such as the Congo, Nigeria, and the
Sudan often find themselves with little in common. At the other extreme,
democracy has survived alongside cultural heterogeneity and geographical
extensiveness in India. Although the cultural explanations of democracy
vary between the countries, they are not necessarily incompatible.

Crowder emphasizes the long tradition of free debate, consensus, and
elite continuity in Botswana (Crowder 1988: 466), while MacDonald and
Payne indicate the ways in which political alliances cut across ethnic cleavages in the West Indies, with elites uniting across ethnic divides to resist

radical challenges in Trinidad (MacDonald 1986: 18, 214), and political affiliations in Jamaica cutting across divisions of class, race, and generation
(Payne 1988: 153). Mauritius, which in 1982 became the first African country to change its government directly through a free election, is another small
but ethnically heterogeneous country in which class and ethnic loyalties criss-
cross one another to prevent "zero-sum politics" (Wiseman 1990: 65–73).

These findings are almost like echoes of Almond and Verba's explanations of democracy in much of the West, but the cultural diversity of a giant
country such as India presents more complicated problems. Whereas ethnic conflicts may be kept in check in smaller countries by the nature of
face-to-face relationships, and with the help of small political elites moderating conflicts when they recognize the danger signals, India presents
democrats with a much greater challenge. Yet the challenge to a would-be
authoritarian would be equally great. Manor and Mitra both suggest that
cultural diversity is so great that no single group is able to dominate the
others. Authority is unavoidably dispersed, and a tradition of accommodation and compromise has emerged. Manor suggests that Indian culture gives
only a limited role to politics, with the implication that the pursuit of political power is not the sole, or main, preoccupation of elites (Manor 1990:
21); Mitra suggests that government at the center provides "just one of
many centres" (Mitra 1992: 10).

Political culture offers a tempting explanation of continuous democracy, although it has often proved to be a slippery concept and one that may
be more useful in describing a situation than explaining it. Crowder's
emphasis on traditions of free debate and consensus seems especially vulnerable, because similar traditions could be ascribed to precolonial culture
in much of Africa. But a willingness to share power within one's own group
does not guarantee a willingness to seek consensus with other alien groups
within a modern nation-state and, even without the dimension of intereth-
nic conflict, the higher political stakes in a modern polity may encourage a
more naked pursuit of self-interest. Indeed, Crowder's belief in the existence of a climate conducive to democracy in Botswana is not shared by
Holm and Darnoff, who speak of a tradition of authoritarian decisionmaking and deference as well as a dislike of public conflict (Holm and Darnoff
2000: 117).

The other cultural explanations of democracy hinge largely on either
the ethnic crisscrossing of alliances at the elite and/or mass level, as in the
smaller countries, or on intergroup bargaining based on interdependence, as
in India (something closer to the consociational democracy model) (see
especially Gupta 2000: 187; and Wyatt and Adeney 2001: 4–5). No one
would deny that these phenomena generally help the democratic process—
though bargaining between groups can also involve an elitist carve-up of
resources, as in Malaysia, rather than a response to democratic pressures.

But there is a danger of regarding democracy as an inevitable outcome of certain cultural conditions instead of seeing these conditions as a reflection of political choices taken within the constraints of particular political structures and economic pressures. Why have Guyana, Sierra Leone, and Malawi not followed the same paths as Jamaica and Botswana? Perhaps there are some significant cultural differences, but practical opportunities and obstacles would have to be taken into account, as well as attitudes to society.

Political Behavior and Political Choices

Is it the wisdom of politicians (and the people who elect them) that has helped to preserve democracy? Crowder extolled the virtues of Seretse Khama in Botswana as a good listener, a man who commanded respect in both traditional and modern society, and who had experience of rural development problems. And as was noted previously, the rulers of Botswana emphasized policies that produced widespread social benefits and thus commanded mass support rather than prestige projects for the benefit of narrow elites (Crowder 1988: 463–466). The willingness of both elites and masses to acknowledge the need for moderation, when crises threaten the foundations of the democratic system, is well documented. MacDonald notes the way in which the middle classes of different ethnic groups in Trinidad united behind the government of Eric Eustace Williams and its policy of "capitalist development" in the face of challenge from the black power movement, thus defusing ethnic tension (MacDonald 1986: 18). Payne suggests a similar retreat from the brink in Jamaica, following the 1980 election in which 600 people were killed and a coup had been attempted (Payne 1988: 149). Manor implies an emphasis on moderation in India, with the argument that the limited extent of reform helped to preserve the liberal order (Manor 1990: 37).

Not only is there a willingness to show restraint in the heat of a crisis, but there is said to be a positive will to preserve democracy on both ascetic and practical grounds. Wiseman suggested that the will to preserve democracy in Africa was helped by the experience of the authoritarian alternative, which had failed to provide stability, development, efficiency, or human rights. In the particular case of Botswana, he indicated the greater efficiency of democracy where, for example, drought relief was readily forthcoming from a government that did not want to lose the votes of the victims (Wiseman 1990: 46–47, 182–183). On a somewhat different note, Hewitt refers to the importance of the existence of opposition groups offering clear alternatives as a means of sustaining democracy (Hewitt 1990: 18–19)—a point to which we shall return.

The political behavior arguments offer the opposite side of the coin to the cultural ones. How far are political actors taking autonomous decisions, and how far is their response to events a reflection of the values of society? Some societies, such as those in Central America or the Middle East, may have less of a tradition of moderation and consensus than others, but it would be foolish to ignore the fact that alternative choices could have been taken in the continuous democracies in relation to economic development and crisis resolution, which could have produced different results. Whether we should share the authors' enthusiasm for moderation as a means of sustaining democracy is a more subjective question. Supporters of black power in Trinidad or a more thoroughgoing socialist program in India might see moderation as a constraint on democratic choice, just as Edie (1991) sees two-party hegemony in Jamaica as a restriction on, rather than an enhancement of, democracy.

The argument that the preservation of democracy is helped by a positive will, on account of an awareness of the less attractive alternatives, is one I have pursued elsewhere (Pinkney 1990: 155–156), but it would seem to be more applicable to countries that have actually experienced homegrown authoritarianism than those that have enjoyed pluralism since independence. Even if we allow for knowledge of events in neighboring countries, one might have expected Ghanaians, Nigerians, and Ugandans to have taken greater care not to allow a restoration of authoritarianism when given a second chance, as compared with West Indians and Batswana, whose knowledge of authoritarianism was less direct. The failure of the former countries to avert a second authoritarian coming might suggest that political will alone is insufficient.

The question of the existence of a distinctive opposition alternative takes us into a different territory, and one that is easily overlooked. A democracy that merely offers a choice between Tweedledee and Tweedledum may be useful as a safety valve to check the abuse of power implicit in indefinite one-party, personal or military rule, but it denies voters any real political choice. Hewitt suggests that India was offered such a choice in 1989, with an opposition manifesto that covered state-center relations, decentralization, electoral reform, the depoliticization of national radio and television, and the alleviation of poverty (Hewitt 1990: 18–19). Whether the contents of any party manifesto have a great impact on the choices made by voters is an open question in any democracy, though it may at least reflect an alternative set of interests, beliefs, and priorities that voters can grasp. In the continuous democracies outside India, the question of what is being contested in the democratic arena emerges less clearly, and outbreaks of political extremism are seen as aberrations to be avoided. Perhaps these countries are small enough to subsist on a relatively parochial diet of political conflict, with rival individuals competing largely on the basis of personal competence rather than ideology, but in this case they may offer only limited lessons to other, larger countries seeking to institutionalize democracy.

Political Institutions and Pre-independence Foundations

In previous chapters we have looked at the impact of preparations for independence, or lack of them, and the literature on the continuous democracies confirms many of the propositions already examined. The advantage of a long preparation for independence in Jamaica is emphasized by Payne. A generation of Jamaicans was, he argues, socialized into democratic values. Many of the political leaders were educated in Britain and genuinely believed in multiparty democracy (Payne 1988: 153). In India, Manor mentions the relatively restrained use of imperial power, which enabled indigenous social groups to flourish, and the Congress Party to establish broad and deep support long before independence. The institutional structure at party and state levels was, he says, strong without being overbearing (Manor 1990: 21–32; see also Currie 1996: 791–793). This leads us toward the Huntingtonian argument that successful democracy depends more on effective institutions than on large numbers of people adhering to democratic values or seeking democratic participation. Political parties are thus singled out as vital institutions by Manor and Payne, while Wiseman emphasized the contribution of honest bureaucracy to democracy in Botswana (Wiseman 1990: 35–36).

The argument that institutions are generally more durable if they have deep foundations in pre-independence history is difficult to refute, though one could dispute the phrase "preparation for independence." If the imperial power consciously prepared nationalist politicians or indigenous administrators for independence at all, this was only done very late in the day. Countries such as India and Jamaica did, however, enjoy the advantage of relative freedom to develop their institutions at an earlier date than many of the others. This might be due to an acknowledgment by Britain that these countries were already more "advanced" than the African colonies, which takes us back to culture and economic development. Outside India and the West Indies, it is not easy to explain the durability of democracy in terms of the length of preparation for independence. Indeed, the preparation was much shorter in Botswana than countries such as Ghana and Nigeria, which succumbed to authoritarianism within a decade of independence. Institutional strength in the former countries may, paradoxically, have been helped by the relative shallowness of the nationalist movement, which left older elites and the bureaucracy more intact and able to provide continuity. If other forces helped the continuity of democracy, these institutions could then help to reinforce it, even if the democracy in question was too conservative for many tastes.

In addition to the institutional support provided by parties and bureaucracies is the obvious importance of an independent judiciary and the rule of law. Crowder (1988: 462) mentioned freedom of speech and the press as well as free elections in Botswana. Edie accepts the importance of open media and a free and impartial judiciary in Jamaica. But both authors are careful to qualify the advantages of these formal structures by noting other forms of elite control, including restrictions on trade union rights and the nomination of ruling party candidates to prevent the opposition from taking control of local authorities in Botswana, and the clientelistic processes already described in Jamaica (Crowder 1988: 462; Edie 1991: 47–48).

What of the postindependence institutions that were built on or in place of the foundations? In some cases the inheritance appears to have been squandered, and Ghanaians and Nigerians in the 1970s and 1980s may have wondered how their countries with their relatively educated populations and extensive administrative structures had degenerated into authoritarianism. In other cases the assets have been used to better democratic effect. In India the federal constitution has maintained checks and balances that enable ethnic, religious, and ideological minorities to enjoy a share of power, and it requires political actors at different levels to negotiate rather than wield absolute power (Gupta 2000: 187; Jenkins 1999: 180). In some countries the foundations appeared less solid, yet postindependence institutions have been developed that have served democracy well. This may involve little more than simple measures to ensure that politicians and officials are held to account through public meetings organized by chiefs and political parties in Botswana (Holm and Darnoff 2000: 134–136) or the more elaborate constitutional devices in Mauritius to guard against both ethnic conflict and authoritarianism. Brautigam highlights the importance of a parliamentary, as opposed to presidential, system to facilitate power sharing, an electoral system that ensures adequate minority representation, and the absence of a standing army (Brautigam 1999: 137–152). One could argue that the nature of institution building takes us back to the choices of political actors, but it may also constrain subsequent actors with weaker democratic credentials. Indira Gandhi inherited an Indian political system that limited any authoritarian tendencies she might have had, and the political system that Khama helped to fashion as the first president of Botswana may have set standards for subsequent rulers.

The Extent of Electoral Choice and Public Participation

Democratic choice may be limited not only by the limited quality and quantity of policy alternatives on offer but also by limited prospects of the ruling party losing office or the limited scope for public participation beyond the electoral process. Payne suggests that the convention of government and loyal opposition sharing in the distribution of patronage in Jamaica is an insurance against the penetration of the system by a radical third party

(Payne 1988: 142–143). Edie goes further in arguing that the two-party system actually deprives people of political choices (Edie 1991: 47). Crowder notes the limited scope for participation in Botswana, where rural voters continued to support traditional elites (Crowder 1988: 472–476). Edie sees participation as being restricted to electoral activity in Jamaica, and even here the contest is between personalities rather than between party programs. The parties themselves have close (presumably undemocratic) links with business and the technocratic elite (Edie 1991: 49). Changing the government through the democratic process is a common occurrence in the West Indies, an occasional one in India and Mauritius, and, according to Wiseman (1990: 63), an unlikely one in Botswana.

There is, of course, nothing intrinsically undemocratic about voters choosing to reelect the same party at regular intervals, but cynics might explain the willingness to tolerate the opposition in terms of its remote prospects of winning or the expectation that it would make only limited changes to the status quo if it did win. Where ruling elites have seen the threats to their policies or their privileges as more serious, as in Sierra Leone, Nigeria, and Pakistan, they have been less willing to tolerate free elections or the results they might produce. A more central question is whether one should see these limitations on choice and participation, self-imposed or imposed from above, as necessary restraints to ensure the orderly functioning of the democratic process (with the prospect of additional democratic increments when the system is strong enough to absorb them) or whether such limitations indicate the limited circumstances in which elites are willing to tolerate pluralism.

Answers to such questions can only be speculative. The fact that elites in some countries are willing to tolerate even limited choice and participation should not be overlooked, bearing in mind the intolerance, ballot rigging, and repression that occur in much of the third world, even when the prospects of an opposition victory are more remote than in Botswana. It may be that social forces or the underlying political culture have reached a stage where repression would be socially unacceptable or costly in terms of resources and political principles (see Dahl 1971), but the social structures and political cultures of the continuous democracies are not obviously different from those of neighboring countries where authoritarianism has flourished. In relatively new states, it is difficult to avoid turning to the attitudes of individual rulers and their immediate followers as explanations of the survival of democracy. Lacking the megalomania, fear, greed, or even inferiority complexes of the leaders who have turned to authoritarianism, they have allowed pluralism to continue. Perhaps the democratic leaders would have been more tempted to tamper with the political process if the initial opposition challenge had been stronger or more extreme, yet the pluralist process may eventually become so institutionalized that rulers cannot suppress opposition even if they want to. The ability of Jamaica, Trinidad, and India to survive major political crises with the democratic process intact might suggest that an important threshold has been crossed.

Is electoral pluralism only possible because of limited party differences and limited participation in the political process as a whole? Such a view would fit neatly with Dahl's prescription of contestation before participation or Huntington's emphasis on order. Raise the political stakes, or the range or intensity of expectations, one might argue, and power holders will be reluctant to relinquish power, while nonelites will be less willing to accept the legitimacy of decisions based on electoral pluralism alone. Look at the gap between the aspirations of the haves and have-nots in Latin America, and one can understand the reluctance or inability of political actors over the years to accept free and fair elections. Extreme polarization certainly makes democracy much more difficult, yet it may itself be blunted by continuous democracy. We have seen that many of the continuous democracies are culturally heterogeneous. Black power was for a time a subject of intense political conflict in Trinidad, and India has faced a range of ethnic and religious conflicts that have involved an authoritarian clampdown elsewhere. Yet the existence of a deep-rooted democratic structure helped each political system to return from the brink. Once again democracy may play a part in determining the nature of political conflict as well as responding to it.

The Armed Forces and Foreign Influence

The military coup is a common means of ending democracy in the third world. If there is no military, there can be no military coup. Democracy survived for many years in the Gambia in the absence of a standing army and was destroyed once such an army was created. The absence of a standing army in Mauritius, in Botswana in the formative years before 1997, and in Costa Rica since 1948 might be an important explanation of the survival of democracy, though one would still have to explain why each government took the exceptional decision not to create, or to dispense with, an army. It might be a reflection of such variables as the perceived stability of the country, the modest aspirations of its rulers, or its remoteness from any international conflict, all of which would themselves augur well for democracy, in contrast to the Middle Eastern countries with their internal instability, megalomaniac leaders, and positions of strategic importance.

Where armies do exist but do not interfere with the democratic process, it is tempting to argue that they have been socialized into values of military professionalism and respect for democracy. Yet if the main evidence for such an assertion is the nonoccurrence of coups, we are only going round in circles. In the early 1960s it was fashionable to argue that the rigors of previous training under the British and French would rule out the possibility of coups in tropical Africa, and this seemed a plausible argument until coups began to occur. It is, of course, possible that soldiers witness the effective working of the democratic process and conclude that elections are a better means of changing the government than coups. In that case, though, nonintervention is a consequence of democracy rather than a cause. It is generally true that armies do not intervene when the democratic process is working relatively smoothly, unless provoked by outside powers, as in Guatemala in 1954, but the converse does not apply so consistently. Armies removed Prime Minister Alahaji Abubakar Tafawa Balewa in Nigeria, President Albert Margai in Sierra Leone, and Prime Minister Benazir Bhutto in Pakistan when their legitimacy was in dispute, yet they remained in barracks during constitutional crises in Jamaica, Trinidad, and India. Although this may be because democracy was more firmly established in the latter countries, can one say with any certainty that the outcome might not have been different if key army officers had made a different assessment of the situation? Was democracy secure, or was it just lucky?

Foreign intervention, like military intervention, is more often seen as a means of subverting democracy than sustaining it. From Hungary to Chile, and Guatemala to Iran, actual or emerging democracies have been brought down through foreign-inspired coups or invasions. The absence of foreign influence in a country may reflect its strategic unimportance, which is generally good for democracy. Countries at international crossroads, such as Egypt, Pakistan, South Korea, and Panama, are unlikely to have as much freedom to develop their own political institutions, and they often suffer the burden of inflated armies demanding more resources and influence. But foreign indifference may reflect a paucity of economic resources, which is generally bad for democracy, though probably not as bad as being someone else's military base.

One twist in the tail is that foreign indifference to democratic experiments in "unimportant" countries may also mean foreign indifference to the removal of governments by unconstitutional means. While there was a loud outcry against the iniquities of military government in Nigeria and one-party rule in Kenya, barely a whisper was raised when the military overthrew an impeccably democratic government in the Gambia in 1994 and then consolidated power through a blatantly rigged election (Wiseman 1999: 216–227). A cynical explanation might be that the Gambia was too small and poor to matter. In a way it was the mirror image of Pakistan, which was so strategically important by 2001 that the West turned a blind eye to continued military rule. If this interpretation is correct, democracy is in the shade in Pakistan because Pakistan matters so much and in the Gambia because the Gambia matters so little.

A Closer Look at the Indian Giant

A nonspecialist such as myself must approach the giant with trepidation, especially if he tries to assess the giant's characteristics in a few pages when others have devoted a lifetime to a study of the subject. Yet it would be inadequate to do no more than try to fit India into a comparative framework with countries that are less than 1/250 of its size. There are, as we have seen, common explanations of democracy that apply to the giant as well as the dwarfs. Like Mauritius, India has found ways of bridging the gaps between different ethnic and religious groups. Like the West Indies, it benefited from a long preparation for independence. Like Jamaica, it has one of the narrowest gaps between rich and poor in the third world. Like Trinidad, its leaders have displayed an ability to step back from the brink of violent confrontations with democracy still intact. But this tells us little about the nature of democracy in a vast, heavily populated subcontinent.

In the smaller countries, we can take their existence as nation-states for granted and concentrate on explaining why they are democratic. Some of them are islands that few people want to split into smaller entities, and others with more artificial boundaries still enjoy the protection of an international community that would not tolerate encroachment by predators. At the same time, none seems likely to merge voluntarily into a larger nation, given the long record of failed federations in Africa, the West Indies, and Southeast Asia. In India we are faced with two interrelated questions: Why is India democratic? And why does India exist at all when so many other large states have been fragmented? Indeed, there is a third question as to what sort of democracy India is, and how far its features are a reflection of the desire to hold the country together.

One theme running, at least implicitly, through much of the literature is the extent to which Indian politics have become more "indigenous" in the half-century since independence. The constitution bequeathed by Britain remains intact, as do many customs and practices in society that endear India to British visitors, but the country has traveled a long road from the prime ministership of the secular, Harrow-educated Jawaharlal Nehru to rule by a party wanting to entrench the Hindu religion. Contrary to what modernization theorists had predicted, "modern" interest groups based on social class or occupation have lost prominence to groups based on caste, religion, and ethnicity (Chadda 2000: 224–225; Jenkins 1999: 216–217). Contrary to what many political scientists would predict, this has not destroyed democracy; in fact, it might even have provided the cement to hold it together. But it is a different sort of democracy from the Western model with its emphasis on the *individual* as a voter and citizen, with distinctive rights, and with an ability to make choices. It is a democracy in which ethnic, caste, and religious groups vie for power and influence at local and national levels, with any "will of the majority" less important than the relative bargaining power of different groups in relation to each other and to the state.

Attempts to explain the rise of primary (or "traditional") groups at the expense of the secondary (or "modern") would divert us too far from our task, but it is clearly a phenomenon that extends well beyond India. Disillusionment with the limited material achievements of politicians has driven many people from party activism to fundamentalist religion, from Latin America to Turkey and Iran, and a greater scarcity of resources has driven many people into ethnic bunkers as they seek to protect "their own" from outsiders. At the same time the global economic climate, and the deindustrialization it has wrought, has either weakened mass movements, as we saw in Latin America, or stunted their emergence. Of more immediate concern is the impact of the greater influence of primary groups on the democratic process. Chadda suggests that democracy becomes less a matter of upholding individual rights than of becoming inclusive through bargains to which the central state and its parts (defined by caste, ethnic, and religious identities) have consented (Chadda 2000: 224–225). Sharma suggests that the state and society have become victims of social fragmentation, with an emphasis on paying off various groups rather than redistributing resources. The state has attempted to expand its power but has failed to expand its capacity as it has become captured by dominant classes and castes (Sharma 1999: 5–13, 235–239). Jenkins, too, emphasizes the rise of ethnic/religious groups at the expense of the modern. Like Sharma, he notes the way in which economic liberalization, and the greater social inequality that it implies as the weak become less protected from market forces, is easier for the government to impose if the political process consists largely of bargaining over payoffs to traditional groups rather than responding to mass demands (Jenkins 1999: 214–217). Chadda suggests that equality and freedom are seen as equality and freedom between and for particular groups, not individuals (Chadda 2000: 230), but this concern with social inequality needs to be set against the United Nations Development Programme figures, which show the poorest 20 percent of the Indian population as receiving 8.1 percent of the country's income, as compared with 3.4 percent in Chile, a country singled out by Sharma for its redistributive policies (UNDP 2001: 182, 184; Sharma 1999: 235–238).

Some of the arguments above suggest a disappointment with Indian democracy, but Chadda takes the stoical view that democracy has adapted itself to the circumstances in which India finds itself and is now well-established, stable, and based on a broad consensus (Chadda 2000: 187). Sharma deplores the capture of the state by dominant classes and castes and demands "a careful nurturing of institutions more conducive to the promotion of developmental goals" (Sharma 1999: 239). Chadda is more willing to take the existing configuration of groups and institutions as given, and to examine the consolidation of democracy within the context of caste/ethnic/religious tensions and the strains that they put not just on democracy but on the survival of the nation-state. In other parts of the world, similar tensions have led to the breakup of the nation, as in the Balkans, or to prolonged violent conflicts, as in Rwanda and the Sudan. In India, Chadda argues, the aim of much violence is not to challenge the state "but to signal the need for a new power sharing agreement" while the coercion used by the state in troubled regions is used "to remove obstacles to the bargaining process," not to impose authoritarianism. The state tries to mediate between antagonistic ethnic and caste communities, and it shows restraint in the use of force (Chadda 2000: 230, 145).

One may question whether the motives of political actors are as clear as this analysis implies and whether the rioter or the politician dealing with mob violence thinks too deeply about the implications of their actions on the nation-state. But there is lurking somewhere a notion that the survival of the Indian nation matters to the vast majority of the population, and certainly to the people who represent them. This might be explained in instrumental terms, with even dissatisfied groups feeling that there would be much to lose if they were no longer part of the national and local bargaining processes that enable them to acquire resources they would not otherwise enjoy. But there may also be a sense of mass identification with the nation that is less prevalent in neighboring Pakistan and Sri Lanka. In Sri Lanka the transfer of power at independence was largely a matter of negotiation between Britain and the indigenous elite, with little mass involvement, and Pakistan is distinguished largely by the fact that it is "not India" rather than by a common culture. India, in contrast, has never lacked a strong sense of national identity, and the mass base built up by the Congress Party helped to spread the sense of identity beyond a narrow elite.

Any fragmentation of India would almost certainly weaken or destroy democracy, as the dominant groups in the secessionist areas would impose their own rules of the political game, unconstrained by the long-established custom and practice of the Indian polity. Any weakening of democracy would almost certainly threaten the survival of India, as the regions or groups gaining least from the center would have little incentive to remain in the fold. In these ways, democracy and national unity may reinforce each other, and explanations of democratic survival have to take into account both the specific interests of the diverse groups that interact in the political arena, and a collective notion that actions that threaten the survival of India as a whole should be avoided. The political arena may remain a violent and often corrupt place, but the imperatives of unity and democracy require the game to be played within rules that do not jeopardize the nation or democracy. We return to Rustow's thesis that democracy comes into being and survives because rival groups can neither defeat each other in battle nor avoid dependence on each other (Rustow 1973: 117–132).

Much of the discussion may suggest that it is the behavior of individual actors, especially those showing restraint in times of political crisis, that has preserved democracy in India; but the ability of India to survive the assassination of two prime ministers, numerous outbreaks of ethnic and religious violence, and the rise to power of a potentially divisive Hindu party suggests that the country may have evolved institutionalized ways of avoiding or defusing crises. The political actors are not entirely free agents; they have to work within accepted constraints if they are to survive. Just as Indira Gandhi could not have used her state of emergency in the 1970s to establish a one-party state, even if she had wanted to, so the ruling party two decades later could not impose Hindu domination without destroying the coalition that it led (Chadda 2000: 174, 183).

It is evident that the international political environment has been favorable to Indian nationhood and Indian democracy. Currie mentions that there has been little external subversion, in contrast to much of Central America, Ethiopia, and Angola, and that India's (not always justified) reputation for competent administration has helped to attract relatively generous World Bank assistance (Currie 1996: 791–793, 799–800). This may be partly because India is too large to be bullied, yet it may also be important that India had become part of the furniture of international politics before much of the third world had gained independence and had become a leader of the nonaligned movement by the time most of the third world solidified. The West valued India for its stability; the East valued it for its anti-imperialism. An India fragmented into unstable, authoritarian states would have served few external interests.

Conclusion

Is it possible to offer any general explanations for the survival of democracy in our varied countries? There is room for argument about whether apparently common features are causes, effects, or symptoms, but at least four variables suggest some common ground: (1) the minimal disruption associated with the transfer of power at independence; (2) the qualities of national leaders; (3) the limited degree of political polarization; and (4) the existence of state structures that were strong enough to maintain stability without being strong enough to suppress dissent.

The conventional wisdom is that a lengthy transition to independence, as in India and the West Indies, during which a strong institutional structure can develop, is conducive to democracy. It is difficult to refute such a contention, but it is easy to overlook countries such as Botswana and Papua

New Guinea at the opposite extreme, where preparations for independence were much more hasty than in countries with a longer history of nationalist agitation, such as Ghana and Nigeria. The former countries were almost free riders that gained independence unexpectedly easily after the independence of the larger colonies had made the preservation of an empire less tenable. Yet their brief preparation for independence gave them the advantage of not having nationalist parties that seriously challenged the older traditional and bureaucratic elites and that elsewhere propelled to the top politicians who were inexperienced in government yet intolerant of opposition. Paradoxically, there appears to have been greater political continuity in the extreme cases of the very long preparations for independence, where politicians and parties had had time to establish effective power bases, and the very short preparations, where older elites were sufficiently confident of their authority to permit dissent. It is in the intermediate cases that democracy has often fared worst, with nationalist politicians who had built up their parties in the 1950s, relying on patronage rather than institutionalized support, then resorting to authoritarianism to retain control as the resources for patronage dried up.

Allied with the "right" circumstances for the transfer of power was the quality of the leaders who took over the reins after independence. Enjoying the support of parties that were either deeply rooted in society or that had not needed to overreach themselves in appealing for mass support, was undoubtedly an advantage. But the qualities of a Nehru or a Khama, or of the broader party elites of the West Indies who commanded public respect and were committed to the democratic ideal, were important in nurturing democracy in its early years.

Limited political polarization is likely to help the democratic process in any country by making the contrast between winning and losing less stark. The question of why polarization is limited is a difficult one to unravel. The smallness of the countries, other than India, may help by making adversaries less remote, as does the inability of any one group to win power without cooperating with others. But the nature of political competition also depends on the perceived interests of different groups and the resources for which they are competing. We have suggested that the developmental position of the continuous democracies, in between the most industrialized countries and the poorest third world countries, has provided governments with sufficient resources to offer something in return for votes, yet without the divisive effects of the sharper class divisions that frequently go with development, as in much of South America. The "right" geographical boundaries, ethnic mix, and economic conditions may thus make democratic development easier, but much will still depend on governments using the resources in what is seen to be an equitable way. Statistics and empirical studies suggest that the leaders of continuous democracies have been more socially concerned and probably less self-seeking than authoritarian rulers, though the evidence is more impressionistic than conclusive. It may be argued that democratic constraints leave rulers with little choice in these matters, but in cases where democracy is not deeply entrenched we return to the importance of political leaders setting the standards that help to sustain democracy.

On the power of the state and political institutions, there is again the argument that the ingredients that can sustain democracy can also destroy it if they are overabundant. The general point is made effectively by Heper in his observations on weak institutions in Spanish Latin America and strong institutions in Turkey, both of which have done democracy more harm than good (Heper 1991: 196–201). Without a broadly and deeply based dominant party and a strong bureaucracy, India would have disintegrated long ago, but if these institutions had been even stronger they might been more tempted to pursue authoritarian solutions. In the case of India, a culturally diverse civil society that contained many nonpolitical centers of power helped to keep such tendencies in check. India may seem out of place in the whole analysis, given its enormous size and complexity, yet the laws of political science may apply to giants and dwarfs alike, just as the laws of gravity do. The giant may make a more spectacular crash if he tumbles, but he may take avoiding action to keep his balance in a way similar to smaller creatures.

In the smaller continuous democracies, as in India, a balance between the relative powers of state and civil society is important for democracy. President Kwame Nkrumah had advised Ghanaians to "Seek ye first the political kingdom and all other things shall be added"—a recipe for a strong, and ultimately authoritarian, state. It is difficult to imagine the leaders of Botswana or the West Indies offering such advice, for they have never been in a position to offer "all other things" given the constraints of societies that contain more autonomous centers of power.

In the end, the search for a cause of the survival of democracy may prove fruitless. Just as we may believe that a cause has been unearthed, nagging doubts set in as to whether it is really a symptom or a consequence or whether a comparable phenomenon elsewhere is not compatible with authoritarianism. Yet there does appear to be a combination of circumstances arising from historical or political accident or political will that helps to reinforce democracy. One has only to look at the opposites to emphasize the point. A major break in political continuity at independence, incompetent or self-seeking leaders, extreme polarization, abject poverty, and a state too weak to regulate political competition or so strong as to suppress competition are all inimical to democracy. A country able to avoid these eventualities in its formative years may, but is by no means sure to, see democracy prosper. The extent of political choice in terms of parties, personnel, and policies may be too narrow for many tastes, and mass poverty and domination by economic elites may continue alongside the electoral process, but at least the structures are in place on which future democrats may be able to build.

7

External Influences on Democratization

While external influences will often be significant causes of third wave democratisations, the processes themselves were overwhelmingly indigenous. (Huntington 1991–1992: 583)

Africans continue to resist international pressures. Donors have encountered considerable difficulty in ensuring that African governments adhere to economic reform agreements. . . . There is no reason to expect recipient governments to comply any more fully with externally imposed political reform commitments. (Bratton and van de Walle 1997: 32)

The proposition that people cannot be forced to be free has long been accepted. Although imposing authoritarian rule on weaker countries, whether directly or by proxy, has seldom been a problem, the notion that one can facilitate the emergence of such a complex process as democracy from outside is more contentious. The experience of decolonization certainly gave democrats few grounds for hope, as most of the democratic constitutions established at independence were torn up or ignored within a decade. Yet the existence of Huntington's "third wave democratizations" is impossible to deny—the first and second waves having begun with the French and American Revolutions in the eighteenth century and with Indian independence in 1947 (Huntington 1991). In the mid-1980s few countries in Africa or Latin America had governments chosen through competitive elections. Today only a minority of governments are not chosen in that way. In Asia, the countries of South Korea, Taiwan, Nepal, the Philippines, Bangladesh, and Indonesia have all emerged from authoritarian rule, and Thailand appears to have moved away from alternation between democracy and military government. I shall postpone any discussion of the quality of democracy, and of whether the occurrence of relatively free and fair elections is sufficient for a country to be characterized as democratic, but the changes that have occurred are significant enough in themselves to warrant explanation.

Bratton and van de Walle suggest that the variations in the nature and extent of democratization have been so great that external explanations by themselves are insufficient (Bratton and van de Walle 1997: 30). Yet one could equally argue that a process so widespread must be explained in terms of something more than different sets of indigenous circumstances in scores of different countries. This chapter considers the scope that existed for effective external influence and the ways in which such influence has been wielded. We shall look at the response of third world countries to external pressures and at the processes by which internal and external forces have interacted. Examples will be taken from tropical Africa, Asia, and Latin America. I have avoided the case of South Africa on the grounds that the issue there was not so much democratization in the narrow sense but the existence of a largely democratic process from which 80 percent of the population were excluded on account of their color.

The Inevitability of Democracy?

The Democratic Ideal

In October 2001 the British prime minister offered to write off much third world debt, practice free trade, and train African soldiers if Africa would practice democracy, end human rights abuses, bad government and corruption, and work to secure peace agreements (MacAskill and Norton-Taylor 2001: 3). A few weeks later, a summit meeting of African leaders demanded more aid and foreign investment and a lifting of trade barriers that were impeding African exports. In return, they committed themselves to establishing clean, accountable government and to ending human rights abuses and internal wars. The communiqué received strong endorsement from the British prime minister, the European Union (EU), and the G8 countries (McGreal 2001: 19). These statements of intent had a pedigree that stretched back at least a decade. In 1999 the African, Caribbean and Pacific (ACP) countries issued the Santo Domingo Declaration of objectives, which included the integration of their countries into the world economy, the protection of human rights, the conservation of the environment, sustainable development, the eradication of poverty, and the consolidation of democracy (ACP Group of States 1999). Four years earlier, the Organization for Economic Cooperation and Development (OECD), representing some of the wealthiest countries in the world, committed itself to combating poverty, reducing social inequalities, good governance, the protection of human rights, the rule of law, sustainable environmental practice, and limiting military expenditure (Mohiddin 1998: 9–10). In the same year the ACP countries and the EU agreed on the desirability of good governance, the rule of law, and human rights (Arts and Byron 1997: 77).

The World Bank had by this time become an enthusiastic friend of the poor and supporter of participation and decentralization. In Uganda it recommended the "delivery of key services to the poor" and emphasized the need to "ensure that the poor are able to participate equitably in [economic] growth" (World Bank 1993: 137). And in 1991 the Commonwealth Heads of Government signed the Harare Declaration that emphasized the promotion of democracy, human rights, and equality for women (Ravenhill 1995: 102). In the Americas, too, rich and poor countries were apparently united in their commitment to democracy. In 1991 the Organization of American States (OAS) agreed that collective action might be taken if there was any interruption of the constitutional order (Steves 2001: 91).

Democracy as Practical Politics

Do all these statements reflect the end of history, when the rulers of rich and poor countries alike reach a consensus on the desirability of democracy and the virtues associated with it? Even if the ideal of democracy was not explicitly rejected in earlier times, the leaders of third world countries might have seen it as less important than such goals as development, socialism, or nation building, while Western leaders might have been more concerned with political stability and checking the rise of communism in the third world. If democracy got in the way of these objectives, democracy might be the loser. Skeptics might question the sincerity of some of the recent commitments. Do third world rulers really believe in democracy, or do they merely need to pay lip service to it in order to attract aid and investment? Are Western countries really concerned about social equality, human rights, and a sustainable environment (none of which had a high priority under colonial rule), or do they need to pay lip service to these objectives to legitimize their continued world domination and the terms on which they offer aid and investment? On these arguments, democracy might emerge as the lowest common denominator, but it is still remarkable that few other common denominators, not even the free market, can attract the same degree of approval.

A less cynical approach might be to echo Winston Churchill's observation that democracy is the worst possible form of government, except for all the other forms. People within third world countries who have experienced the brutality of authoritarian rule, and the greed and vanity of the rulers, might regard even the worst form of democracy as preferable, while Western leaders with doubts about the feasibility of democracy in the third world might still feel that authoritarianism is a recipe for the continued misuse of aid. The survival of an authoritarian government depends not on the votes of the masses but on satisfying a clientele of businesspeople, soldiers, and bureaucrats. It is therefore rational for authoritarian rulers to spend money on lucrative projects for building hotels, ministerial residences, or factories relying on imported raw materials rather than on providing clean water, feeder roads, or agricultural education. The former projects did little to promote economic regeneration, so aid and investment contributed to growing debts and diminishing ability to repay them (though the worsening terms of trade exacerbated the problem in many countries). In the absence of public accountability, corruption was able to flourish, and this led to the further unproductive use of resources.

It is no coincidence that the earliest Western pressure on third world governments, especially from the international financial institutions (IFIs), was not directly for democratization but for good governance, which implied a competent, prudent, and honest use of resources to ensure that foreign aid did not seep away. This was implicit in many of the International Monetary Fund's (IMF) structural adjustment programs (SAPs) in the 1980s, which required a more careful monitoring of the disbursement of funds. Given their nominally nonpolitical status, the IMF and the World Bank could only demand sound administration rather than democracy, but Western governments began to see the link between authoritarian government and misspending, corruption, and lack of accountability. Democratic governments, in contrast, have to face the wrath of parliaments, a critical press, or voters wanting value for money, so democrats are less able to misuse resources. Democracy thus became a basic ingredient in prescriptions for good governance. Whether democratic governments do actually perform better is another matter, though one could at least make a case that no democratic leader has devoted as much of a country's resources to self-aggrandizement as General Bokassa in the Central African Republic or General Mobutu in the Congo, and few have dissipated human resources (quite apart from any humanitarian considerations) by slaughtering as many of their citizens as General Amin in Uganda or General Pinochet in Chile.

Democracy and the Demise of the Second World

While the West was losing patience with authoritarian governments in the third world, developments in the second world helped to tip the balance further in favor of democracy. The disintegration of the Soviet bloc left not only a power vacuum but also an ideological vacuum. There were few third world governments that really tried to emulate the Soviet model, if only because they lacked the resources for building an all-embracing totalitarian party or a state-controlled command economy. However, several third world leaders defended the institution of the one-party state on the grounds that it was a driving force for rapid development, free of the divisive effects of opposition and dissent. This defense looked increasingly threadbare as the actual plight of the Eastern European countries was revealed. Opposition politicians within third world countries were quick to exploit the nakedness of the one-party state, as we shall see in the next chapter.

As far as the external impact was concerned, Western countries favoring a capitalist economy at home and abroad now had less to fear from the challenge of actual or incipient left-wing parties that might threaten the economic order. Such a challenge had seldom been a problem in Africa, where the social structure was not generally conducive to the rise of radical parties, but it had been a Western fear in much of Latin America and parts of Asia. Authoritarian governments had been openly or tacitly supported in the 1970s and 1980s—for fear of the election of a pro-Soviet alternative—in most of Central America, Brazil, Chile, Indonesia, and the Philippines. The repugnance of these governments, whether in terms of brutality or incompetence, needs little elaboration, and by the late 1980s and early 1990s there were few reasons for the West to continue to sustain them now that the "communist threat" had gone.

Many historians might see the fall of the Berlin Wall in 1989 as marking the end of the Cold War, yet the plausibility of the Soviet Union fermenting revolutions in third world countries had looked increasingly remote by earlier in the decade. Even those opposition activists who favored a socialist economy recognized that, to end authoritarian rule, they would have to work within a broader coalition and join in demanding the bourgeois institution of free elections. Burgess notes the emergence of a pro-American opposition in Latin American countries in the 1980s (Burgess 2001: 62–63), and Drake notes that as early as Ronald Reagan's presidency, the United States was more willing to accept the growing democratic tide in Latin America (Drake 1994: 18). If costly support for repression or civil wars against insurgents could be abandoned with minimal risk of free elections producing governments hostile to the United States, support for democratization made good sense. None of this is to underestimate the strength of pro-democracy movements within the third world countries, but the unwillingness of the West to continue to underwrite the dictators often hastened their demise. It also made a peaceful transfer of power more likely than a fight to the death, which might have been less conducive to any subsequent democracy.

Democracy and Globalization

A further explanation of the external impact on the rise of democracy is economic. Indeed, there are at least three strands of economic change that have become interwoven: globalization, the growth of free market policies (sometimes confusingly referred to as neoliberalism, though they are opposed by many who regard themselves as liberals), and the manipulation of the global economy by the most powerful countries and the institutions that they dominate.

What is significant about globalization from our point of view is that national frontiers can now be crossed more easily and subject to a diminishing

ability of national governments to control such movements. The questions
of whether the volume of world trade has increased to a greater extent than
the level of production, or whether countries are more dependent on the
world economy than formerly, are less important. Most third world countries have always been heavily dependent on foreign trade, often relying on
the export of a few primary products such as coffee, cocoa, or copper, and
importing most of their manufactured goods. What is new is their diminishing ability to control movements across their frontiers—movement not
just in the form of conventional trade but of mass media, fundamentalist
religions, illicit weapons and drugs, terrorists, and fashions in clothing and
music. People may gain access to opinions their leaders do not wish them
to hear and acquire a taste for "decadent" lifestyles that do not conform to
their leaders' wishes. Such access is helped by satellite television and foreign newspapers. At the same time, those who wish to challenge authority
now have greater access to weapons that may help them in this process.
Many countries in the 1970s and 1980s had undergone civil wars that were
subplots within the Cold War, using arms supplied by rival Cold War pro-
tagonists. They have subsequently been destabilized by armed groups with
less coherent objectives, using weapons that are now supplied largely from
Eastern Europe out of the motive of profit rather than ideology. None of
these developments are necessarily good for democracy, but they are almost
all bad for authoritarianism, as they imply a loss of state control over society—a theme in Chapter 5.

By themselves, the freer movement of ideas, fashions, and weapons might
be a source of annoyance to authoritarian rulers without necessarily precip-
itating their downfall, but when the freer market in conventional trade and
investment is added, the impact can be fatal. The free market ideology
existed long before globalization, having found its first major prophet in
Adam Smith in the eighteenth century. It was perfectly plausible to believe
that society would benefit from a minimum of state regulation of manufacturing and trade even in the days when foreign competition was constrained
by the speed and capacity of sailing ships. If one can have a free market
without globalization, the question of whether one can have globalization
without a free market is more complicated. One could conceivably have a
global economy in which trade was mainly between state corporations that
used their profits to promote infrastructural development and social welfare, but it seems implausible in practice.

The global economy increases citizens' awareness of the goods and
services available in other parts of the world, and it increases the ability of
businesses to trade and invest beyond their shores. The whims of a consumer in Britain can be satisfied by a South African company growing
flowers in Tanzania and flying them to London in a matter of hours. In earlier times the Tanzanian government might have decided that such a use of

resources was less sensible than using the land to grow food for an impoverished population, but it is now unlikely to turn away the employment and investment opportunities that the foreign company brings. If a government accepts the desirability of foreign investment in principle but tries to regulate it out of concern for working conditions, public health, the conservation of the environment, or the protection of indigenous production, the foreign firm is likely to take its business to a country where such restrictions are less onerous. In these ways, formerly authoritarian governments find that their control over events within their frontiers is now much more limited. Power is lost to foreign businesses, and governments are less able to build support through patronage in such areas as disbursing import licenses, employing favored individuals in state corporations, or locating production in areas that suit the ruling party or favored ethnic groups. I am not arguing that the power has been lost altogether, and some governments like that in Kenya continue to fight a rearguard action to control the flow of resources, but the general trend is for large sectors of third world populations to become less dependent on the decisions of their political masters.

In some cases the greater integration of the third world economies into the global market was the result of deliberate decisions by third world authoritarians, especially the military governments in Latin America. In Chile, for example, there was a wholesale privatization of manufacturing industries, health care, pension funds, and education; state regulation of investment and business was reduced, the economy was increasingly opened to foreign competition, and long-established labor and welfare laws were repealed (Pinkney 1990: 59). Yet even where the free market policies were apparently homegrown, the external element was present in the sense that many of the military rulers had been socialized through training in U.S. military academies and employed "Chicago School" economists who had imbibed the free market gospel in the United States.

In most of tropical Africa and Asia, the market policies were undertaken more reluctantly as a requirement of the SAPs. This brings us to the third strand of the economic changes. The "free market" may be nominally free in the sense that decisions on industrial location, investment, production, and prices depend on market forces, but behind these forces there is often the invisible (or sometimes not so invisible) hand of Western governments and the institutions that they dominate, such as the IMF, the World Bank, the World Trade Organization (WTO), and the EU. The conditions imposed by the IMF might look like little more than the prudent conditions that any creditor would impose to ensure the repayment of debts, though even these conditions can have a substantial effect on the power bases of governments if they require privatization and cuts in public services and public sector employment. But the edicts from the other institutions may constrain national governments still further. The WTO demands its own version of "free trade" in which third world countries are required to dismantle import restrictions, while Europe and North America continue to subsidize the production of crops such as sugar beets to the detriment of third world exporters. The weak bargaining position of third world countries leaves them with little influence over these decisions and often drives them into deals that worsen their position still further. The Mauritanian government raised funds to pay its debts by selling its right to fish its own waters to the EU. Even then the government was too weak to enforce the details of the agreement so that European boats (subsidized by their own governments) allegedly used illegal nets that trawled everything on the seabed and thus endangered the survival of any remaining fish stocks (Willsher 2001: 15).

There may be no obvious link between these developments and the demise of authoritarian governments. Such governments might, especially in the short term, act as collaborators with powerful external forces without relaxing their grip on their own citizens. But the loss of state powers of patronage, as power is lost to foreign businesses, foreign institutions, and the indigenous private sector and nongovernmental organizations (NGOs), is likely to take its toll. Privatization may have the immediate effect of enabling a government to decide which clients to enrich, yet this, too, may ultimately add to the range of new centers of power autonomous from the state.

A freer media facilitated by globalization exposes people to information and opinions their government does not wish them to hear, at least in urban areas, and the legalization of opposition parties often becomes mandatory as a condition of continued aid. Against this background, the dispersion of economic power may then provide the means for the actual creation of opposition parties and pressure groups, as people's livelihoods depend less on the state. But, rooted in the private and voluntary sectors or the professions, these are not likely to be the sort of radical groups that formerly displeased Western governments in countries such as Chile, Guatemala, and Indonesia. What has emerged in much of the third world is a series of moderate multiparty systems that pose little threat to business or to the global order and therefore meet with the approval, and often encouragement, of external powers. This implies party systems dominated by the middle class.

For the poorest sections of society, the immediate effect of globalization and subservience to market forces was to plunge them into greater poverty as unemployment rose, wages fell, and welfare benefits were lost. But even among the poor, such deprivation did not generally give rise to revolutionary movements, as the Marxist alternative was now under a cloud. It did make for greater dissatisfaction with the current authoritarian rulers who seemed unable to provide either bread or freedom. Authoritarianism was now under attack from yet another quarter, but it was an attack that was blunted by new realities.

While the move from interventionist economies to freer markets frequently undermined authoritarian rule, there is more room for argument about whether a market economy is an essential basis for democracy. Proponents of this view point out that no command economy has ever existed alongside democratic government and often suggest that choice in the polling booth and choice in the marketplace are complementary elements in a free society. On the first point, one might respond that there are now very few countries in the world beyond Cuba and North Korea that have tried to remain outside the global market, yet many countries still lack democratic polities, including China and most of the wealthy Arab oil kingdoms. Authoritarian rulers, as well as democrats, have been able to claim the market as part of their moral high ground. Whitehead suggested that the free market had an appeal to military rulers in Latin America because it offered a clear system of rewards and punishments, with the latter falling mainly on the enemy, and a redistribution of resources from vanquished to victor (Whitehead 1985: 12–15). The market could echo the discipline of the parade ground, with defaulters penalized for their improvidence, as well as echoing the freedom of the bazaar. What probably matters more than the largely obsolete conflict between capitalism and socialism is the diversity within the (now overwhelming) capitalist world. Countries such as Botswana and Mauritius can work within a capitalist framework to secure a degree of social provision that may give democratic legitimacy to their governments, while others such as the Central American republics (excepting Costa Rica) or Indonesia may use the economy to enhance elite privileges and may have to rely more on coercion than democratic consent.

Full Circle: From Policies Back to Ideology

In economics, as in politics, external pressures do not imply that only one path may be followed, but they do suggest that many paths are now ruled out of bounds. Countries wanting Western aid may occasionally stray along these forbidden paths if their bargaining position is strong enough, but most will be punished with loss of aid if they stray too far. For the most part, acceptance of the free market and the global economy—and a pluralist political system—are minimal requirements, even if variations are possible within these guidelines. As we saw in the opening quotes of this chapter, not even the third world leaders offer any radical alternatives to the agenda of economic and political liberalization. For the West, the imposition of democracy may be seen as part of the spoils of victory in the Cold War, just as the imposition of Christianity represented the spoils of victory in the Crusades. The rejection of democracy in the third world, whether in rhetorical terms or in practice, might give greater aid and comfort to antidemocratic forces in the West. There is no longer the obvious communist alternative, but the growth of religious fundamentalism, violent nationalism, or the implosion of states into anarchy, as in Liberia, Sierra Leone, and Somalia, are all possibilities. These in turn can lead to greater international instability, the loss of markets, and attempts at mass migration out of third world countries to avoid chaos or persecution. Attempts to inculcate democratic values and practices may make sense from a Western point of view as a means to more competent government making better use of Western aid, but beyond that looms the larger question of legitimate bases of authority. Those who claimed that the terrorists who bombed the World Trade Center in New York in 2001 were motivated by a hatred of Western democracy may have overlooked a complex range of motives and values. Nevertheless, the conclusion might still be that any attempt to strengthen the hold of Western values on the rest of the world would make the West more secure from any further backlash from those who are dissatisfied with the current global order.

From Exporters of Democracy to Importers:
The Third World Reception

The official pronouncements from third world governments, individually and collectively, suggest enthusiasm for democracy. Yet are the commitment and the ability to put democracy into practice really there? An immediate response might be that many communities in Africa and Asia functioned in a democratic way long before European colonization and that Europeans have no business lecturing the third world on the subject, especially in view of the ways in which they suppressed popular participation during colonial rule and supported authoritarian rule afterward. But as was suggested in Chapter 3, the experience of a democratic ethos in nomadic communities or small settlements in earlier times offers only very limited guidance as to how to run a modern nation-state that is normally much larger, is culturally more heterogeneous, and provides a more complex range of services. The juxtaposition of precolonial experiences (or myths) and the current predicament of the third world can lead to a variety of expectations about third world responses to recent external attempts to encourage democratization. One response is to point to the inappropriateness of what is crudely called the "Westminster model," though similar models may be found in other European capitals and in Washington.

> Democracy by debate/vote/majority rule presupposes Western individualism; democracy by dialogue/consensus/common rule would be more compatible with non-Western we-cultures. (Galtung 2000: 145)

Sandbrook defined liberal democracy as "a political system charac-terised by regular and free elections in which politicians organised into parties compete to form a government, by the right of virtually all adult citizens to vote, and by guarantees of a range of familiar political and civil rights." Others would prefer a broader definition of democracy so as to involve key ideals such as political choice, social equality and empower-ment. Other sources of democratic ideals, and institutions, within Africa include the democratic aspirations of some key nationalist figures, such as Leopold Senghor who evoked the African idea of democracy as involving the *palaver,* dialogue or discussion, followed by unanimity of decisions. More contemporary academic annals have pointed to the positive effects of ethnic heterogeneity, and the surprising resilience of democratic politi-cal culture or a democratic ethic underneath the authoritarian model. (Riley 1992: 540, quoting Sandbrook 1988)

Ake was another writer who saw the Western version of democracy as too individualistic and confrontational. His vision of African democracy included greater control over decisionmaking beyond electoral choice; a greater decentralization of power; social and economic as well as political rights; and collective as well as individual rights (Ake 1996: 132.) In Asia, Shin suggests that Confucianism does not endorse individual freedom, human rights, or the rule of law. It emphasizes the rule of man, the supremacy of the group over the individual, family over community, duties over rights, and personal wisdom over impersonal law (Shin 1999: 254); while Diamond argues that liberal democracy in Asia does not require "the exalted status of individual rights that obtains in Western Europe and . . . the United States" (Diamond 1999a: 15.)

An appeal to African or Asian tradition can, of course, be used by the demagogue to justify a range of authoritarian practices, just as democratic values can be invoked to justify antisocial behavior or appeals to the low-est human instincts if they are deemed to be matters of individual freedom or a reflection of the wishes of the majority. Politicians who wish to pervert the political process are seldom short of justifications. Chan emphasizes the need to distinguish between violations of human rights motivated by the self-interest of rulers and violations motivated by ideological or cultural beliefs shared by much of society on matters such as religious freedom, marriage rights, the death penalty, homosexuality, abortion, freedom of expression (in the nonpolitical sphere), and minority rights (Chan 1998: 29–30). This brings us to the question of whether recourse to indigenous values and myths can help to build a model of democracy different from that offered by the West, for those who genuinely want it, and whether they will be able to reject or modify Western pressures in the process. In contrast to Galtung and Riley, Allison suggests that Africans have had enough of "the legend of the palaver tree," or the myth of monolithic consensus evolved by debate and requiring no party competition. They reject the claims of purely African ideas of democracy in favor of universal (Western) forms. In short, he argues, what they want is what the West has already got (Allison 1994: 15–16). Austin, too, sees contact with the West as a necessary point of departure rather than the reconstruction of an earlier culture: "The colonial state is the indispensable framework for any prospect of democratic government that may emerge. There is no alternative in either African tradition or pan-Africanist sentiment" (Austin 1993: 204.)

While African and Asian states wrestle with the relative merits of precolonial tradition and postcolonial reality, such a debate is missing from Latin America where the vast majority of the population is descended from migrants from other continents. Such democratic tradition as Latin America enjoys evolved not from either the palaver tree or the colonial office but from the interaction between groups within well-established nation-states. One can argue about which groups were crucial at which time and place, but for the most part the expansion of democracy was a means of resolving conflicts between old-established and rising social groups, as it was in much of Western Europe (see especially Stephens 1989: 281–352; and Diamond et al. 1999: 38). The problem for aspiring democrats since the 1970s has been not so much one of choosing between traditional indigenous and Western values as of trying to reconcile well-worn democratic structures with a new socioeconomic environment in which the previously dominant social groups are now in decline. With deindustrialization, corporatism has largely disappeared, but a democracy based around the affluent, educated, assertive citizen has not arrived.

What does all this tell us about the prospects for "imported" democracy, or at least imported components of democracy, when it arrives at the frontiers of third world countries? Which parts of the package will be accepted, which will be discarded, and which will be used for purposes very different from those intended by the exporters? The responses to these questions are summarized under the headings of "Perversion," "Adaptation," and "Rejection."

Perversion

> The Danish Government . . . has been sponsoring visits to Copenhagen by Nepalese parliamentarians so they can observe a democratic legislature at work. . . . When I asked a senior staff member of the Nepalese Parliament what he saw as the effects of these trips, a different view emerged. With every trip to a foreign parliament in an affluent country, he said, the members of Nepal's Parliament are more impressed by the luxurious offices, cars and fancy equipment, and they return to Nepal yet more determined to increase still further their own perquisites and benefits—or simply to steal more money—so that they can live like "real" parliamentarians. (Carothers 1999: 201)

In such ways are Western attempts to foster democracy transformed into means of strengthening third world elites. Increasing the wealth and privileges of Nepalese members of Parliament (MPs) may not, by itself, be a threat to democracy, but Western political structures exported to third world countries can often be used as instruments of authoritarianism. The U.S. presidential system, with its separation of powers and checks and balances, has been used in much of Latin America as a means of concentrating power in the hands of one man, with no adequate civil society or independent judges or legislators to curb his authority. Parliamentary or quasi-parliamentary systems such as those in Europe—which ensure that an elected legislature can scrutinize and ultimately remove the executive—have been used in Africa to ensure effective executive control over docile parliaments. A "first past the post" electoral system has enabled President Daniel arap Moi to continue his rule in Kenya with the support of less than 40 percent of the electorate. In Zanzibar a similar system left the opposition party with 49.8 percent of the vote in 1995, after a count had been hotly disputed and the ruling party had rejected any suggestion of power sharing—a far cry from the myth of seeking consensus rather than counting heads.

Among the informal political institutions that the West may seek to encourage, political parties might be seen as an essential bridge between the government and the ordinary citizen. Yet in Thailand, McCargo speaks of the rise of professional rather than mass membership parties, dominated by professional politicians and technocrats, with few members, personalized leadership, funded by interest groups, campaigning around particular issues, and adhering to no ideologies (McCargo 1997: 130). In Ghana a military government was able to justify the banning of political parties on the grounds that "historical data and journalistic accounts abound as to the acrimony, the near disintegration of Ghana and the fanning of discordant ethnic feeling as a result of party politics" (Ghana 1977: 33). In Uganda, the current rulers continue to prohibit party politics in view of the violence that parties based on ethnic and religious affiliations had allegedly created in the past. In Latin America, Espindola suggests, "Political parties can hardly be active components of civil society, articulating demands, channelling participation, influencing decisions; they become state institutions to legitimise the regime, socialising decisions in which they have had little influence, managing electoral processes as system maintaining mechanisms" (Espindola 1997: 14).

None of this is to argue that it is wrong for external powers to encourage the adoption of presidential or parliamentary constitutions or to support the development of political parties and competitive elections, still less to argue that the prospects for democracy would be enhanced if these institutions did not exist. But experience does suggest that exporting or encouraging the indigenous growth of such institutions will be insufficient in the absence of at least some of the cultural, social, and economic requisites for democracy that earlier writers such as Lipset and Rustow highlighted.

Adaptation

More optimistic democrats might see the imported packages or raw materials as useful complements to indigenous cultures and structures. President Léopold Sédar Senghor of Senegal, whose views on palaver, dialogue, and discussion were quoted earlier, may not always have practiced what he preached, but his rule was certainly less autocratic than that of many of his neighbors. Similarly, President Julius Nyerere's rule in Tanzania might be criticized for its economic ineptitude and its intolerance of organized opposition, but Nyerere did attempt to use his single party to encourage mass participation and the choice of MPs through intraparty competition. If this was consensus politics at work, it might have been a consensus that was too much imposed from above to suit many purists. But, coupled with an egalitarian ethos that prevented party and government leaders from amassing large fortunes, it did help to hold a large country together with a minimum of coercion. President Yoweri Museveni's no-party state in Uganda, legitimized by an 80 percent vote in a referendum in 2000, might be seen as seeking similar objectives to Nyerere's one-party state. Whatever the ulterior motives in terms of the current rulers wanting to retain power, one could see the no-party state as an attempt to avoid the violence and divisiveness of previous multiparty competition, while still keeping open the channels of electoral choice and political participation, especially at the local level.

In the case of India, we have noted the way in which political parties, pressure groups, and governmental structures have become increasingly "indigenized" since independence, with secular pressure groups based on class and occupational interests giving way increasingly to demands based on caste, ethnicity, and religion. And throughout most of the actual or aspiring democracies of Asia, the parts of the democratic package regarded as most relevant have been retained or adapted, while those that are considered less compatible with indigenous culture, such as individual rather than collective rights, have been put to one side or discarded. Our concern here is neither to approve nor to condemn such adaptations but merely to note that political actors who accept the broad principles implicit in democracy, in terms of electoral competition, political participation, and accountable government restrained from arbitrary power, may from choice or necessity deviate from the forms of democracy generally favored in the West. This may then lead to friction if Western powers decide that the deviation has gone beyond acceptable limits, whether it is Uganda's refusal to permit party politics or Malaysia's imprisonment of an allegedly homosexual minister.

Rejection

It is unusual for a country committed to pluralist democracy to reject outright what the West regards as basic democratic institutions, though political parties have sometimes been an exception. What happens more frequently is that little positive attempt is made to adapt the institutions to what might be regarded as the requirements of democracy. This is different from, though it may blur into, what we have termed "perversion." Perversion implies deliberately using an institution to strengthen undemocratic forces, such as using the election of a president to give greater legitimacy to his authoritarian tendencies. Rejection is used here to mean that the institution remains largely oblivious to the democratic tide lapping around it, without necessarily using the existence of democracy to advance its own ends. An obvious example would be third world bureaucracies, which often pay scant regard to any mandate from the people that politicians claim to enjoy and whose members may have little notion of a role as servants of the wider public. It would be unduly harsh to tar all bureaucrats with the same brush, especially for an academic who has tried the patience of many bureaucrats yet come away with invaluable information and insights. But most third world bureaucracies were created before the democratic institutions, and in many colonies they enjoyed substantial power long before elected politicians came on the scene, let alone citizens with a sense of their own rights. Two quotations from Ghana suggest the free-floating nature of the bureaucracy:

> Authority is . . . a basic problem in the sense that many officials do not always do what they are told. They do not comply with the routines of their official duties, and do not accept the goals or the hierarchy of the organisation as, at least, the parameters within which they might pursue their interests. (Crook 1983: 188)
>
> Heavy sums have been voted annually by previous governments for road maintenance. No one knows how such maintenance votes have been used in the past and it may be asking too much of the Ghana Highways Authority to justify the expenditure made and also their very existence. (*Legon Observer,* 21 November 1980, quoting President Hilla Limann)

An Indian civil servant was asked by a television interviewer whether, as a human being, he felt concerned about the closure of a refuge for street children who had nowhere else to go. He replied, "I am not a human being. I am a public employee."

Other groups on the state payroll may also see democracy as an intrusion that should make only a minimal difference to their daily lives. An occasional judicial verdict may remind politicians that they are not above the law, but it requires a courageous judge to trespass too far into political territory. Under colonial rule, little distinction had been made between upholding the law and upholding the authority of the state and its officers, and there has been no major departure from this trend. In the case of the police, we have noted O'Donnell's description of the torture and execution of crime suspects from poor or otherwise stigmatized sectors in Latin America

(O'Donnell 1993: 1358–1359). It would be unfair to condemn police forces as a whole, but again there does not seem to have been much consideration of how the role of the police might require adaptation to democratic conditions. In the case of both the civil service and the police (though probably not the judges), the problem has been exacerbated by falling, and irregularly paid, real wages. This has encouraged the extraction of bribes, often from the poorest sections of the community, in order to make ends meet, and this does little to enhance any notion of public service.

Having explored the role of the armed forces in previous chapters, it would be foolish to say that nothing has changed with democratization. Very few countries now live under military rule, and any threats of further military intervention will ring increasingly hollow as few soldiers now appear to want the burden of political office, few civilians want them to bear the burden, and many Western governments would cut off aid if the burden were taken up. Yet soldiers, like civil servants, often have a free-floating role that shields them from democratic control, whether in taking a large share of the national budget with minimal justification, exercising a free hand in dealing with internal rebellion, or using the occupation of other countries (whether as invaders or peacekeepers) as a lucrative source of income.

These apparent rejections of democratic norms are not necessarily a matter of deliberate defiance. It might be better to think of the word "rejection" in the same sense as a human body rejecting an organ transplant. There may be no malicious intent, but the institutions may see no reason, or may lack the means, to behave differently. This poses yet another set of problems for external powers hoping that free elections and new constitutions will set a democratization process in motion.

The Marketplace for Democracy: Exporters and Importers Meet

The marketplace for democracy has been entered by a variety of traders. On the exporting side, IFIs have demanded good governance as a condition for aid, and Western governments have been more explicit in insisting that this governance be based on the ballot box. Much of the work on the ground is done by quasi-governmental, or arm's-length, agencies such as the United States National Endowment for Democracy or the Swedish International Development Agency. The democratic ingredient may be part of a larger package concerned with aid and self-help. These official bodies are joined by voluntary organizations that have their own visions of democracy.

Many Western political parties seek to promote democracy on the basis of their own ideological slant, notably via the German *stiftungen,* which are offshoots of the main German parties. NGOs are sometimes open in their desire to promote democratic values, as in the case of bodies such as Amnesty International; others, such as Oxfam, may smuggle democratic values in as part of the process of dispensing aid. There is no guarantee that these nonofficial groups will promote a version of democracy compatible with that of their parent governments, and they may often take a more radical line on issues such as political participation and challenging elite power. There are also attempts by third world governments to influence each other, such as the communiqués of pan-African and pan-American conferences insisting on compliance with democratic norms. Words are not always translated into deeds, but there have been some cases of action such as the Nigerian attempt to restore democracy in Sierra Leone and the attempts by South African presidents to put a restraining hand on President Robert Mugabe in Zimbabwe.

On the importing side are third world governments and NGOs, together with specific political structures that may be offered aid or advice, including political parties, legislatures, judiciaries, and electoral administrators. The "transactions," like the exporters and importers, can take a variety of forms. At the formal end, SAPs and other aid packages may lay down in detail what the recipients are expected to do, in the political as well as the economic sphere. At a less formal level, the traders may enter into ad hoc negotiations. External donors highlight particular alleged nondemocratic malpractices, such as police brutality or the rigging of an election, and hint that further aid may be conditional on righting these wrongs. Western diplomats, including those from the EU, play an important role in this process. Moving to the more informal processes, exhortation, encouragement, and support will all play a role. In the previous authoritarian era, it was often contact between dissident groups in the third world, including members of churches, trade unions, academics, lawyers and other professional groups, and their counterparts in the West, that helped to keep resistance alive. With democratization the contacts may not be so vital, but external support may still help to stiffen the resolve of groups whose activities meet with government disapproval. Beyond that, there is the question of the transmission of a more intangible democratic ethos as civil society becomes more diverse and more autonomous from the state.

It would be very difficult to say which pressures or which groups in which places have been most effective, for any one of them cannot easily be separated from the others. The explicit tying of aid to the expansion of democracy is often important in making the initial breach in the authoritarian wall, as with the restoration of multiparty politics in Kenya in the early 1990s, yet the fine detail may depend on more subtle pressures and fine-tuning. The Ghanaian elections of 1992, 1996, and 2000 each marked a step along a road away from authoritarianism. The results of the first election were disputed by the opposition, but the succeeding elections were generally regarded as free and fair. External institutions would not take all the credit for this, and the growing autonomy of groups in civil society was an important factor, as was the more conciliatory behavior of rival politicians. But more careful monitoring of elections, as experience was gained, helped to ensure an acceptable outcome. In other cases the opponents of democracy grew bolder on the basis of what they had previously got away with. The narrow and possibly falsified majority won by the ruling party in Zanzibar in 1995 may have encouraged it to secure reelection five years later with a greater degree of violence and intimidation. External aid to specific political parties may be regarded as illegitimate by some people with moral scruples about interfering in internal politics. In contrast, Southall and Wood argue that it was such aid that helped to end one-party rule in Malawi and Zambia (Southall and Wood 1998: 205–206), and Burnell justifies the aid on the grounds that the external powers that helped to destroy authoritarian regimes have a duty to help build something in their place—especially to build civil societies that facilitate more even contests for power (Burnell 1998: 15–16).

At a more general level, Carothers raises the important question of the relative merits of aid to forms (structures) and aid for processes. Aid for structures such as parties, legislatures, or electoral commissions has the advantage of being targeted at clearly visible entities whose performances can then be evaluated. The disadvantage is that resources may be wasted on trying to imitate inappropriate foreign structures or on actually strengthening the grip of nondemocrats who control the structures. Aid for processes implies concern about such democratic virtues as consensus, tolerance, accountability, and participation, though it is not immediately clear who should be the recipients of the aid (Carothers 1999: 92, 101–108, 207–252). One can speak vaguely about strengthening civil society, but because money cannot simply be thrown at an abstract entity, one needs to discriminate between different NGOs. This takes us back to the problem of how far it is considered ethical for outsiders to manipulate internal institutions and how far indigenous rulers will tolerate such manipulation once they realize what is going on. Once again, the scope for external influence has to be balanced against the indigenous ability to pervert, adapt, or reject the democratic pressures from outside.

The Genuine Article or a Cheap Trinket?

Much of the discussion above assumes that there is a genuine external attempt to promote democracy and, if the outcomes are inadequate, that this is largely attributable to the limited timescale of democratization pressures so far or the unwillingness or inability of indigenous governments and societies to respond adequately. Yet there is an alternative view that either Western interest in democratization was just a passing phase, and that it might be set aside if it conflicted with other objectives, or that democratization was never more than a means to the end of continued economic exploitation.

It is certainly not difficult to find inconsistencies in Western policies. Military government is deplored in Myanmar (Burma) but condoned in Pakistan. The Kenyan government is pilloried for its treatment of opposition parties, yet Uganda receives only a mild rebuke for not permitting parties at all. France supported a military coup in Congo (Brazzaville) and gave aid to a military government in Niger, despite policy pronouncements favoring democratization. The United States supported democratization in Haiti but imposed no sanctions on Zanzibar after the apparently rigged election in October 2000, and it intervened actively in support of one party in the Nicaraguan election of 2001. The United States provided money, free food, and explicit support from the U.S. ambassador to influence the result, though this did mark a departure from the earlier U.S. policy of supporting mass terrorism to secure the desired result (Campbell 2001: 17).

Many of these policies might be attributed to realist foreign policies in which the quest for democracy was not abandoned but was suspended when democracy conflicted with other objectives. Pakistan was important to the Western powers wanting to invade Afghanistan; there were French oil interests in the Congo (Baker 2001: 17); and the Niger state needed to be shored up to reduce the risk of Libyan influence spreading to Nigeria and beyond (Olsen 2001: 323). Britain needed Uganda as a stable ally on the edge of an unstable Central Africa. The United States did not want to rescue an opposition party in Zanzibar, which it saw as Islamist, and was in no position to sermonize on the competent administration of elections after the count of presidential votes in Florida a few weeks after the Zanzibar election (Cameron 2001: 286). In Nicaragua, a former left-wing bogeyman was standing for the presidency. Yet some critics would argue that it is not just a matter of deviations from a generally pro-democracy position but of using apparent support for democracy to maintain Western economic domination. Abrahamsen speaks of a good governance agenda that legitimizes the power of the West and the economic policies it imposes (Abrahamsen 2000: 1), and Hearn perceives an emphasis by donors on "polyarchy" (namely, minimal democracy) to legitimize an unjust social order with socioeconomic inequality (Hearn 2000: 15). Unlike Carothers, Hearn sees aid to civil society not as a broad-based attempt to inculcate democratic behavior and values but as a selective means of promoting those groups that favor free market economics and limited electoral democracy, while giving little help to rural groups or the "popular sector" (Hearn 2000: 3–4, 15–22). There are echoes here of Tornquist's concern that the West is not supporting genuine campaigners for democratization (Tornquist 1999: 168).

Is there any middle ground between the models of the West as the bringer of a new democratic order and the West as an exploiter using democratization as the latest fig leaf for covering exploitation of the third world? We may be in danger of assuming the existence of more clearly thought-out policies and objectives than is really the case. Western support for democratization evolved in a piecemeal way, influenced by such factors as a growing awareness of incompetence, corruption, and brutality under authoritarian rule, a reduced fear of left-wing electoral victories with the demise of the Cold War, and a growing realization of the strength of pro-democracy movements in third world countries. It seems unlikely that any politician or bureaucrat ever drew up a grand plan for advancing democracy that took into account all the potential points of influence or hazards along the road. The carrots of aid and exhortation, and the sticks of sanctions and condemnation, were expected to tip the balance in favor of democrats, but there appears to have been little assessment of exactly how far various policies, individually or collectively, might advance democracy, or of what alternatives might be deployed if these attempts failed. After all, the whole venture of trying to promote democracy in a country very different from one's own had hardly been attempted previously, with the possible exception of Allied attempts in Germany and Japan after 1945.

Given this background, it is hardly surprising that the actual objectives were often unclear and the results patchy. Sometimes democracy has suffered setbacks because Western powers have pursued policies inimical to democracy, as in our examples of Pakistan, Congo (Brazzaville), Niger, Zanzibar, and Nicaragua. In other cases, as mentioned earlier, there were varied forms of indigenous resistance or inertia, whether from incumbent elites, bureaucrats, the military, or civil society. There may be elements of the altruistic motives cited by Carothers and the economic motives cited by Abrahamsen and Hearn, but consistency and single-mindedness have not always been in evidence. We need only to compare the number of authoritarian regimes in the third world in the 1980s with the number today to remind ourselves of what external pressures have achieved, yet the road ahead looks hazardous for democrats of both radical and conservative persuasions.

For those who take a conservative (or realistic?) view of democracy as requiring little beyond periodic elections and the protection of basic civil liberties, there is the question of how far populations will value democracy if incumbent rulers can usually manipulate elections to ensure their survival, if governments take little notice of public opinion, and if democracy does little to arrest falling living standards. There is the danger that not just the rulers, but the whole (nominally?) democratic system will lose legitimacy and that few people will offer much resistance if the system is challenged either by an aspiring dictator or by creeping anarchy. For the radical who believes that democracy should incorporate social justice, equality, and mass participation, warnings of what should not be done are often clearer than prescriptions for the right remedy. A "night watchman" state that sheds a range of social and economic functions and is thus unable to implement policies for which the electorate is deemed to have voted is the wrong solution. But what guarantee is there that a state with a greater capacity and more resources would behave in a democratic manner? Hearn and Tornquist both suggest that the wrong groups have been aided rather than those that would contribute most to democratization, yet how does one find the right groups? And if they can be found, how far can or should outsiders support groups that may come into confrontation with indigenous governments, to say nothing of foreign businesses?

Many radicals would welcome the growth of groups defending oppressed minorities or resisting deforestation or pollution by foreign mining companies. In philosophical terms they might argue that support for such groups does not imply interference in internal politics any more than external governments and businesses are interfering by encouraging privatization and foreign investment. This brings us back to the reality of international politics. Those who favor egalitarian, participatory democracy may enjoy the resources of some influential NGOs and may sometimes be able to appeal to the consciences of Western politicians, but those who favor a largely uncontrolled free market, and the more limited form of democracy that it implies, hold most of the trump cards. They are the ones who control most of the Western governments and IFIs, with all the sanctions that they can deploy, and they control the rules by which international trade and investment are conducted.

The balance of power may shift one day, or Western countries may decide that the economy and the environment at home and abroad should be subject to greater democratic control. But for the immediate future, the external impact on democracy depends on something more than the sum total of aid for democratic institutions and practices. It also depends on a broader external notion of the boundaries of democracy within and between countries. External aid has given democracy in the third world an enormous lift over the past two decades, yet it has also imposed a formidable ceiling on its further growth.

8

Transitions from Authoritarianism to Democracy

Some third world countries are democratic today because, as we saw in Chapter 6, they have preserved and developed the democratic systems that they inherited at independence. But for the vast majority of today's third world democracies, power had to be wrested from indigenous authoritarian rulers, or at least these rulers had to be made to conform to democratic standards. Although such changes could be brought about by a revolution, social structures in third world countries are seldom conducive to revolutions, and revolutions are seldom conducive to democracy, as the victors need to wield substantial force to prevent the vanquished from regaining power. In the absence of revolutions, the move from authoritarianism to democracy requires a period of transition.

The term "transition" is open to criticism on the grounds that it may imply a recognizable process with a beginning and an end, and with an interaction of different forces in between. It might also imply the resolution of conflicts between distinctive groups or individuals that can be categorized as pro- or antidemocratic. Politics in the real world are clearly more complicated than that, with democracy and authoritarianism often a matter of degree, and with the pursuit of, or resistance to, democracy frequently emerging as a secondary consideration for political actors pursuing other goals. Were General Francisco Franco's immediate successors in 1975 authoritarians who had to be bullied into accepting democracy, or were they democrats who were merely awaiting the right conditions for democratic restoration? Did Spanish communists who favored democratic elections really give a high priority to pluralist democracy? Have all heads of one-party and military governments been implacable foes of democracy, or have they been victims of circumstances in which democracy has failed to work? And beyond the formal political structure, there are innumerable groups in society for whom democracy may be of only marginal interest but who may support or oppose moves toward greater democratization according to whether it is seen to enhance their wealth, status, or security.

Yet it is difficult to discuss the moves from authoritarianism to democracy without the concept of transition. Countries are not, except occasionally in a very formal sense, authoritarian one day and democratic the next. The intervening period is likely to be a matter of years, even if we cannot easily plot the exact beginning and end. Indeed, the process may not be a linear one. Sometimes, as in much of Central America, it is more like trench warfare, with democracy gaining a few miles of territory only to be driven back again following a rigged election or the misuse of presidential power. Or there may be a series of transitions, as in Pakistan and Thailand, with democrats having to regroup repeatedly after being ousted by the military.

How do we know when a transition has been completed? Linz and Stepan suggest that this moment is reached when there is sufficient agreement about political procedures to produce an elected government; when a government comes to power by a free and popular vote; when the government has authority to generate new policies; and when the executive, legislative, and judicial power generated by a new democracy does not have to share power with other bodies (Linz and Stepan 1996: 3). This may be a desirable state of affairs, but one wonders whether most third world countries have really undergone a transition if such rigorous tests are applied. Even if the hurdle of a free and popular vote can be cleared—and the fairness of elections is often disputed—the ability of governments to generate new policies is frequently circumscribed by limited capacity and resources and the constraints of the military, transnational corporations, and foreign donors. Mere electoral democracy may be a less desirable state of affairs, but its establishment after long periods of authoritarian rule is surely significant enough to be regarded as marking the achievement of a transition, irrespective of whether further democratic gains then follow. I shall therefore use the term "transition to democracy" to denote any shift from an authoritarian political order to one in which there is democracy, however imperfect, in the sense that governments are chosen and legitimated by competitive elections, and citizens enjoy a degree of freedom of expression and association together with freedom from arbitrary arrest and imprisonment.

In this chapter we shall consider the extent to which a transition requires certain preconditions and then seek to identify the main actors involved in the transition. We shall consider the opportunities and constraints created or imposed by underlying economic conditions, political cultures, and ideologies and then examine the dynamics of the actual process of transition as pro- and antidemocratic forces interact.

Preconditions:
An Exclusive Democratic Club or an Open Door?

Chapter 3 looked at the arguments that democracy was much more likely to emerge if certain preconditions were fulfilled. These included not only

economic development but also the existence of the right political attitudes, behavior, and institutions. There is room for argument about
whether these variables are a cause of democratic evolution or whether
they flourish as a result of a democratic environment. But advocates of
the preconditions approach would probably argue that if the economic,
social, or institutional requisites either do not exist initially, or are not
easily generated by a changing political system, then the prospects for
democracy are bleak. The transition school, in contrast, places the emphasis on the ability of political actors to reach a consensus on the rules of
the political game; it may note the advantages of economic prosperity, a
culture of tolerance, or strong institutions, but it does not see their
absence as an insurmountable barrier. When Lipset was writing in 1959
(Lipset 1959: 69–105), it seemed plausible to believe that only a few
wealthy countries possessed the necessary qualifications for membership
in the democratic club. Politicians and citizens in poorer, more socially
and culturally divided countries might want democracy, just as they might
want greater prosperity, but wanting alone would not be enough. Yet the
transitions we have witnessed since the 1980s indicate that some of the
world's poorest countries can gate-crash the club. Whether they can sustain their membership is a matter we shall consider when we look at democratic consolidation.

Przeworski et al. suggest that the statistical probability of dictatorship
being replaced by democracy is random with regard to per capita income
but that the subsequent survival of any newly created democracy is much
more likely with greater prosperity (Przeworski et al. 2000: 273). So the
would-be democrat in a poor country is embarking on a hazardous journey,
though most of the democracies created since the early 1980s (using our
minimal definition of democracy) have so far survived. In Africa it was
Benin, one of the poorest countries and one that had suffered considerable
ethnic tension between north and south, that was the first authoritarian
country in the third wave to reach a consensus on the rules for free elections and the first to displace a government through the ballot box. In Asia,
Bangladesh is a democracy and Singapore is not, and in Latin America the
relatively wealthy Mexico lagged behind most of its poorer neighbors in
institutionalizing multiparty competition. All this suggests that human will
and skill can contribute to democratization even when many of the alleged
preconditions are barely visible.

The Players in the Game

Having argued that the interaction between political actors can facilitate a
transition to democracy, one immediate problem is to decide how to classify the actors. Table 8.1 suggests a range of possibilities.

Table 8.1　Forces Stimulating or Resisting Democratization

Approach	Elements Involved	Possible Hypotheses
Institutional	The state; government; organized opposition; the military	• Single parties lose cohesion and claims to legitimacy. • The military seek to cut their losses through exit from government. • Personal rulers are limited by mortality. • A growing number of opposition groups seek democratic transition.
Class interest	Social classes, especially middle class	• With economic development, the middle class becomes less dependent on the state, and the state's justification for authoritarianism becomes weaker. • In few third world countries are economic conditions conducive to collective working-class pressure.
Pluralist	Elites; counterelites; masses	• Inconclusive struggle and interdependence lead to elite compromise, which provides a framework of rules for political competition.
Group theory	A range of groups	• Specific groups are more important than social classes or even elites. • Democratization depends on building a winning coalition of groups.
Communitarian	Civil society	• Democratization is helped by growing sectors of society becoming less dependent on state patronage and welfare.
Globalization	External environment	• Democratization is helped by external support and pressures and by a freer flow of information.
Behaviorism; agency	Individual actors	• When political structures are weak or fluid, individual choices have a major impact.

It is not a question of establishing which of the elements listed does or does not exist but of assessing which are most useful in analyzing any transition. A trade union leader may be classified as belonging simultaneously to several groups, including the working class and the counterelite. He will also be part of civil society and may be an individual negotiator in the transition. Yet we want to know which of the hats worn will be the most significant. Is transition best viewed as a process in which formal institutions change their roles, or is it better to view the process as one of class conflict, challenges to elites, or interaction between groups? Or is it something that is set in motion by the emergence of civil society, the impact of the external environment, or the behavior of individual actors?

Previous chapters have been devoted to civil society and external influences, both of which are better seen as contributing to the preconditions for democracy rather than influencing the shorter-term process of transition. Civil society, by its nature, can only evolve gradually, and the course of any transition will depend on what its members actually do rather than its mere existence. External factors can make democratization easier or more difficult, but the actual transition will depend on the ability of internal actors to utilize the opportunities offered. The gradual withdrawal of U.S. support for General Augusto Pinochet helped democratization in Chile because there were already strong pro-democracy forces on the ground, whereas the withdrawal of Western support for Saddam Hussein did little to advance democracy in Iraq in the absence of any strong pro-democracy movement. This leaves us with recognizable entities within the countries initially under authoritarian rule.

State Institutions and Opposition

A starting point for many scholars is the formal machinery of state and its response to those who confront it. The growing confrontation may arise from a variety of forces we have already discussed, including economic hardship, the brutality of authoritarian rulers, the emergence of power bases autonomous from the state, and examples of successful democratization elsewhere. It may also be important that more dissatisfied groups are now committed to democracy (rather than violence or secession) as a means of advancing their interests. Barkan suggests that more opposition groups in Africa are now "transition seekers" rather than being merely "anti-regime" or "patronage seekers" (Barkan 2000: 241), although their true intentions may turn out to be different if they ever win power. Violence became a less effective strategy after the Cold War, as the United States, Russia, Cuba, and South Africa withdrew their support for rebel movements in different countries, while the ideological preferences of opposition groups became less of a barrier to negotiation with governments as Marxist positions were abandoned. For authoritarian governments, their response to pressures for democratization has been influenced by their own structures. Table 8.2 distinguishes between military, one-party, and personal regimes. Huntington summarizes neatly the prospects of each type being supplanted by democracy, and some of his ideas are pursued in the table (Huntington 1991–1992: 579–616).

Military rulers are the ones best able and most willing to retreat, provided there are sufficient personal safeguards from prosecution for the soldiers and institutional safeguards for the resources and autonomy of the army as a whole. But displaced armies find it easier to return to power than other authoritarians because the army as an institution is more likely to remain intact than a displaced authoritarian party or the entourage of a displaced

Table 8.2 Types of Authoritarian Governments and Opportunities for Democratic Transition

Type of Authoritarian Government	Prospects for Transfer of Power	Analytical Problems
Military	• Few institutional barriers to democratization. • Military governments generally see themselves as only temporary. • Conflict between political and professional functions may encourage a return to barracks. • Military governments have a narrower power base of people and groups dependent on authoritarianism.	• The army as an institution is likely to remain intact and may therefore intervene again. • Left-wing military governments frequently reject bourgeois democracy. • The successor government will not necessarily be democratic. • Is the existence of a military government a cause or a symptom of the nature of political conflict?
One-party	• One-party regimes often claim exclusive legitimacy and ideological purity. • Broader power base with a vested interest in retaining power. • Party leaders show greater skill than soldiers in devising a viable successor regime.	• Many third world ruling parties are less tightly structured or ideologically coherent than those in the totalitarian model.
Personal	• Personal rulers seldom want to surrender power, but they have a limited lifespan. • They may leave few viable authoritarian structures behind.	• Is personal rule a reflection of political polarization, which might make democratization more difficult?

authoritarian ruler (Huntington 1991–1992: 582–583). This is generally borne out by experience, though one could make a distinction between right-wing or largely apolitical military governments with relatively modest objectives of restoring order or retaining or restoring the power of dominant elites—as in most of Latin America, tropical Africa, and South Asia—and left-wing governments. The latter seek a more thoroughgoing social transformation, as in North Africa and the Middle East. Soldiers in the former group will often prefer an early return to barracks as the army faces a growing strain of reconciling its professional functions with the process of government (Bratton and van de Walle 1997: 270; Lee 2000: 190; Linz and Stepan 1996: 66–67). This does not guarantee that the successor government will be a democratic one, but the impending departure of the military at least creates an opportunity for democrats. Left-wing military governments are likely to cling to power for much longer and have little time for bourgeois democracy. A transition to democracy is less likely than a transition to Huntington's other authoritarian types: one-party rule, through an army-created party to give the soldiers a greater legitimacy (as in Egypt), or personal rule (as in Libya). Of the more conservative military governments, those in Indonesia and Paraguay are the only obvious ones that have gone along a similar road.

One-party and personal rule both present greater institutional and ideological barriers to democratization. Institutionally, there are problems of disentangling the party from the state and resisting the antidemocratic pressures of party functionaries who have a vested interest in the status quo. Ideologically there is the question of why people who have previously insisted on the party's exclusive right to determine the nation's destiny should cease to proclaim such a right. Huntington (1991–1992: 582–586) focuses more on countries closer to the totalitarian model than on the flimsier one-party states of Africa, but even the latter are likely to embrace a wider range of powerful interests than a government relying on the army as its main constituency.

Personal rulers are even more reluctant to retire than military rulers or party politicians. Their departure is more likely to depend on death, whether from natural causes, assassination, or revolution. In the former case, the ruler's successors may seek a democratic transition if no other viable political structure appears to be available. Huntington cites the case of Spain. In some instances, personal rulers have sought legitimation through the ballot box in elections or plebiscites of varying degrees of freedom and fairness. Blatantly rigged elections bring democracy no closer, as with General Pinochet's first appeal to the people of Chile, but more open ones, such as his second, may enable the electorate to take advantage of the leader's miscalculation of his popularity and bring his rule to an end.

One danger in focusing on the structural form of authoritarian government is to assume that it is an independent variable. Was it only a matter of chance whether earlier attempts at democracy were suspended by military, one-party, or personal rule, or did the outcome depend largely on the country's culture, history, and recent political structure? The one-party states closest to the totalitarian model, which are Huntington's main concern, are generally devices for imposing authority on the more economically advanced societies, as in Eastern Europe, where a relatively complex political structure and a relatively plausible claim to legitimacy are considered necessary for effective authority. In contrast, a handful of soldiers can take and retain control of a less "advanced" country, such as Togo, through a rudimentary political structure with little coherent ideology. The non-totalitarian one-party state, as found in much of tropical Africa, frequently emerged gradually and by default—rather than through a dramatic event such as a coup, revolution, or invasion—and has reflected the failure of democracy to flourish in a hostile environment.

Personal rule is, at first sight, more difficult to explain. It has emerged in both relatively advanced third world countries, such as Chile, and relatively backward ones, such as the Congo, in countries where much of traditional society remained intact, such as Ethiopia under Haile Selassie, and countries where both "traditional" and "modern" structures have broken down, such as Uganda and the Central African Republic. Insofar as there is a common thread linking the emergence of personal rule in these countries, it appears to begin with a period of extreme polarization, whether along ideological lines as in Chile (and possibly Spain) or ethnic lines as in Uganda and the Congo. Such polarization makes any institutionalized resolution of conflict, by a party or a disciplined army, difficult, with the result that a leader is able to break free from the political structure that initially put him in power.

If we treat the type of authoritarian rule as a dependent variable, largely dependent on the type of society the authoritarians have to rule, rather than an independent variable, any discussion of the prospects and nature of a transition to democracy must bear in mind the broader environment. Of the third world countries cited by Huntington as undergoing democratization between 1974 and 1990, the only ones to begin that process from a starting point of personal rule were Chile, the Philippines, and the dubious case of India (Huntington 1991–1992: 583). One might infer that the small number of cases reflected not only the reluctance of personal rulers to depart but also the difficulty in establishing any consensus for democracy in the divided countries that had given rise to their emergence.

When Huntington was writing, he discovered a dearth of one-party regimes undergoing a transition to democracy, in contrast to the retreat of military rulers. While single parties were initially more reluctant than the military to risk sharing or losing power, they provided for a more stable democratic polity when they did eventually depart. Although the ending of military government requires a new constitutional settlement, with rules that may be subject to varied interpretations and degrees of support, the single party can simply decide to allow multiparty elections with only minimal amendments to the constitution, as in much of East and southern Africa. This might raise questions about the authenticity of the subsequent democracy if the single party is merely transformed into the dominant party, with little prospect of electoral defeat and little respect for the minority who have voted against it, yet at least the door is ajar for further democratic developments. The ability of opposition parties to win power in Senegal and Zambia, and to deprive the ruling party of an overall majority in Kenya, indicates what is possible.

There have, of course, been cases of viable democracies succeeding military regimes, especially where there has been a premilitary model as a point of reference, as in Argentina, Chile, Uruguay, and Ghana. But the military's lack of political skill, or the lack of consensus in society that facilitated military intervention in the first place, may make for a stormier passage. An extreme case was the attempt by the Nigerian military in 1992 to prescribe not only the number of permissible parties but the ideologies and policies they should espouse. Brazil, Guatemala, and Peru have all had problems in constraining presidential power within a nominally democratic system. The Pakistan military have been unable to abandon the habit of subverting elected governments that do not come up to their standards, and postmilitary democracy in Indonesia has yet to build a stable base. The restoration of a defunct one-party regime is virtually impossible, so post-single-party democracies have an opportunity to work out their own salvation. But there is the all-too-apparent possibility of the restoration of the military, or at least of its influence behind the scenes.

Social Classes

An obvious objection to the emphasis on regime types is that it places undue emphasis on those who wield power and those who aspire to take it from them to the exclusion of the wider society. At other times and places, the struggle for democracy might have been interpreted more in terms of social class, with lower classes challenging the privileges that authoritarianism was preserving; yet little of the literature on recent transitions focuses on this variable. The nearest one gets is in East Asia, where democratization is linked to reduced middle-class dependence on the state. In the early days of industrialization, the manufacturing industry depended on import restrictions and state subsidies, but these had been largely swept away by the late 1980s, and the middle classes wanting to live in a freer environment now had less to lose by offending the state authorities (Amsden and Euh 1993: 300; Thompson 1996: 637–638). In South Korea it is not clear whether there was a ruling class in the traditional sense or merely military men and their clients who held onto power for as long as they controlled the means of coercion. But the party leaders in Taiwan with their mainland Chinese background might be seen as a more exclusive group. In Latin America the poorest people are often those of indigenous Indian and African stock, and this has sometimes given rise to challenges to authority that look more like class struggles based on distinctive identities. Yet it was a partial renunciation of class politics that often facilitated transition, as Marxist demands for a command economy and a redistribution of wealth were replaced by demands for free elections and civil liberties. Collier makes a plea for greater recognition of the role of labor in democratization in Latin America, but even here the issue is largely presented as labor as an organized group rather than a class. This group was not so much concerned with labor representation on the nineteenth-century European model as with the unprecedented harshness of authoritarian rule, human rights, and honest, competent government—all issues on which labor could campaign alongside a variety of other groups (Collier 1999: 179–180).

Elites, Counterelites, and Masses

A more common starting point is to focus on elites, counterelites, and masses. This terminology suggests more transitory groups whose power depends on their tenuous influence or control, or potential control, over the machinery of state. Rustow was one of the pioneers of the "democratization via elite pact" school, arguing that democracy emerged after a serious but inconclusive conflict forced rival elites to agree on the rules of the political game—rules that ultimately provided the checks and balances that democracy required (Rustow 1970: 337–363). Deegan's study of South Africa implicitly follows this approach. Few of the contenders for power, she suggests, initially believed in democracy, but most ultimately saw little alternative, so that Marxism was abandoned on one side and racial superiority on the other (Deegan 2001: 89–92). Wood's comparative study of El Salvador and South Africa points in the same direction. The elites in El Salvador, whose wealth was derived from coffee growing and sustained by the coercion of the masses by the military, found that the war against Marxist insurgents made the coffee plantations more vulnerable and the military protection less effective. These elites were then displaced by, or transformed into, elites investing in manufacturing and commerce and seeking compromise rather than confrontation with the masses. In South Africa, she argues, business elites were hit by crises of investor confidence and political instability as the apartheid regime became increasingly isolated, and the business elites were ahead of the political elites in demanding universal suffrage (Wood 2000: 52–57; 169). These examples illustrate the ways in which apparently powerful elites may have to accept democratization as the price they pay for survival, though they also suggest the primacy of "the political." It was not so much a matter of rising or falling economic groups, as in eighteenth-century Britain, but of the political pressures of nonelites damaging the economic bases of the elites and forcing them to reconsider their positions.

In other parts of the third world, elite pacts are also said to have been the key to democratization, as incumbent rulers fearful of the loss of their wealth and status (and possibly their lives or liberties) have sought to bargain with what we might regard as counterelites in moderate (and often underground) political parties, and sometimes with representatives of nonelites among the poor and disadvantaged (see especially Peeler 1998: 190 on Latin America). In Africa, Bratton and van de Walle speak of the importance of mass protests, but when the "masses" turn out to include students, parastatal employees, doctors, nurses, and teachers, as well as discontented party activists (Bratton and van de Walle 1997: 101, 176, 268–269), one wonders whether "counterelites" would not be a better term.

Groups

Uncertainty as to who belongs to an elite, a counterelite, or the masses might suggest limits to the value of such categories. If the term "social class" is inadequate to classify political actors in East Asia, Africa, and much of Latin America, do people fit much more easily into elite and mass categories if the implication is that there is some coherence, interaction, and a sense of identity within each category? Does the groundnut grower in northern Ghana have much in common with the street vendor in Accra, or the human rights lawyer with the army officer? It might ultimately be useful to consider people's elite or mass status in terms of their resources and degrees of access to centers of power, but an additional way of viewing third world societies is to see them as consisting of a wide range of groups, each of which has its own interests (and possibly ideology) and will make shifting alliances with other groups, sometimes supporting an authoritarian government and at others resisting it. Some groups will have a formal organization, such as opposition parties, trade unions, and professional organizations; some will actually be formal organizations, such as the army, the civil bureaucracy, or the ruling party; while others will be less formal, including villagers cooperating in development projects, ethnic and religious groups, and urban mobs and guerrillas. The Catholic Church in Latin America is an example of a group that does not appear to have a fixed position in the social or political hierarchy. It was once seen as a conservative force, but priests frequently took the side of the oppressed under military government, even if it was difficult to speak of the church as a whole having an explicit stance. There is nothing new in group theory as an explanation of political outcomes in Western democracies, with ample literature on the relative power of farmers, businesses, and bureaucracies, but it seems especially relevant in third world countries where broader social groupings are often difficult to detect.

To which groups do we need to look? In some cases it may be the sheer diversity of groups that is important in facilitating the transition, with the whole being greater than the sum of the parts. In Ghana it was a loose grouping of opposition politicians, professional groups, and impoverished workers that turned General Ignatius Acheampong's no-party state referendum in 1978 into a moral defeat for the military, and in South Korea Shin speaks of a united front of churches, parties, trade unions, and students (Shin 1999: 1–2). The groups that have most frequently been highlighted are presented in Table 8.3.

Table 8.3 Groups in Society and Prospects for Democratic Transition

Group	Possible Contribution to Democratic Transition	Possible Weaknesses
Social movements	Ability to articulate interests and participate in protests when more formal groups are outlawed	Extreme demands; limited formal contacts with authority
Intermediate associations	Autonomy from the state; socialization of the people into political participation; strength of bases in society; moderate nature of demands	Limited sanctions
Guerrillas	Ultimate sanction of force against recalcitrant authoritarians	Violence makes dialogue with authoritarians difficult; violence may be used as a pretext for retaining authoritarian rule
Political parties	Provide a bridge between groups in society and formal political structures	Dangers of: subservience to the state; parties increasing polarization; and parties restoring the status quo ante, and its inherent weaknesses

Social movements have been especially prominent in Latin America, and Tornquist hints at their importance in Indonesia and the Philippines (Tornquist 1999: 142). Many authors use the term but few define it. Cockcroft (1990) writes of the urban poor in Peru protesting against austerity imposed by the International Monetary Fund, as well as slum dwellers and urban strikers in Brazil hastening the end of military government and shantytown dwellers leading the first popular uprisings against General Pinochet. Munck refers to varied social movements in Chile covering producers, consumers, health, and education that fueled the protests of 1983 and 1984 (Munck 1989: 90–92), and Petras speaks of social movements in Central America encompassing a broad array of social classes and occupational, professional, civil, and human rights associations that dominated the process of redemocratization in the pre-democratic phase. These groups included trade unions, the self-employed squatters, the professions, and universities (Petras 1990: 88).

In terms of activities, as well as the range of membership, the social movement seems to be equally ubiquitous. According to Grugel, the popular sector (which presumably embraced social movements) was involved in street and neighborhood protests in Chile as a result of economic crises, and it galvanized political parties into action, while mass participation was important again in the plebiscite that removed Pinochet and in the subsequent election campaign (Grugel 1991: 367–368). The works of Cockcroft, Munck, and Petras imply a similar range of activities against authoritarian governments, but what does all this tell us except that "the masses are revolting"? What is distinctive about social movements, as opposed to other vehicles of protest at other times and places, and are their objectives or their means of advancing them conducive to the process of transition?

The description so far suggests a certain informality about the organization of social movements (as compared with more tightly structured pressure groups), with no fixed membership, few rules, and few contacts with authority. Yet their ability to offer the oppressed mutual support, to embarrass governments through what, in other contexts, we would call direct action, and to make governments fear an enlargement of such action if their demands are not met, are signs of strength. If opposition to authoritarianism came mainly from political parties, governments could (and they frequently do) outlaw the parties and detain their key members, but the more spontaneous uprisings of social movements are more difficult to control. But can the undermining of authoritarianism be translated into the building of democracy? Cockcroft describes the aims of social movements as the redistribution of income and opportunity and the punishment of military rulers, and he notes the absence of any organizational network to bring the groups together as the left did in earlier times (Cockcroft 1990: 25–29). Even if the description of objectives is exaggerated or overgeneralized, there is clearly a problem with a black-and-white view of society, which is hardly conducive to negotiating a transition to democracy, quite apart from the absence of any formal organizations to carry out the negotiation. Social movements can shake the foundations of authoritarianism. Whether this then leads to a democratic transition will depend on the willingness or ability of more articulate or better connected groups to support their cause, including intellectuals, political parties, the Catholic Church, and ultimately members of the elite, and the government itself.

The term "social movement" is not used so frequently in Africa. Sandbrook prefers to speak of "intermediate associations." These include professional groups such as the Association of Recognized Professional Bodies, which was instrumental in hastening the demise of the second military government in Ghana, trade unions, cooperatives, and ethnic unions (Sandbrook 1988: 259–262). Sklar, too, refers to "the high degree of autonomy for diverse non-party and extra-governmental organisations" (Sklar 1987: 698).

> Rural development associations and co-operatives resourcefully guard against attempts by governments and party officials to circumscribe their autonomy and subordinate them to outside powers. In Zimbabwe, the future of democracy appears likely to turn on the question of respect for the autonomy of demonstrably accountable organisations of small farmers. Similarly in Kenya "peasant-initiated self-help development projects" are rural "schools for democracy" that might be expected to foster its revival and growth nationally. (Sklar 1987: 699)

These appear to be more conservative groups than the social movements of Latin America, in societies where class conflict is much less polarized and the moderate nature of their behavior and demands may be reas-
suring for the authoritarian rulers who are contemplating democratic
restoration, though the reverse side of the coin is the more limited sanctions
available if such democratization is not contemplated. But what is important is that on both continents we need to guard against the caricature of the
powerful government and state confronting a powerless, unorganized population. The political subsystem may be less complex than in the West, but
when authoritarians ban formal opposition they may find that a varied
range of less formal groups can ultimately engineer their destruction.

We have so far concentrated on groups that, for the most part, live
within the law of the land, even though they sometimes resort to violence
against persons and property. Nothing has been said about the contribution
to democratic transition of guerrillas or terrorists who resort to violent
resistance as a way of life, and there is little in the literature to suggest that
they make any contribution. Violent antigovernment groups are more likely
to be blamed for the reactions against them, which give authoritarians a
pretext for displacing soft democratic governments that fail to maintain
order, as in Argentina and Uruguay, and such groups have usually remained
at the margins of politics in any transition. The main exceptions have been
in Central America, although one's interpretation of if and when democracy
was established may depend on one's ideological standpoint. In Nicaragua,
the Sandinista guerrillas overthrew the dictatorship of Anastasio Somoza
and established a pluralist system (according to some), and the Contra terrorists (aided by the U.S. government) subsequently forced the Sandinistas
into conceding more genuinely free elections (according to others) in which
the Sandinistas were defeated. In El Salvador, years of guerrilla warfare
forced the government to move from semi-competitive elections confined
to right-of-center parties to competitive elections open to the former Marxist guerrillas. But observers of a conservative persuasion might argue that
the initial democratic openings, and the departure of military governments,
had already been achieved on account of the moderation of other political
actors. It is, perhaps, a matter of degree. Realists would not expect a challenge to an authoritarian government to be mounted without a degree of
violence, whether from stone-throwing mobs in spontaneous demonstrations or from organized guerrillas in the bush, but in the end it is the willingness to renounce violence, by government and governed alike, that
makes a democratic dialogue possible.

Individuals

In a relatively stable political system we normally recognize the limits of
individual action. Persuasive leaders may get the electorate to vote for new

policy departures or win over key figures to steer their policies through cabinet or parliament, but well-established institutions and procedures generally force the leaders to work within the confines of a recognizable system. In the twilight of authoritarian rule, the institutions and procedures are less clearly defined and accorded less legitimacy. While opposition parties may be banned, it is difficult to frame laws that will prohibit the expression of every opinion the government dislikes or prohibit every gathering of individuals at which dissenting opinions might be expressed or autonomous actions initiated. Much may therefore depend on the willingness of particular individuals to test the water by either risking official disapproval for an action that is not actually illegal, such as preaching a sermon on human rights, reporting corruption in high places, or going beyond the law to organized resistance. Once there is a recognizable set of pressures for democratization (i.e., a transition has begun), the fluidity of political structures and rules may become increasingly apparent, so that determined individuals with sufficient support may be able to impose their own will. This is implicit in Tornquist's demand for support for "genuine actors in real processes of democratisation" (Tornquist 1999: 168) and Wyatt and Adeney's observation that human agency may be important in the rapid transformation of political structures in South Asia (Wyatt and Adeney 2001: 5).

With the authoritarian mold broken, if not yet destroyed, but with the new democratic mold not yet set, it may be individual behavior that shapes the structures rather than the other way round. Would the transition in South Africa have taken the same form without Nelson Mandela? And would a democratic consensus in El Salvador have taken the form that it did without the emergence of individuals on both the government and opposition sides who were willing to compromise? Indeed, actors within, or close to, the government can be as crucial as opposition figures. Former President Julius Nyerere kept up the pressure on his successor to permit multiparty competition in Tanzania, and Nyerere's charisma helped him to win the day.

Inescapable Contexts:
Economics, Political Culture, and Ideology

A difficulty with the human agency argument is that the fluid state of political structures and the rules of political behavior may blind us to the subtle constraints that do actually exist. Individual actors have their own skills and groups have their own resources, but the ways in which these resources are deployed will be influenced by certain unwritten rules of political conflict that may vary between different times and places. Democratic and authoritarian governments may come and go, and written constitutions, where they exist at all, may provide only a limited guide to political behavior, but accepted political and social practices may prove more durable. To take some obvious examples, no government in Ghana would be able to survive very long without coming to terms with the chieftaincy, few governments in Thailand have threatened the monarchy, and few in Latin America would want to go too far in alienating the church. This is partly a recognition of the strength of enduring institutions and partly a reflection of political cultures that value these institutions and the beliefs and customs they symbolize. Tropical Africa's shorter experience of nationhood may make the unwritten rules less clear and binding than in Asia or Latin America, though some outlines are still visible. A degree of ethnic balance, and not merely weight of numbers, is generally important for any group attempting to win or consolidate power, whether it is a political party or a military junta; technocrats tend to be respected to a greater extent in the third world than in the West, where party politicians are more confident of their own prescriptions, and technocrats are frequently co-opted into high positions by authoritarian governments. At the same time, various niceties may be observed by authoritarian governments in relation to actual and potential opponents, even though the governments have the physical ability to crush them. Despite the horrors that have occurred in countries such as Burundi, Liberia, Rwanda, and Sierra Leone, where authoritarian government merged into near anarchy, or praetorianism in the language of political science, many African governments have imprisoned rather than executed their opponents and have tried to avoid confrontations with religious groups or universities even when these have been major sources of opposition. There have been exceptions, but generally it seems that respect for religion and education outweigh the politician's desire for conformity, while the nonexecution of opponents may reflect a code of "do as you would be done by" in relation to past, present, and future rulers and dissidents, which tends to break down mainly when government ceases to be a regularized process, as in Ghana in 1979.

In Latin America, too, long-accepted practices and values may be suspended under military rule, but not destroyed. Mainwaring has shown how South American countries that appear similar in terms of socioeconomic development have vastly different party systems, which have made for different patterns of transition (or nontransition). In Brazil's top-down political system, parties have always been heavily dependent on the state, and the state allowed them to continue to function even after the military had taken over, albeit with attempts by the military to tilt the party system in their favor. Such continuity also implied the continued existence of an elected congress and state governors. The transition to democracy was less abrupt than elsewhere, with the military gradually retreating in the face of a succession of electoral setbacks. The Chilean system, in contrast, was one of strong, autonomous parties, in a powerful legislature, less willing to moderate their behavior for the benefit of the head of state. This autonomous, polarized system was deemed incompatible with military government, and parties suffered a long period of suspension. Uruguay is different again, with the main parties largely frozen in the narrow elitist mold of an earlier generation and sufficiently conservative to facilitate negotiation with the military (Mainwaring 1988).

The constraints on political behavior will not, of course, remain static. Social and economic change will give rise to new groups with new resources and different values from those that previously predominated, and this may influence both the pace and nature of democratization. Linz and Stepan make the general point that economic improvements under authoritarianism may produce a larger middle class, a more skilled workforce, greater contact with other societies, and a more diverse range of protests (Linz and Stepan 1996: 77). In South Korea, Flanagan and Lee mention a changing political culture influenced by economic change. Deference, conformity to traditional social norms, and suspicion of new ideas have been replaced by individual autonomy, open-mindedness, tolerance of a range of life-styles, and a search for self-improvement, self-fulfillment, and self-indulgence (Flanagan and Lee 2000: 626–659). Few third world countries have undergone as radical a social and economic transformation as South Korea, and many of the changes that have occurred have been in the direction of decline rather than development, but the impact of the changes on the political process is still visible.

In Latin America we have noted the ways in which deindustrialization inhibited the reemergence of radical mass parties. In Africa, economic decline and the curtailment of state welfare provision are said to have made for more individualistic societies where there had once been a greater sense of communal obligation (see especially Mung'ong'o and Loiske 1995: 176–177; and Githongo 1997: 43). Whether this augurs well for democracy depends on whether one sees democracy as emerging as a consequence of the rise of enterprising individuals more autonomous from the state or as a result of a stronger sense of commitment to society.

Dynamics of Change:
Rival Teams and the Different Arenas

The Teams

Having established that a variety of groups exist with varied resources, but subject to constraints imposed by political culture and by custom and practice, I now want to plot their positions in relation to attempts at, or resistance to, democratization. An outline is suggested in Table 8.4.

**Table 8.4 Sources of Initiative for Democratization:
Government and Opposition; Elites and Masses**

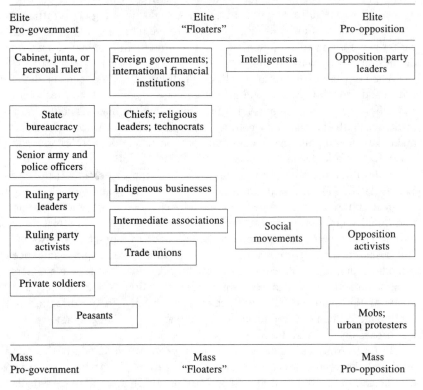

Elite Pro-government	Elite "Floaters"		Elite Pro-opposition
Cabinet, junta, or personal ruler	Foreign governments; international financial institutions	Intelligentsia	Opposition party leaders
State bureaucracy	Chiefs; religious leaders; technocrats		
Senior army and police officers			
Ruling party leaders	Indigenous businesses		
Ruling party activists	Intermediate associations	Social movements	Opposition activists
	Trade unions		
Private soldiers			
	Peasants		Mobs; urban protesters
Mass Pro-government	Mass "Floaters"		Mass Pro-opposition

The horizontal axis suggests a continuum that groups may occupy between membership in, or support for, the government and support for the opposition; the vertical axis suggests their positions on an elite-mass continuum. The latter continuum is important on account of the different resources that various groups will employ in pursuit of their demands. The table therefore brings together the different approaches emphasizing structures, elites and masses, and groups, which we explored earlier in this chapter. I argue that most third world societies are better viewed as consisting of groups rather than social classes. Many of the groups have little formal organization and the boundaries of their membership may be unclear, but there can still be a clear perception within a group—whether it be a group of soldiers, clergy, or the urban unemployed—of where their interests lie and what their ideological position should be. Whether a particular group belongs to an elite, in the sense of a body of individuals whose wishes generally prevail in a particular area of policy or in decisionmaking in general, is not always clear. Table 8.4 suggests a continuum from the most to the least influential on the vertical axis, though there is obviously room for argument as to where each group belongs at any given time or place.

Elites may be able to use formal authority, control over the machinery of state, or manipulation of their followers, while the masses will be more dependent on weight of numbers, whether in casting votes, violence, or civil disobedience. The use, or threatened use, of such resources might therefore produce a different type of transition from that initiated at the elite level. Table 8.4 might suggest the layout of a battlefield, but it is a field in which several battles may be going on simultaneously, with the contestants not necessarily remaining on the same side throughout. There is a configuration of issues as well as a configuration of interests, and democracy may be only one of several outcomes being sought. The more immediate interests of groups may be with such matters as higher wages for trade unionists, better equipment for soldiers, more foreign exchange for businesses, higher commodity prices for cooperatives, or adequate roads for farmers marketing their crops. The government may be under pressure, but people are not necessarily seeking its removal. Even when they are, they are not necessarily seeking democracy. Members of tribe A may want to displace the authoritarian government dominated by tribe B to ensure that more of the benefits of political patronage are diverted to them. Middle-ranking army officers may want to displace a government run by senior officers in order to enjoy the spoils of office. But none of these changes would necessarily imply any shift to democracy (see especially Herbst 1994: 190).

Yet within this kaleidoscope of varied groups with varied demands, there will be some groups that can normally be identified as supporters of the status quo and some that are likely to be proponents of democracy, with a large middle band of "floaters" whose role may be crucial in determining the outcome. Members of the ruling party or state bureaucracy are unlikely to turn against the government, whereas students and academics are seldom enthusiastic supporters of authoritarian rule. The position of soldiers is slightly more problematic, but the plotting of coups is generally a minority activity occupying very little time, in contrast to the long periods during which the military sustain authoritarian governments. Businesses prefer not to be too openly involved in politics and prefer to be on good terms with whoever is in power, but they may begin to look to opposition groups if these appear to offer a better deal without creating instability.

These different positions are more frequently taken for granted than explained. We are used to the peasant dutifully supporting the government no matter what hardships the government imposes, the sociology professor and the lawyer demanding democratic rights despite their apparently privileged positions in the existing order, and the opportunist businessman changing sides when it seems expedient to do so. Nyong'o explains "African bourgeois" demands for democracy in terms of expectations of less corruption and a more efficient allocation of resources (Nyong'o 1992: 99), and it may well be that the longer authoritarian government lasts, the more corruption and inefficiency are exposed, so that there is a general bourgeois stampede toward democracy. But even here a rational calculation of what is best in terms of value for money may merge into broader ideological or even philosophical considerations about what form of government is socially desirable. We should not underplay the importance of political conviction and the way in which it can gather momentum.

Alternative explanations might be sought in terms of the disciplines that an occupation highlights, though at the risk of creating rigid stereotypes. Academics and lawyers expect the truth to emerge through allowing the flow of conflicting evidence, whereas technocrats and soldiers perceive incontrovertible solutions and are less tolerant of dissent, while business-people seek a "best buy" with less concern for the processes by which the policies they favor have emerged. But we need to be careful to distinguish between the pursuit of democracy as a desirable end and actions that have the effect of easing the transition. Technocrats, and even soldiers, may turn against an authoritarian government if they feel it is straying from the correct path, and they may make common cause with opposition groups concerned more specifically with democracy.

We are still left with the floaters whose position may be crucial in achieving or blocking the transition. Religious groups, chiefs, trade unions, and self-help groups are not primarily concerned with the advancement of democracy, although individuals within these categories will have their own preferences. Like businesses, they may be more concerned with the impact of individual policies than with whether the government is democratically elected; unlike businesses, they are more likely to be adversely affected by the policies of retrenchment and economic liberalization that are the government's response to economic decline, as employment, real wages, and social provision are reduced. The effects on churches are less obvious than on the other groups, yet they may be used as vehicles for protest if more formal means of protest are prohibited. Embryonic opposition parties will want to incorporate the floaters into a broader challenge to authoritarianism, but the government will be equally eager to contain them within its sphere of influence. Many will already exist as "wings of the party" in a one-party state, and a military government may try to bring them under its umbrella as revolutionary committees or as bodies dependent on state patronage.

On the face of it, a government with powers of patronage, coercion, and financial inducements holds the advantage in winning the middle ground. But if the groups are hostile to the policies that have affected them adversely, the government may have to pay a price for their allegiance in terms of a greater willingness to consult and permit a greater degree of criticism and autonomous activity. The government may ultimately retain enough support from the key groups to win a competitive election, but the fact that democratization has advanced to a point where it is deemed necessary to hold an election is a reflection of the ability of the floaters to create new openings.

The Arenas

We now turn to the types of ground on which the contests in the battle for democracy are fought. Occasionally the battle scene will be a dramatic one, with the red flag raised in victory for democracy, as in Nicaragua with the ousting of Somoza, or the white flag raised in humiliation, as with the departure of military governments in Argentina and Greece after failed foreign adventures. But more often there is a process of negotiation. The negotiating table may be a literal and not just a metaphorical one, as in Uruguay in 1981 when members of the military government sat down with their adversaries to secure a smooth exit from politics, or in South Africa between 1992 and 1994 when the dismantling of apartheid was agreed. In other cases the authoritarian rulers and their opponents refuse to talk to each other directly, but each side reads the signals coming out of the rival camp and from the broader political forces at home and abroad. Huntington sketches out a typical sequence in which the government begins to lose its authority after allowing some liberalization and then finds that the opposition exploits this, expands its support, and intensifies its actions. The government reacts to contain the opposition, and government and opposition then begin to explore negotiation (Huntington 1991–1992: 608–609). Karl elaborates on the "foundational pacts" that then follow. These make pluralist democracy conditional on the contending forces not harming each other.

> The pacts serve to ensure survivability because, although they are inclusionary, they are simultaneously aimed at restricting the scope of representation in order to reassure dominant classes that their vital interests will be respected. In essence, they are anti-democratic mechanisms, bargained by elites, which seek to create a deliberate socio-economic and political contract that demobilises emerging mass actors while delineating the extent to which all actors can participate or wield power in the future. (Karl 1990: 11–12)

At this extreme end, the process of transition depends on a small number of people who can fit into one room, even though they may claim to represent larger segments of society; in other cases it has been necessary to establish more broadly representative bodies. Two devices frequently used are the national conference and the constituent assembly. The conference was common in Francophone Africa, and was also used in Ethiopia,

Somalia, and South Africa. It does not necessarily have any formal powers of decisionmaking, but it has the advantage of bringing an authoritarian government face-to-face with representatives of various sections of civil society and opposition parties and may therefore make the ultimate settlement less elitist. It might be compared with a jury, passing a verdict on the survival of an authoritarian government, but with the disadvantage that it tends to be a "yes" or "no" verdict, leaving little room for compromise. Bratton and van de Walle suggest such a "winner takes all" contest enabled authoritarian rulers to survive in the Congo (then Zaire) and Togo, while incumbent rulers collapsed in Benin, Congo (Brazzaville), and Niger (Bratton and van de Walle 1997: 172–173; see also Baker 2001: 91.)

The creation of a constituent assembly implies that even the incumbent regime acknowledges the need for a new constitutional order. One-party regimes are generally reluctant to do this, having for years claimed a legitimate mandate from the people, but military rulers only claim a mandate to tackle immediate problems in the absence of competent politicians. They eventually need to convert themselves into civilian rulers or to usher in a new order. This may amount to no more than a cynical ploy to legitimize continued authoritarian rule, as with General Pinochet's referenda in Chile in which he sought to regularize his position. His defeat in the second referendum in 1988 showed the danger in such a strategy, as did the moral defeat of General Acheampong in his referendum on the no-party state in Ghana in 1978, when he had to depart after 45 percent of the electorate had voted against him despite every attempt to rig the poll. The constituent assembly is a safer strategy, leaving scope for the rulers to influence the composition of the body and the agenda it considers, including the immunity of the outgoing rulers from prosecution. The assembly can include representatives not only of geographical constituencies but of a variety of groups, from soldiers and lawyers to hairdressers and canoe fishermen, thus giving a role to civil society, but the rulers will normally reserve the right to nominate a substantial proportion of the members. While the rulers may lose some of the arguments, there is less risk of losing control altogether, compared with the zero sum games implicit in the national conference and the referendum. Constituent assemblies enabled the military to hand over power to their favored civilians in Ghana in 1969 and enabled Flight Lieutenant Jerry Rawlings to transform himself into President Rawlings in 1992 after hastily creating his own political party. President Yoweri Museveni enjoyed similar success in Uganda in transforming his insurgent movement into an elected government.

In the case of one-party regimes, the strategy is frequently to accept internal and external pressures for democratization but to insist that this requires little more than permitting opposition parties to contest elections without making any major constitutional changes. Lacking any doubts about their own legitimacy, the rulers do not feel the need to negotiate with the opposition or civil society representatives through a national conference or a constituent assembly (though foreign donors did force President Hastings Banda to hold a referendum, which he lost, on the maintenance of the one-party state in Malawi). Kenya and Tanzania both underwent government-controlled transitions, as opposition groups were kept waiting outside while their rulers decided when, and under what rules, they would be permitted to contest elections. Such a strategy does not guarantee that the erstwhile authoritarians will win a democratic election, as the defeat of President Kenneth Kaunda in Zambia shows, but it will normally handicap the opposition both strategically and ideologically. Strategically, the government can devise rules that will enhance its own prospects of success, whether it is in permitting a presidential candidate to win on a minority vote or in maintaining state domination of broadcasting. Ideologically, an election can be presented to voters as an opportunity to reaffirm their allegiance rather than as a new political departure.

Conclusion

Running through much of this chapter has been the paradox that transitions to democracy in the third world in recent years have apparently been easier and more rapid than they were in the West in the nineteenth and early twentieth centuries, despite the handicaps of severe poverty, economic decline, and cultural heterogeneity, when earlier literature had suggested that democracy required social and economic development, a civic culture, and national unity. Various favorable circumstances have helped the process. There are functioning democratic systems in existence in the West that, in modified form, may serve as models to emulate, in contrast to the absence of any such models when Western societies began to challenge authoritarian rule. The ending of the Cold War has reduced ideological polarization, which has made rival contenders for power less incompatible with one another and reduced Western attempts to discourage democratization for fear of the "wrong" side winning. There is generally less of an entrenched ruling class, compared with nineteenth-century Europe, to resist the demands of the lower orders, and a more fluid social structure makes it possible to build a winning coalition of groups that want to challenge an authoritarian government. The fluidity also provides scope for the choices and influences of individual actors such as Mandela or Nyerere to play a significant role. There is, for all the talk of economic dependency, a sense in which political will can triumph over economic power. Our examples of El Salvador and South Africa showed that economic elites could have their power bases undermined by political challenges to the government, whether through civil war or the withdrawal of foreign investment, and that these elites then sought conciliation with pro-democratic forces. To say that democracy has become the only game in town would be an exaggeration, but the unattractiveness of alternative games such as religious fundamentalism, genocide, and bandit capitalism might make the quest for democracy seem more worthwhile.

Problems begin to arise when we look at "grasp" rather than "reach." There may be a functioning Western model that many—though by no means all—democrats in the third world would like to emulate, and some foreign practices can obviously be imported. But what is feasible in the political system as a whole is likely to depend more on the indigenous cultures, values, ideologies, institutions, and power structures, not all of which will be conducive to democracy in a contemporary nation-state. Uruguay may be able to achieve a transition to something close to the tried and tested form of democracy that the country had experienced for much of the previous century, but Kenya and Indonesia cannot. Some institutions in third world countries may be conducive to democracy, but bureaucracies, armies, religious leaders, and chiefs will not necessarily fit easily into any democratic consensus. There might once have been a hope that mass movements would facilitate wider participation and social justice, but deindustrialization or the absence of industrialization make this unlikely for the foreseeable future.

Finally, there is the distinctive role of the state in third world countries. It may not be strong in terms of capacity, and any stranglehold over civil society may have been weakened by economic liberalization, yet control over the machinery of state, and access to those who control it, are important to personal prosperity or sheer survival. This is in contrast to the earlier democratization process in many European countries where there were more sources of income that were not dependent on the state. Third world rulers who have lost their grip on the state when they are unable to maintain order or pay the wages of their soldiers or civil servants have often had to pay a heavy price, and they have lost control over the process of transition. Those who have maintained a minimal grip have been better able to control the process of transition to their advantage, whether through orchestrating the proceedings of constituent assemblies or simply ignoring the opposition and imposing their own settlement. However, even if we retain our minimal definition of democracy, we may find that what emerges is a fledgling democracy whose survival is threatened from different sides. There may be the disorder that the outgoing rulers failed to control or the authoritarian tendencies that those who retained control of the transition are reluctant to abandon. Our next task is to examine the ability of these fledgling democracies to survive, or even to prosper, in the harsh environment into which they have been born.

9

Democratic Consolidation or Democratic Decay?

> It is difficult to identify and analyse . . . what I propose to call *unconsolidated* democracies. Regimes trapped in this category are, in a sense, condemned to democracy without enjoying the consequences and advantages that it offers. They are stuck in a situation in which all the minimal procedural criteria for democracy are respected. Elections are held more or less frequently and more or less honestly. The various liberal freedoms exist—multiple political parties, independent interest associations, active social movements, and so on—but without mutually acceptable rules of the game to regulate the competition in the formation of governments and policies. Each party considers itself uniquely qualified to govern the country and does what it can to perpetuate itself in power. Each group acts only in the furtherance of its own immediate interests, without taking into consideration its impact upon the polity as a whole. Whatever formal rules have been enunciated (in the constitution or basic statutes) are treated as contingent arrangements to be bent or dismissed when the opportunity presents itself. (Schmitter 1995: 16)

Schmitter's description of unconsolidated democracy suggests a survival of "business as usual" in many countries, despite the completion of transitions that have replaced authoritarian rule with nominally democratic structures. Consolidated democracy, in contrast, implies not merely the existence of new structures but of attitudes, behavior, and processes that reflect the spirit as well as the letter of democracy. Linz and Stepan suggest that consolidation has been achieved when (1) no significant political actors try to achieve their objectives by creating a nondemocratic regime or encourage violence, foreign intervention, or secession; (2) the vast majority of the population believe in democratic government, and supporters of antidemocratic alternatives are few and isolated; and (3) conflicts are resolved within specific laws, procedures, and institutions sanctioned by the democratic process (Linz and Stepan 1996: 6).

There is ample scope for creating models of consolidated and unconsolidated democracy, but is the concept of consolidation of any value in helping us to understand what happens once a transition to democracy has been completed? Baker and Hughes reject the utility of the concept on the grounds that it assumes that democracy is permanent and cannot be destroyed (Baker and Hughes 2000: 7); and Aguero and Stark object that the concept skirts around the question of how incomplete, contradictory, and disjointed the actual regimes are (Aguero and Stark 1998: 373). These may be valid criticisms of the ways in which some writers have employed the concept, but does one have to believe that the existing political systems should be measured against some perfect and permanent form of democracy, or reject the concept altogether? The experience of fascism in the 1940s and neocolonialism from the 1950s onward should be sufficient to dispel any illusions of permanence. As for the imperfections, these can be the lifeblood of democracy, as rulers in even the most long-standing democracies are challenged on such matters as bypassing legislatures, politicizing the civil service, or evading ministerial responsibility, and are forced either to win support for their behavior or to change their ways. Without seeking perfection, one can recognize the contrast between the behavior in Linz and Stepan's model, which implies the observance of democratic norms, and the behavior in Schmitter's model, which indicates a frequent desire and ability to evade such norms.

There is still the question of what sort of democracy one has in mind when assessing whether it has been consolidated. If one's expectations do not go far beyond the survival of an electoral democracy, the criteria for assessing the extent of consolidation would include the fairness of the electoral process, the opportunities for freedom of expression and association, and possibly the protection of civil liberties. If, however, the goal was a more participatory, social democracy, one would want to look at the opportunities for effective involvement in political parties and pressure groups, the responses of the government to mass public opinion, and its willingness and ability to redistribute power and wealth away from the elite. Whether consolidation of one of these forms of democracy is necessarily conducive to the other is a question that has seldom been asked directly. It is tempting to believe that the achievement of relatively free and fair elections is a necessary step toward any broader or deeper democracy, but Burnell warns that the factors encouraging formal democracy in Africa may impede the growth of a more egalitarian democracy, as economically entrenched groups try to retain their positions (Burnell 1998: 22–23). It certainly seems to be the case that many ruling politicians and elites are now in a more secure position than they were under authoritarian rule, as they can claim a democratic mandate that reduces any pretext that the military or foreign governments might have for seeking their removal.

Most of the literature, however, seems to see democracy as one large entity rather than a set of subtypes, and the extent of consolidation is measured by examining such variables as the working of political institutions, the attitudes and behavior of citizens, the scope for political choices, and the ability to achieve outputs that reflect the wishes of the majority, including greater social equality and reduced poverty. There are obvious objections to such an indiscriminate approach. Not only does it make it unclear what sort of democracy is (or is not) being consolidated, but it may impose the criteria of an outsider, or a member of a minority group, in assessing success or failure. Should we, for example, accept Shin's view that consolidation in South Korea has been limited by the underrepresentation of the masses and by intolerance toward any policy alternatives that smack too much of communism (Shin 1999: 39–40, 262), or should we judge the effectiveness of consolidation by standards that most South Korean political actors would accept? There are no entirely satisfactory answers, but in this chapter we consider consolidation in terms of any processes that broaden or deepen democracy, whether at the basic level of ensuring a consensus on the administration of elections, or in terms of establishing a range of institutions, attitudes, and processes that extend opportunities for political choice and participation and reduce the scope for the arbitrary exercise of power or discrimination.

In this chapter, we shall look at examples of alleged successes or failures in consolidation, the relevance of the preconditions for democracy to consolidate, and the extent to which the processes of transition have laid the foundations for consolidation. We shall then explore the contribution of evolving political institutions and public attitudes to the process of consolidation.

Consolidated and Unconsolidated Democracy: Some Successes and Failures

Despite the rapid rise in the number of democracies since the 1980s, very few third world countries are regarded as enjoying consolidated democracy. The continuous democracies that were described in Chapter 6 qualify, almost by definition, even if they are not sufficiently participatory or egalitarian for some tastes, or are too dominated by social, business, or religious elites. For all these imperfections, they have evolved working systems in which any exercise of arbitrary power is severely limited in scope and duration and in which a variety of means of articulating interests and opinions have remained open. Of the countries that have emerged from authoritarian rule, Uruguay is the only one that appears to enjoy universal acclaim as a consolidator, despite the continued ambiguous position of the military and the relatively poor performance of elected governments (Linz and Stepan 1996: 151–165; Diamond et al. 1999: 61; Stockton 2001: 108). Behind Uruguay, less enthusiastic claims might be made for Argentina, Chile, South Africa, and even Ghana. The performances of Argentinian governments have been substantially worse than those in Uruguay, which makes it all the more remarkable that voters are still able to change their governments through the ballot box, that the military remain under civilian command, and that nondemocratic alternatives attract little support. But Waisman reports that presidential power remains excessive, and respect for the rule of law is unstable and conditional (Waisman 1996: 122). Chilean democracy emerged with the handicap of an army departing from power from a position of strength, which was reflected in the appointment of General Augusto Pinochet as "senator for life" and the subsequent inability to put him on trial, but none of this has prevented orderly changes of government and a general reluctance to act outside the democratic process (Diamond et al. 1999: 61).

South Africa appears to have a weaker case in that there is little prospect of a change of government through the ballot box, given the extent of voting along ethnic lines, and there are signs of a greater intolerance toward opposition (Giliomee 1999: 140–154). There is also the criticism that the state is largely closed to popular influence while open to the corporate and professional sectors (Lowe 1999: 429). This may reflect disappointment with a regime initially created on a wave of popular support, but such a criticism could equally be directed at many Western democracies. Against this, South Africa has maintained most of its democratic institutions intact and practiced a form of power sharing rare in Africa (see especially Southall 2000: 147–170). Ghana's case has fewer advocates. Haynes is pessimistic about consolidation on the grounds that there is still no agreement between the political actors on the principles of cooperation and competition in the formulation of government policy. Moreover, the pursuit of power is a zero-sum game, with control of the state as a highly prized goal (Haynes 1999: 5–22). Yet Sandbrook suggests that a party system with a long history has been consolidated (Sandbrook 2000: 126), and this may set Ghana apart from many of its neighbors. There is almost a microcosm of Rustow's rival elites first fighting each other but eventually realizing that they must live together. The rivalry goes back to the 1940s and has involved substantial violence and repression, but there have also been relatively free elections in 1969, 1979, 1996, and 2000 that provide some foundation for democratic competition, with the latter election producing a peaceful transfer of power. Apart from their mature years, the major parties contribute to democracy because, beyond their ethnic and ideological cores, they need to build broad coalitions of support so that no one party is guaranteed indefinite power (Rustow 1970: 337–363).

Any attempt to extend the list of consolidated democracies still further would be to strain either the concept or the interpretation of the facts. Observers would probably disqualify most of tropical Africa, Central America outside Costa Rica, most of South America, and most of Asia outside India. (A case might be made for Bangladesh with its ability to change governments through the ballot box, but this is in a context within which severe poverty limits any government's room for maneuver). Sieder's description of the democratic deficits in Central America could be applied to different degrees to many of the other unconsolidated democracies. The military are still involved in politics, the judiciary is still politicized, and political parties are unstable and unable to mediate and represent different interests. There is a lack of accountability and transparency, structural adjustment programs make it difficult to control economic policy, and there is inadequate representation of women, marginalized urban groups, and indigenous groups (Sieder 1996: 274–276). The emphasis in this account is on the state rather than society, but the evidence suggests that civil society is frequently unable to constrain or cooperate with the state and that there is often an absence of deeply held democratic values. Even in a prosperous country like South Korea, the attitudes and social institutions that nurtured democracy in the West do not appear to be so abundant (Shin 1999: 39–40; Im 2000: 21–52).

How does one explain the small number of successes and the larger number of failures in consolidation? An immediate reaction might be to explain the relative successes in terms of previous democratic experience before the third wave. Argentina, Chile, and Uruguay all have long histories of democracy based on multiparty politics, even if this has been punctuated by military intervention and populism and strained by social polarization. South Africa had a pluralist system before and during the apartheid years, albeit one open only to the European minority, which could be adapted with the coming of majority rule. In contrast, most of the current unconsolidated democracies have had a less propitious history. Even when they have had nominally democratic government, this has been constrained by the influence of the military, rigged elections, and a mixture of patronage and coercion to minimize any opposition.

If we focus on the adjective "consolidated," it is clear that the consolidated democracies are those with the richest democratic history, but if we focus on the verb "to consolidate," there is more scope for examining the fine detail. Most third world democracies are not consolidated, but specific actions may have been taken, by accident or design, that consolidate *particular aspects* of democracy and thus make the survival of democracy as a whole less precarious. The actions may range from the disqualification of corrupt members of Parliament in Tanzania through steps to ensure the more impartial administration of elections in Ghana, or the adoption of proportional representation in South Africa, to public demonstrations to prevent military rulers from winning a bogus election in Côte d'Ivoire and public pressure to remove the corrupt President Fernando Collor in Brazil. In the pages that follow, we shall explore the various actions that contribute to or retard consolidation, even if they leave countries far short of any completely consolidated utopia.

Background:
Preconditions and the Processes of Transition

Why should many third world countries have democratic constitutions but day-to-day political processes that frequently fall short of democracy? The traditional road to understanding the existence of democracy was via a search for preconditions such as economic development and a civic culture that embraced democratic values. The more modern road has often been via a search for favorable transitions, where authoritarianism can be undermined and judicious political behavior can achieve democratic outcomes. The road to democracy traveled by Britain (considering the revolution of 1688 as the starting point and the 1884 Reform Act as the culmination) required a journey of nearly two centuries in which the various preconditions gradually nurtured democracy. In Ghana and Tanzania the transition lasted less than a decade. These countries had apparently followed the bypass while Britain had followed the packhorse route, but perhaps the African countries failed to pick up some of the necessary baggage on the way.

It is not simply a matter of arguing that democracy, like whisky, improves with age. Japan developed a relatively successful pluralist system from a standing start in 1945, while South American countries, which began their first attempts at democracy much earlier, have had more checkered careers. Spain was a late starter and had had only limited democratic experience before 1975. No doubt greater democratic maturity is an additional asset, but Japan and Spain did appear to enjoy many of the generally accepted social and economic preconditions that most of the third world lacks. While indigenous intellectuals and external powers may continue to insist on preserving the freedoms that Schmitter describes, the establishment or enforcement of his "mutually acceptable rules of the game" remains a difficult task. At an abstract level, most significant political actors would probably prefer democracy, however loosely defined, to any other set of political arrangements, but the immediately rational course of action in preserving or advancing one's interests may lead to behavior that is detrimental to democracy. Yet such behavior is not subject to the sanctions that it would be likely to face in the West. Bribery, patronage, election rigging, and voting for politicians who are more interested in trading benefits for votes than in observing democratic norms are all manifestations of such behavior. This can be attributed partly to the immaturity of democracy but also to conditions in which poverty makes for a more desperate struggle for power and in which civil society provides inadequate counterweights to undemocratic behavior. There may also be sins of omission, as well as commission, that inhibit the growth of democracy. These include a reluctance to jeopardize one's career or wealth by criticizing authority, and a reluctance to devote one's energies to building up pressure groups or opposition parties if their prospects of power or influence seem remote in the face of a government that controls the key resources (Schmitter 1995: 16).

If the culmination of the democratic transition in Britain was 1884 (though some people might prefer 1928), the democratic consolidation over the following century can be seen in an acceptance of the legitimacy of participation in the political process by business, trade unions, professional, and later environmental groups, and in the responsiveness of the state to public demands for extensive social provision, especially in relation to education, health, housing, working conditions, and social security. At the same time, new avenues were opened up, through such devices as administrative tribunals, public inquiries, and ombudsmen, to enable the aggrieved citizen to seek redress against the state. This is not to suggest that perfection was achieved, but the legitimacy that the state enjoyed, in the eyes of the newly enfranchised population, owed much to its willingness and ability to respond to the demands of society. Civil society attracted more adherents largely because it could be seen to be shaping the political environment and, as it grew, it became better able to impose checks on the state. What is the relevance of this to the third world? There are clearly few immediate prospects of any great expansion of social provision, and states seem ill-equipped to improve channels of redress. In the face of economic constraints and a tenuous hold on the administrative process, mere survival might be regarded as an achievement, without any attempts to build a welfare state or a participatory democracy. As Schmitter points out, democratic transition and attempts at consolidation often occur at times when there are pressing parallel problems such as civil control over the military, the efficiency of the fiscal system, the fate of inefficient state enterprises, and the stabilization of the currency (Schmitter 1995: 27).

The process of transition may be constrained not only by the absence of adequate preconditions but by the ways in which the process occurred. The groups that dominate the transition are seldom interested in democracy solely as an end in itself and may often shape the new structures to enhance their own privileges. Table 9.1 lists various types of transition and their possible implications for any subsequent consolidation.

Who? Groups Dominating the Transition: Government, Opposition, and Transplacement

The classification of transitions according to the nature of the group dominating the process is brought out especially clearly by Huntington, who suggests processes of transformation (initiated by governments or elites), transplacement (involving joint actions by government and opposition), replacement (initiated by the opposition), and intervention (initiated by a foreign power) (Huntington 1991–1992: 582). Of the countries normally

Table 9.1 Classification of Democratic Transitions, and Their Possible Implications for Consolidation

Criteria for Classification	Possible Implications for Consolidation	Examples
1. Who? Groups dominating the transition (Huntington 1991–1992)		
Government	Veto by old elites or military	Most of tropical Africa
Opposition	Old elites are weaker	Argentina; Greece
Balance between government and opposition	Consensus between elites and counterelites	El Salvador; Honduras; South Africa; South Korea; Uruguay
External	External veto	Germany and Japan 1945
2. How? Processes of transition (Karl 1990)		
Pact	Veto by old elite; consensus; stability	Chile; South Africa; Uruguay
Imposition	Veto by old elite	Most of tropical Africa; Brazil; Ecuador
Reform or revolution	Limited consensus or stability; greater popular participation; equality	Bolivia; Nicaragua
3. With whose support? Compatibility of objectives (Share 1987)		
Consensus	Consensus; stability	South Africa; Spain; Uruguay
Conflict	Instability	Kenya; Nicaragua
4. At what pace and to what magnitude? The extent and pace of change (Karl 1990; Share 1987)		
Moderate	Veto by old elite	Most of tropical Africa; Uruguay
Radical	External veto	Nicaragua; Spain
Gradual	Consensus	Most of tropical Africa; Brazil
Rapid	Indeterminate	Argentina; Greece; Nicaragua; Spain

regarded as belonging to the third world, the only example Huntington offers of democracy through foreign intervention is the dubious one of Grenada, and only Argentina and the Philippines achieved democracy through an opposition initiative. The remaining cases are divided evenly between those of a government initiative and a joint government-opposition initiative.

The qualifications we need to make to such a classification should be clear from previous chapters. Governments and oppositions are not monolithic groups with clearly defined boundaries, and there is room for argument about how far these different modes of transition are independent variables that shape subsequent consolidation or whether they are merely reflections of the reality of power in the countries concerned. Thus, one might attribute the relative stability of (but limited participation in) Brazilian democracy, and the high potential for military or elite veto in the democratic process, to a government-controlled transition. But this would ignore Brazil's long tradition of a strong state that casts its shadow over both transition and subsequent consolidation. The limited number of opposition-dominated transitions also requires comment. Unless a regime suffers military defeat (Argentina and Greece), internal collapse (the Philippines), or the loss of a powerful foreign backer (possibly the Philippines), it is difficult for the opposition to exercise much leverage against an intransigent government unless it does so by proxy through the military, as in Ghana in 1966, or through a full-blown revolution. Revolutions are also a rarity in the third world, for reasons beyond the scope of this study, though the absence of a large urban proletariat is obviously one factor. And when revolutions do occur, they seldom facilitate the consensus necessary for democracy.

It would require an extremely deterministic approach to attribute government control, or lack of it, over transitions simply to immovable traditions or power structures. The countries in which, according to Huntington, governments have initiated transitions include (1) relatively integrated ones such as Brazil, (2) fragmented ones such as Guatemala and Nigeria, (3) countries with relatively professional armies in government such as that in Pakistan, and (4) countries with factionalized armies such as in Nigeria. Similarly, the countries experiencing joint government-opposition initiative vary from the stable Uruguay to the unstable El Salvador and from the wealth of South Korea to the poverty of Honduras. This might suggest that the source of initiative depends at least partly on the choices made by political actors and not just on preordained conditions. But what difference does the source of initiative make for subsequent consolidation? Table 9.1 hypothesizes that the variables of stability, nondemocratic veto, and inequality might be influenced by the extent to which the transition was government-dominated or sponsored jointly by government and opposition. One would expect joint government-opposition action to usher in greater stability if the democratic settlement takes into account the interests of a wider variety of groups, whereas a government-initiated transition may be more the result of unpopular rulers running for cover (Nigeria and Pakistan) or seeking the least harmful means of preserving their interests (Brazil and Chile).

In some cases, there is the problem, noted in Chapter 8, of outgoing military governments prescribing constitutions that are incongruent with political reality and therefore break because they cannot be bent—hence the precariousness of civilian governments in Nigeria and Turkey. In other cases, the government may freeze out groups considered to be politically unacceptable, but they cannot be wished away, such as Marxist guerrillas in Guatemala. Where opposition groups have played a larger part, as in Uruguay, South

Korea, and perhaps El Salvador, a more even balance between rival groups may contribute to a more stable and lasting democracy.

The prospect of a veto on the democratic process appears to be greater in democracies built on government-dominated transitions. Such vetoes can be found in even the most "advanced" democracies, where elites try to prevent public debate on the privileges they enjoy, but they are much more immediately apparent in the third world, where elected governments challenge big business, landlords, the army, or foreign investors at their peril. The veto is a matter of degree, but a government, and especially a military government, that has kept the process of transition largely under its control is more likely to be able to build in mechanisms for veto, whether constitutionally or informally. The privileges preserved by the Brazilian and Pakistani military, for example, have at best made a large defense budget sacrosanct in countries where the poor might have different priorities with regard to public expenditure and at worst left the military as the final arbiter of what is politically acceptable. Even where opposition groups have played a large role in the transition, as in Uruguay and the extreme case of Argentina, armies have secured amnesties for the misdeeds they perpetuated when in power, yet that is a more defensive form of veto and has less bearing on day-to-day politics. A recognizable elite, of which the military is only a part, may nonetheless cast its shadow over most of the fledgling democracies discussed here. This point emerges again when we look at moderate and (less numerous) radical transitions, but it seems clear that where the government is either the dominant force or a significant force in the transition, we are not going to find participatory or socialist democracies at the end of the road. Governments concede to democratic demands in the expectation that competition for power will not threaten the unequal social and economic structure of which they are the beneficiaries.

How? The Process of Transition: Pacts, Imposition, and Reform

Pacts, as hinted in the previous chapter, may be metaphorical—a series of unwritten understandings rather than a sealed document—but they will reflect a relatively stable settlement, irrespective of whether the terms were initiated mainly by the government, the opposition, or half-and-half. Considering the outcomes in Table 9.1, transitions by pact score highly in terms of consensus—at least at the elite level—and in terms of stability but poorly in terms of prospects for equality and mass participation. They also leave a built-in elite veto in place. This does not mean that the new democracy is different only in name from the authoritarianism that went before. Apart from the likely ending of arbitrary arrests, torture, and executions, trade unions may enjoy recognition and voters will at least be able to remove the most unpopular politicians. But capitalists are likely to enjoy guarantees against expropriation, and little is likely to be done to relieve the plight of the poor. Such a description would fit much of postauthoritarian Latin America and Pakistan until 1999.

Democracy by imposition, in Karl's terminology, occupies the "force" end of the compromise-force continuum (Karl 1990: 11–12). It may coincide with Huntington's "democracy by transformation" in which the government takes the lead, but the imposition could come from other sources, such as a foreign invader, the victor in a civil war, or an older elite that fills the vacuum left by a discredited military government, as in Greece after the failed invasion of Cyprus. The varied forms of these imposed transitions make it difficult to generalize about the nature of the democracy that will emanate from them, except to predict that the elites who facilitated their creation are likely to wield a powerful veto in the absence of countervailing forces.

Reforming and revolutionary transitions differ from the previous two types in that they are shaped more by the masses and less by elites. Karl distinguishes between the two by associating reforming transitions more with compromise and revolutionary ones with force, but for our purposes we can take the two types together. In Karl's definition (though with some qualifications), Argentina from 1946 to 1951, Guatemala from 1946 to 1954, and Chile from 1970 to 1973 were democracies established through reform, whereas Bolivia after 1952 and Nicaragua after 1979 (or possibly 1990) were democracies established by revolution. To seek social and economic reform while preserving or extending pluralist democracy and civil liberties may be a laudable objective, but it is likely to leave the door open to deposed elites wanting to return, so that consensus and stability will be under strain and the democratic experiment may have only a brief life, as Karl's chronology shows. Although the former civilian elite may have been politically disabled as a redistribution of resources weakened it, the army may still impose the ultimate veto. And foreign powers may feel that the revolution has gone too far in threatening their economic or strategic interests, as with the U.S.-supported invasion of Guatemala in 1954. For a brief spell, the radical democracy might evoke the praise of idealists for its pursuit of popular participation, equality, and social justice. However, like a desert flower, its vivid colors may last only briefly until its bloom fades as inclement conditions return.

With Whose Support? Compatibility of Objectives: Consensus and Conflict

Share, like Karl, offers a two-dimensional classification that enables him to produce four "boxes." In this case the dimensions are consensus and nonconsensus, and rapid change and gradual change (Share 1987: 530). The tempting inference from the former continuum would be that consensual transitions are a good thing because, like transitions based on pacts, they will lay down the rules and conventions for a lasting pluralist democracy, in contrast to the nonconsensual transition in Nicaragua, where the incoming regime was intolerant of its predecessors and reluctant to concede them democratic rights. A similar point was made by Weiner, who spoke of the need to win over a sufficient section of a military government by showing the moderate or right-wing credentials of its potential successors (Weiner 1987: 863), though doubts creep in at two points.

First, we need to know something about the breadth of the consensus. Hooper (1990) refers to the acceptance of the need for national unity by members of the departing Franco regime in Spain as an influence on their willingness to secure agreement with the opposition. The priority given to national unity would seem to imply a willingness to accommodate a variety of adversaries, even if they subscribe to radically different ideologies and represent radically different interests. This in turn might provide a basis for an inclusive democracy that is both broad, because it is reluctant to freeze out any significant group, and deep, because it is seen as necessary to maintain a long-established nation. In contrast, transitions from military government in some African states may only appear to be consensual. Few people are actively opposing the restoration of pluralist democracy through a given settlement. But this consensus is often a reflection of the convenience of soldiers who have found politics too tiresome and civilian elites who are thirsty for power. There may not be any deeper concern with the beneficial effects of maintaining the new democracy or with threats to other objectives, including national unity, in not maintaining it. As a result, the subsequent democracy may be unstable and short-lived.

Second, on the question of depth of the consensus, there is the danger of focusing on consensus between elites and ignoring the dissent of the masses, whose opinions on the democratic settlement may not have been sought. Gillespie (1990: 53–54) raised the question of the legitimate social order, as well as the political order, in South America. What are the positions of business, the educational system, professional elites, or the patriarchal family within the settlement? Even these questions are concerned with counterelites as much as nonelites, and the latter receive surprisingly little attention in the literature on transitions, beyond the observation that they may disrupt the consensus by making unacceptable demands or harboring unrealistic expectations.

It may be true in the third world, as it was true in the West in the formative years of pluralist democracy, that the transition is smoother if it is not overloaded with mass demands for increased participation or a wider distribution of wealth, but that is different from believing that it is possible to ignore such demands. Supporters of the "transition through elite consensus" hypothesis might point out that many countries have achieved relatively stable democracy through this route in recent years and that the masses have apparently been willing to accept poverty with political liberty as preferable to poverty without such liberty. Whether they will continue to do so, or whether political liberty will merely be regarded as a first installment of emancipation, is another matter. And if mass pressures do increase, how well equipped will the political system and society be to respond to them? In much of Europe it was possible to channel mass challenges through trade unions and political parties and thus to retain relative stability while extending equality and participation. But we have seen that in the third world the era of the mass party, and in many cases the powerful trade union, has been largely bypassed—these may be regarded as postindustrial societies that have not experienced full industrialization. If this is true, then mass pressures may be exerted more through social movements, and we have noted the difficulties of integrating these into the political process. While few people would prescribe political conflict as a desirable means to achieving stable democracy, we must avoid the assumption that recent or current transitions will establish such stability because they are built on consensus, if the consensus turns out to lack breadth or depth.

At What Pace and to What Magnitude? The Extent and Pace of Change

The moderate-radical axis might appear to be similar to the consensus-conflict one. Moderation will frequently go with consensus and radicalism with conflict, but not invariably. In Spain after the death of General Franco, there was a broad consensus in favor of what many would regard as radical changes in the political system, whereas the attempts to restore democracy in Nigeria were generally characterized by an absence of desire for radical change, in the sense that there was broad agreement on the desirability of checks and balances and a continuation of the mixed economy and the role of the chieftaincy. Yet there was intense conflict between different ethnic groups over constitutional provisions that would affect their relative strength.

Much of the literature praises moderation, just as it praises consensus, emphasizing both its existence in the minds of the key political actors and its desirability as a goal. Bermeo argues that it is important to keep the political stakes low. Authoritarian rulers may not surrender power if a left-wing party wins an election, and anyway the experience of authoritarian rule makes voters moderate. They do not want to vote for parties raising the political stakes (Bermeo 1990: 362–371). We are concentrating, of course, on transitions from non-left-wing forms of authoritarianism to democracy, which constitute the vast majority of transitions in the third world. Levine, focusing on Latin America and southern Europe, also argues that transition is helped by the moderate demands of the civilian population, which ensure the election of right-of-center parties without any need for the outgoing rulers to rig the ballot (Levine 1988: 381–382). Two pertinent questions must be asked here. First, is moderation an attitude of mind, or something for which people vote in the knowledge that a radical vote would not be acceptable? Second, are the initial elections at the end of authoritarian rule as free as they appear at first sight?

Several key politicians were disqualified from contesting elections in Turkey and Uruguay, and the military's manipulation of the electoral system in South Korea ensured a narrow victory for their candidate on a minority vote. The Pakistan military helped to prevent Benazir Bhutto from winning an overall majority by preventing people without identity cards (generally the poorest citizens) from voting. In Central America, even when elections are not rigged blatantly, the main contenders have been expected to declare their opposition to nationalization or punishment of soldiers for violating human rights. Voters have come to understand that, if they elect a left-wing party, it will not be allowed to take office and that it might therefore be more prudent to restrict their choice to parties acceptable to the outgoing authoritarians. The pattern may be less one of authoritarians and voters (and the parties representing them) subscribing to the same right-of-center consensus than of each calculating how far they can go without antagonizing the other to such an extent that the whole transition venture is shelved. The Pakistan military thus allowed an election to be held in 1988 on the tacit understanding that the Pakistan People's Party would tone down the policies it had favored in the 1970s, and Argentinian parties were careful not to jeopardize the prospects of a free election by promising over-rigorous prosecutions of soldiers who had served under General Leopoldo Galtieri.

What are the implications for democratic consolidation of this willingness to vote for moderation? Optimists might point out that in Argentina, Brazil, Chile, Uruguay, and Turkey, voters at least elected parties not favored by the outgoing authoritarians, even if these parties were not considered to be so radical by the latter as to be banned or harassed. And in Greece and Spain, cautious votes for "acceptable" parties were followed in subsequent elections by votes for parties further to the left. On the face of it, moderation made the transition to stable democracy easier and opened the door at least a crack to further installments of democracy. These installments might reduce the scope for military or elite vetoes and widen the range of ideological choices, but perhaps moderation is a necessary rather than a sufficient condition.

The extent to which perceived radical politicians were handicapped or outlawed in El Salvador, Guatemala, and Pakistan may have made for unstable forms of democracy circumscribed by a strong military veto, when a sweeping coup against the authoritarians, whether within the military or through a civilian revolt, might have ushered in a less constrained democracy. The obvious example here is Nicaragua, in which a fierce dispute was waged over the country's democratic credentials. Among the minority who see the prospects for democracy enhanced by a more radical transition, Cammack suggested that democracy might work better in Nicaragua than elsewhere because reforms had gone beyond mere institutional measures and had empowered the poor (Cammack 1991: 544). If radical changes reflect a broad consensus within society, as appears to have been the case with the transitions from authoritarianism in Eastern Europe and Spain (and an acceptance of liberal democracy in place of fascism does seem to be a radical political change, even if the economic changes were less dramatic), then perhaps a new democratic equilibrium can be achieved. But if—to return to the continuum of the previous section—the changes are the outcome of a fiercer conflict in which older elites reject the new order, the survival of the new order may be more precarious, with a prospect of armed rebellion together with external subversion if an international as well as a domestic consensus has been broken.

On the gradual-rapid continuum, the immediate problem is whether to make comparisons between different places or different times. We have noted that the transition in Britain took two centuries. The German transition that culminated in the Weimar Republic could be measured in decades rather than centuries and ushered in a much less stable system, although it was still a gradual transition compared with Brazil, where barely twelve years elapsed between the first concessions to democracy by the military government and the free elections that marked the end of military rule. Yet Brazil is regarded as a case of gradual transition by modern standards. As Baloyra (1987: 88) points out, less than seven years elapsed between the deterioration of authoritarianism and the installation of democracy in Latin American countries outside Brazil. In South Africa the dismantling of apartheid took barely five years. As with so many aspects of modern society, what was once regarded as indecent haste is now considered slow, and, as in other aspects of society, this has much to do with modern technology. Mass media and the ability of political leaders (and sometimes followers) to visit countries where pluralist democracy has already arrived make people living under authoritarian governments more aware of the alternatives available and more impatient to liberalize their own countries.

Conservatives might see gradual change as necessary for stability, and rapid change as a recipe for instability, with threats to democracy from ousted elites and the military. But as Share (1987) points out, much will depend on whether the rapid change is based on a broad consensus, as in Spain, or on the old regime being removed against its will by a popular uprising (Nicaragua), an invasion (Germany in 1945), a coup (Portugal), or an implosion as a result of its own incompetence (Argentina). In Spain most of the old elite was carried along, albeit reluctantly, in the rapid whirlwind of democratic change. In the other countries mentioned it was not, and much then depended on its willingness or ability to resist the new order.

One danger with the rapid-gradual axis is that it may imply that democratization is a relatively smooth process, whatever its duration. But what of the countries where the gradualness involves not slow, steady progress but a form of trench warfare between authoritarians and democrats in which a few miles of democratic territory may be gained in one battle, only to be lost in the next? This has been the case in much of Central America. Or there are cases, as in West Africa, where the war is actually won in the sense of free elections being achieved, only for democracy to be attacked again and defeated a few years later. One could argue that the occurrence of such battles is significant more for what they tell us about the underlying society than for predicting the nature of any democracy that ultimately emerges. But it seems useful to distinguish between a gradualness that allows a steady consolidation of democratic gains, whether in Britain in the nineteenth century or Brazil in the 1970s, and what is merely a lengthy time interval between the initial challenges to authoritarianism and the final democratic outcome, brought about by the ability of authoritarians to retreat and then regroup.

Political Institutions and Consolidation

A transition to democracy provides an opportunity to create or modify political institutions to minimize the risk of an authoritarian restoration, a descent into anarchy, or the tampering with the democratic process for undemocratic ends. We shall consider institutions under the headings of "Institutional Design," "Capacity," and "Accountability" and then look at two specific institutions, namely, political parties and the military.

Institutional Design

If we are looking for adventurous constitutional innovations, such as those of the American Founding Fathers, the Allies in Germany in 1945, or General Charles de Gaulle in France in 1958, we shall be disappointed. But institutional design in one country, even if it appears to be only marginally different from that of a neighboring country, can still make a significant difference in terms of governmental innovations. Amundsen et al. draw attention to the differences between South Africa and Zambia. South Africa has a system of proportional representation that makes inflated parliamentary majorities less likely, a president elected by Parliament and directly answerable to it, and a judiciary that is better able to keep the executive in check (Amundsen et al. 2001). Such innovations might be seen partly as building on the narrow democracy that existed under apartheid, but they could also be seen as reflecting a desire to protect the civil liberties that had been flouted under that regime. In Ghana, Gyimah-Boadi and Oquaye draw attention to post-transition innovations that made for fairer elections, following the boycott of the 1992 parliamentary election by the opposition on the grounds that the previous presidential contest had already been fixed and that further electoral participation would be pointless. If the opposition had continued to reject the legitimacy of elections, democracy would have been in serious trouble. By insulating the electoral commissioner more from political interference, and by developing a system in which civil society groups monitored elections, it was possible to hold elections in 1996 and 2000 that were acknowledged as fair by all sides (Gyimah-Boadi 1999: 105–121; Oquaye 2000: 54–55).

In other cases, institutional design appears to have lessened the prospects for consolidation because the elites dominating the transition process have entrenched their own positions. This has been achieved more through sins of (probably deliberate) omission rather than commission. In most of Africa, Baker points to the continued strength of the head of state and the security forces, the protection of private enterprise, and the subordination of the press and political parties. Not only have nineteen erstwhile autocratic leaders survived as heads of elected governments, but the personnel heading the civil service, the judiciary, the churches, the military, the media, and the ruling party are largely survivors of the previous authoritarian era, so that many authoritarian habits persist (Baker 2000: 10–11). Although recent elections in Ghana have been acknowledged as fairer than formerly, Bratton suggest that the general trend in Africa has been for the second election after transition to be of "lower quality" than the first, with more opposition boycotts, fewer changes of leadership, lower turnouts, and a larger share of votes and seats for the incumbents (Bratton 1999: 20–31). Such outcomes might be interpreted as reflecting voter satisfaction with the current rulers, yet a more skeptical view would be that the erstwhile authoritarians had learned how to manipulate the political process more effectively to minimize criticism and dissent.

In Latin America, changes of government have been more frequent since the restoration of democracy, but the institutional innovations to hold rulers and their officials to account have been minimal. In particular, persistence with the U.S. style of presidential constitutions, without the reality of U.S. checks and balances, has left extensive discretionary power in the hands of presidents and, in the cases of Guatemala and Peru, to periods of plebiscitory presidential rule. Everyday politics fall a long way short of consolidated democracy, but the ability of the legislature and judiciary to engineer the removal of the erring presidents in these countries, and in Brazil, is clearly a gain for democracy.

Capacity

Capacity is a problem both in the micro sense of states having difficulty in carrying out basic administrative functions and in the macro sense of lacking the autonomy to tackle the massive social and economic problems that most third world countries face. Even in a relatively "developed" country such as Argentina, there are said to be problems of tax evasion, corrupt judges, criminal policemen, and low standards of public health, education, and welfare (Waisman 1996: 71–130). In a poorer country like Uganda, a contrast can be drawn between the greater openness and free criticism, which had been facilitated by democratic transition, and the inability to punish those who had been found to transgress democratic norms (Furley 2000: 79–102; Tangri and Mwenda 2001: 117–133).

At the macro level, a minority of writers see the elimination of political extremism following the end of the Cold War as something that helps democratic consolidation by making for greater consensus.

> The Southern Cone demonstrates an underlying transition in the ideological stance of political elites across the region from a world view dominated by state-centred, conflict-dominated conceptions of domestic and international politics, to a world view in which democracy, the rule of law, liberalism, free markets, and regional co-operation structure domestic political agendas. (Steves 2001: 93; for a similar view, see also Green 1999: 21–22)

As was noted in previous chapters, the notion that free markets and globalization are good for democracy is one of opinion rather than fact. At the opposite extreme to Green and Steves are writers such as Abrahamsen who see the Western practice of linking good governance with economic liberalization as making for unstable, exclusionary democracies, with governments more concerned with satisfying foreign donors than their own constituents (Abrahamsen 2000: 139–140; see also the similar views of Hawthorn 1993: 1299–1312; and Peeler 1998: 154). Our concern here is not to assess the relative merits of free market and dirigiste economies but to consider whether free markets and globalization have limited the capacity of third world governments to deliver policies that reflect the wishes and needs of their citizens. In most cases, it would be difficult to deny that they have imposed substantial limitations, especially when the inability to protect the indigenous economy from global competition is added to the specific directives from foreign donors and creditors as to how the states' resources should be used. It has long been asserted that no country with a command economy has ever been democratic, yet few third world countries following the more extreme versions of free market economics have achieved democratic consolidation. Continuous democracies such as India,

Botswana, Costa Rica, and Mauritius are closer to the social democratic model—or were at the time when consolidation was achieved.

Accountability

In a mature democracy, capacity and accountability are often viewed as complementary. If policies can stand up to the rigorous scrutiny of legislatures, the media, and public opinion, they are far less likely to be misconceived or based on naked self-interest. That assumes that any scrutiny carried out is at least partly based on a search for the truth and the common good. There are, of course, many cases of reports on governmental inadequacies in Western democracies gathering dust once the initial shocks have subsided, but the problems of holding third world governments to account are made more difficult by the limited resources of legislatures, ombudsmen, and the media. Democratization has certainly made it easier to bring cases of maladministration to light without fear of punishment, but if those who reveal maladministration suffer limited personal inconvenience, the same is also true of many of the politicians and officials whose misdeeds are revealed. This may be attributed partly to the slow and creaking administrative and judicial processes (capacity) and partly to cultures in which corruption and maladministration do not always lead to public disapproval (see especially the case studies of Uganda by Furley 2000: 79–102; and Watt, Flanary, and Theobald 1999: 37–64.)

Specific Institutions: Political Parties and the Military

Of the third world institutions that deviate most markedly from their Western counterparts, political parties and the military are frequently singled out as major causes of the malfunctioning of democracy. In an ideal consolidated democracy, we are told, parties will represent a range of interests in society, provide ideological coherence, and enable voters to pass judgment on past and future policies, while the military remain obedient servants of political authority, defending the nation when necessary, but not using their weapons to press political demands. In most third world countries, the roles of parties and the military are very different from this.

Stockton offers a useful checklist of factors that are likely to make for "the institutionalization of political parties." These include the longevity of the parties, consistency in voting, parties not being based on personalities or regions, parties having strong links with organized groups but remaining autonomous from them, adaptability to change, and smooth successions to party leadership. In Latin America, he cites Chile, Costa Rica, and Uruguay as coming closest to these criteria (Stockton 2001: 102–108). Most studies of individual third world countries suggest that parties are inadequate in performing the textbook function of linking government to governed. Interludes of authoritarian government, in which many parties were outlawed and many leaders were arrested, have made the longevity of parties difficult and have made it hard for them to build and maintain mass support. A survey conducted in Latin America found that the percentage of voters who regarded themselves as "close to a political party" reached a maximum of only twenty-one in Uruguay and fell to six in Peru (Espindola 1997: 22). Hagopian found a steady fall in party identification in the 1980s and 1990s, from 44.4 to 24.6 percent in Argentina (1989–1995), 80 to 50 percent in Chile (1988–1996), and 62 to 49 percent in Mexico (1987– 1990), compared with a drop from 75 to 70.3 percent in Britain (1979– 1992) (Hagopian 1998: 116).

The absence of mass support is also highlighted in Thailand, where McCargo sees the likely future pattern as one of parties dominated by professional politicians and technocrats, with few members, personalized leadership, funding by interest groups, campaigning around particular issues, and carrying little ideological baggage (McCargo 1997: 130). Such a pattern would also be recognizable in much of tropical Africa, though the ideological baggage there tends to be even lighter and the interest groups are more likely to be based on ethnicity. Although ruling parties in Botswana, Kenya, and Tanzania have enjoyed unbroken rule since the 1960s, few opposition parties have enjoyed a similar longevity, so identification is again weak and support shallow. Funding is frequently a problem, and the expectation of state subsidies or foreign support reduces the incentive to deepen indigenous bases (see especially Southall and Wood 1998: 202– 228). In East Asia, money is said to be a problem for a different reason. Ferdinand suggests that consolidation is set back by the corrupt funding of parties, which again points to the absence of a broader base of support (Ferdinand 1998: 180–201).

The absence of clear party ideologies is a recurring theme. McCargo's description of nonmass, nonideological parties in Thailand is echoed by Kim in South Korea, where he observes that there are few ideological differences between the parties, which rely more on the charisma of party bosses to mobilize support, so that the party system has failed to transform electoral democracy into "a more responsive and participatory system" (Kim 1998: 117, 127). Shin also refers to weak party loyalty and the failure to consolidate democratic values (Shin 1999: 116, 219). In Central America, Cruz speaks of a de-ideologizing process, so that there are few differences between the parties, and the public interest is subordinated to the sectarian and personal interests of party leaders (Cruz 1996: 49).

The traditional party functions of articulating and aggregating interests was never going to be easy in preindustrial and postindustrial societies. Some of the Latin American parties went through a "mass" phase before the

1980s, when society was more organized into corporate groups and the state was more amenable to corporate pressure, but we have seen how dein-dustrialization and economic liberalization have destroyed many of the old corporate structures. In more atomized societies, populist leaders belonging to small fringe parties, notably in Guatemala and Peru, have been able to win power without finding the absence of a mass base any great handicap. In South Korea, as in the West, parties have found that the media and inter-est groups undermine their role in articulating interests and molding opin-ions (Shin 1999: 166) but with the difference, as in most of the third world, that the parties did not have a head start before such competition emerged.

Finally, few third world parties have been able to sustain support on the basis of their records in office. The worsening terms of trade since the 1980s, the growth of debt, and the need to comply with the strictures of for-eign donors and the World Trade Organization leave little room for vote-winning policy innovations. There may be periods of generous spending in the run-up to elections, as in Ghana and Kenya in the early 1990s, which pay electoral dividends, but this puts the emphasis on instrumental voting rather than deepening party loyalty.

Napoleon remarked that you could do anything with a gun except sit on it. Few soldiers have sat on power since the 1980s, but many have contin-ued to find ingenious ways of influencing political events, often to the detriment of democratic consolidation. Hunter's study of Latin America suggests that the significance of the military can be assessed in terms of both power and behavior. The military may enjoy legal or constitutional privileges, as in cases of exemption for prosecution for human rights vio-lations, or representation in the senate in Chile. But how they actually use their power will depend heavily on their perceptions of their role and inter-ests, which may be clouded by the setbacks and tensions suffered when they were previously in power, and by an awareness of the support, or lack of it, that they enjoy from the population. Soldiers in Argentina, who had relinquished power in disgrace after the Falklands War, might thus be more wary of intervening in politics than soldiers in Brazil where there is still some nostalgia for the days of military government (Hunter 1998: 299–322).

The continued presence of the military as a political force is in little doubt. In Pakistan the army imposed limitations on the scope of its civilian successor regime after 1988, before recapturing power in 1999, and Wilkin-son attributes the more precarious position of democracy in Pakistan, com-pared with Bangladesh, to the strength of the army as an institution that had a lot to lose if it lost control of events (Wilkinson 2000: 203–226). In Latin America, Linz and Stepan perceive a continuation of military constraints on politics in the Southern Cone (Linz and Stepan 1996: 219), and Fitch em-phasizes the continued influence of the military, even though all the mili-tary governments have now departed. If free market policies lead to greater

civil unrest, civilian governments could depend increasingly on the support
of the military (Fitch 1998: 162–163). In Peru, Mauceri attributes the
strength of Fujimori's "plebiscitory democracy" to the support of an army
and a politicized technocracy owing loyalty only to the president (Mauceri
1997: 899–911).

Yet one could equally remark on how little armies have done. The military have generally been reluctant to take power directly, influenced no
doubt by the chastening experiences of previous military government, public unpopularity in many countries, and a post–Cold War international climate hostile to military rule. It is a sign of changed times when an army is
hostile to a populist president who flouts the constitution in Guatemala and
keeps a relatively low profile at such flashpoints as the arrest of General
Pinochet, the fall of Presidents Fernando Collor and Alberto Fujimori in
corruption scandals, and the economic crisis of 2001 that brought down the
Argentine government. In Africa, military coups have also been few since
the 1980s, and civilian protesters succeeded in chasing the military out of
office in Côte d'Ivoire. In both Mali and Malawi, the military took the side
of civilian democrats against authoritarian rulers (Baker 2000: 24).

If soldiers are neither ruling countries directly nor passively obeying
their political masters at all times, this raises the question of exactly what
roles they are expected to perform and with what consequences for democratic consolidation. As was noted in Chapter 5, soldiers are often given—
or they take—largely autonomous roles in policing internal order and security, and this can ultimately take away yet another item on the political
agenda from elected governments, in addition to the partial loss of control
over social and economic policy to foreign donors. There are also dangers
in the well-meaning policy of "finding something useful for soldiers to do"
in areas such as the control of drug trafficking or crime generally. As Malan
points out, involvement in such areas may alienate soldiers from society
(Malan 2000: 157), especially if the methods used involve a disproportionate amount of force.

Our concern with both armies and political parties is not to praise or
condemn their behavior but to assess their contribution or otherwise to
democratic consolidation. Both institutions are frequently victims of circumstances rather than autonomous actors. It would be very difficult for
any political party in the current third world context to perform the textbook roles that enhanced consolidation in the West, though more leaders
like Mandela, Nehru, Nyerere, or Senghor might have made the task easier. The legacies of authoritarianism, economic hardship, post–Cold War
ideological convergence, and culturally diverse societies all make the task
a formidable one. The mere fact that competing parties are allowed to exist
and provide the opportunity or threat of a peaceful change of government

can be seen as a gain, but most countries are still a long way from a form of democracy in which clear alternative political choices are available and in which parties can be forged, or opinions influenced, in the cut and thrust of political dialogue.

Regarding the military, the signs are rather more helpful for democratic consolidation. One has only to look at the ways in which the governments in Ghana of Busia from 1969 to 1972 and Limann from 1979 to 1981 were dogged at every stage by the possibility of a military restoration to appreciate the greater freedom that democratic rulers now enjoy. The existence of the army as a pressure group that can behave in unpredictable ways, and which demands greater autonomy and resources than are really its due, has to be acknowledged, but the democratic process or the force of public opinion may now be making the military less of a threat to consolidation.

Political Culture and Public Attitudes

If the modes of transition and the political institutions, created or evolved, present challenges to democratic consolidation, what of public attitudes and the cultures in which they are rooted? In the absence of extensive survey data, I will offer merely an impressionistic sketch.

There seems to be little opposition to the general principle of democracy, if only because of the paucity of alternatives after experience of authoritarian rule and the collapse of the Communist bloc. Yet there are occasional concerns that an unhealthily large minority would not be averse to authoritarianism in certain circumstances (see especially Shin 1999: 90 on South Korea; and Linz and Stepan 1996: 222–226 on Chile). When it comes to the actual practice of democracy and its feasibility in individual countries, the doubts are somewhat greater. While references to South Korea might provoke the charge that it has no place in a study of the third world, it is instructive to contrast Flanagan and Lee's observations on the growth of a culture that is now less deferential, more critical of institutions, more receptive to new ideas, and more tolerant of a range of lifestyles and beliefs (Flanagan and Lee 2000: 26–59), with Steinberg's account of intolerance in the political sphere. Heterodox views on the virtues of capitalism or sympathy with North Korea are not so readily accepted (Steinberg 2000: 203–238). South Korea may be a special case in view of its former frontline position in the Cold War, but the suspicion remains that in much of the third world, and quite possibly beyond it, there is a contrast between permissiveness in the social sphere and greater conformity in the narrower economic and political spheres. Societies may be more tolerant of drugs, alcohol, abortion, promiscuity, and a variety of personal eccentricities, and more sympathetic toward racial and sexual equality (though there are parts of the world where religious constraints continue to be powerful). But political choices are narrowed as globalization and pressures from donors constrain any departure from the current free market orthodoxy. It is not so much that people are locked up for questioning the teachings of Adam Smith but that politicians and officials who advocate even mild departures from the orthodoxy are likely to be branded as unrealistic and may well jeopardize their careers. The orthodoxy has gained some legitimacy because it has been presented as part of the good governance package that goes with democratization. But it is often the least popular part of the package and we do not yet know how far even a grudging acceptance of it will extend (see especially Bratton, Lewis, and Gyimah-Boadi 2001: 231–259 on Ghana).

There remains a gap between a generally expressed preference for a democratic order and the political behavior that is necessary to sustain such an order. As regards the low and falling levels of party membership, participation, and identification, does this reflect a socially irresponsible citizenry that has either withdrawn from politics altogether or who prefer the quick fix of a protest march, demonstration, or riot to the long haul of building support for, and shaping the policies of, a political party? Or does it reflect the unattractiveness of the parties themselves, with their lack of clear principles or policies, their preference for wealthy donors over mass membership, and their inability to implement such policies as they have proclaimed?

These are questions that have a familiar ring in the West, but parties in the West are better able to live off their fat, having built up a measure of support in the past. Democrats might prefer to blame the parties rather than the citizenry on the premise that it is the producer's job to satisfy the consumer, but social and economic reality leave parties with little room to maneuver when it comes to seeking distinctive policies or mass support.

Policy choices are constrained by poverty, debt, and donor demands, and developing party loyalty is constrained by the strength of loyalty to primary groups. As debates on principles and policies become increasingly academic, the temptation is to seek votes on the basis of ethnic or religious appeals or to project individual leaders as national saviors. Diamond notes that most voting in Africa is on the basis of ethnicity rather than issues, and Peeler suggests that elections in Latin America are more about the selection of rulers than policies (Diamond 1999b: ix–xxvii; Peeler 1998: 199). The presidential models adopted in Latin America encourage the personalization of elections, and Hagopian writes of the rise of leaders like Collor, Fujimori, and Carlos Menem who promise to solve national problems almost single-handedly and without parties and who treat congress and the courts as a nuisance (Hagopian 1998: 104). Taken to extremes, this descent of democracy into populism can end in the suspension of the democratic constitution by the president, as in Peru (Cameron 2001: 219–239).

Conclusion

The failure or inability of third world societies to strengthen democratic institutions might suggest a move toward democratic decay rather than consolidation, but how far has decay been allowed to go? Presidents such as Collor in Brazil, Fujimori in Peru, and Jorge Serrano in Guatemala were eventually driven out of office for their misdeeds. Their removal owed much to public protest, whereas in earlier times such removals would have depended more on the army or machinations at the elite level. In Africa, protests in the streets brought an end to a military interregnum in Côte d'Ivoire, and the combined if uncoordinated efforts of opposition parties and civil society have helped to end the ruling parties' overall majorities in Kenya and Zambia. Some people might see such developments as part of the unfinished business of transition rather than consolidation, but they have all occurred after the initial stage of authoritarian rulers conceding multiparty elections. This brings us back to the distinction between the adjective "consolidated" and the verb "to consolidate." It is clear that few third world democracies are consolidated, especially if we use the rigorous criteria suggested by Linz and Stepan, which allows for little political behavior outside the bounds of democratic norms and institutions. But many countries have taken specific steps (beyond the holding of free elections and providing basic civil liberties) that have replaced authoritarian or anarchic behavior and institutions with something closer to democracy. These include facilitating public criticism, governmental accountability, and the redress of grievances; restraining the power of armies; and establishing means of removing rulers, not just on the grounds of unpopularity but for reasons of constitutional violation. In all these ways, particular aspects of democracy have been consolidated, even if these developments do not add up to a consolidated whole.

On the question of why consolidation has made such progress as it has, and why not more, it is difficult to escape the explanation that some democracies, even if not born with silver spoons in their mouths, have enjoyed advantages in terms of social and economic preconditions—and in terms of transitions based on consensus between the different actors, moderation, and gradual change. Some of the earlier works of Diamond and Huntington could give the impression that there was little hope for democracy unless transition was negotiated in a conservative way (Diamond 1989: 145; Huntington 1991–1992: 608–609). But that is rather like saying an empty house is made habitable more easily if it requires only spring cleaning and interior decoration rather than structural alterations. It may be good news for the occupant of the structurally sound house, but does it necessarily imply that the occupant of the structurally unsound house next door should either make do with a broom and a pot of paint or give up altogether?

Where there are underlying conditions that favor cooperation, consensus, and gradual, moderate change, and where political actors exist who are willing to give a high priority to democratic objectives and have the skills to know how to pursue them, it would be foolish to dismiss these assets. But if many of these underlying conditions are absent, it would be dangerous to pretend otherwise. There is a danger in freezing counterelites or the masses out of any democratic settlement, on the grounds that their heterodox views will threaten consensus, or prescribing gradual change when more rapid change might remove an obstructive elite that could otherwise undermine the democratic process, or in failing to remove blatant social injustices in the interests of moderation. Such moves could perpetuate injustices that might infect the body politic for years to come. They might also reflect an attempt to build on unsound foundations while pretending that the structure was basically sound.

In countries such as El Salvador, Nicaragua, and South Africa, where the quest for democracy arose from a sense of social injustice, and not just as a fad of a small counterelite, efforts have been made to reconcile groups that were previously poles apart. But where students of democratization, including the present author, appear to have been wrong is in anticipating that a modicum of social justice and poverty relief were either prerequisites of democracy or issues that democracies would have to address if they were to survive. The indignities imposed by apartheid have gone, as have many of the humiliations imposed by fraudulent elections, torture, and execution, but any pact between the haves and have-nots has generally been concerned with constitutional rather than social rights. Consolidation has not, to anywhere near the same extent as in the West, been built on assumptions that the ballot paper is a currency that can be exchanged for better health, education, welfare, and employment conditions. Indeed, one could argue that any attempts by the masses to secure such a contract would strain democracy to the breaking point. Ruling elites, constrained by limited state capacity, the demands of foreign donors, and their own pursuit of self-preservation, would be unable or unwilling to deliver.

For how long the current distribution of resources, both within third world countries and between the third world and the West, will be accepted as legitimate is a matter for speculation. As far as democratization is concerned, any observer looking at developments from the vantage point of the late 1980s and who returned to the scene today would be surprised that the process has been both so broad (in terms of the number of countries achieving transitions) as well as so shallow. Most of the democracies have survived, and many have made innovations that help to consolidate particular democratic practices, but it is significant that much of our attention focuses on the smoothness or otherwise with which the democratic machine works, rather than on what the machine is able to produce. And this brings us back to speculation on how far that machine will be able to continue functioning if dissatisfaction with the end product grows.

10

Third World or Three Continents? The Geography of Democracy

The discussion so far has allowed for differences in the experience of democracy between individual countries on account of their different resources, histories, cultures, and political actors. It has also emphasized that there have been global trends that have transcended national boundaries, such as pressures for the ending of colonial rule after 1945, the rise and fall of communism and the Cold War, changing ideological fashions, and globalization itself. Why complicate matters by moving to an intermediate level and searching for authentically African, Asian, or Latin American manifestations of democracy? Could one not argue that a well-established democracy like Botswana has more in common with Costa Rica than with neighboring Angola, that India with its institutionalized system of party competition is politically closer to Uruguay than to Pakistan, or that Nigerians freeing themselves after long periods of authoritarian rule would feel at home in Indonesia?

An immediate answer would be that many people who live in, and write about, the individual continents believe their own region to be distinctive, and that such claims require investigation. Another answer would be that, as we saw in earlier chapters, the three continents were colonized at different times and in different circumstances and that these varied types of colonization—and the decolonization that followed—have left their mark on the nature of states, societies, and relations with the outside world. In this chapter, we shall therefore consider the extent to which the fact of belonging to Africa, Asia, or Latin America may affect the nature of democracy in an individual country. But first let us digress briefly to look at a region where it is the absence of democracy that is more the center of attention.

205

An Empty Chair in the Democratic World:
The Middle East

Haynes's study of *Democracy in the Developing World* includes a chapter on the Middle East, in addition to chapters on Africa and Latin America. Yet his use of Freedom House data reveals a stark contrast between the Middle East and the rest of the third world, as indicated in Table 10.1. No Middle Eastern country is classified as "free," and only four of the twenty-one are "partly free." In contrast, no African or Latin American country is classified as "not free," and 37 percent and 53 percent, respectively, of the countries on each continent are free (Haynes 2001a: 54, 137, 165).

Table 10.1　Democracy in the Middle East, Africa, and Latin America

Region	Free Countries	Partly Free	Not Free
Middle East	0	4	17
Africa	6	16	0
Latin America	8	7	0

One can point to individual Middle Eastern countries where elections are freer, or human rights better respected, than in the recent past, but most of the discussion of democratic transition and consolidation in this book would find few echoes in Middle Eastern politics.

Independence came to most Middle Eastern countries earlier than in Africa and Asia, at a time when even nominal democracy based on universal suffrage was not considered desirable. Political institutions were largely dominated by monarchs and landed elites. When these groups were eventually challenged by lower social groups, the demands were not for extended parliamentary democracy, as in Western Europe, but for more revolutionary changes that would sweep away aristocratic and bourgeois democracy and transfer power to "modernizing" groups such as soldiers and technocrats. These groups often favored a redistribution of wealth, but under authoritarian forms of government that did not want to risk any counterrevolution. Where such challenges succeeded, as in Egypt, Libya, Iraq, and Syria, military governments emerged. Where they failed, as in many of the Gulf States, authoritarian governments under kings and aristocrats survived, but nowhere did pluralist democracy emerge. There was no evolutionary route to democracy, with industrialization and rising middle and working classes gradually gaining representation. Neither was there an introduction of planted democracies, which was the pattern in countries that became independent after 1945 when only the emancipation of the entire adult population was acceptable (on the historical background, see Cammack, Pool, and Tordoff 1993: 41–49). Once the undemocratic forms of government had been established in the Middle East, they proved difficult to dislodge. Regimes might change from military to one party, or from monarchies to theocracies based on Islamic law, but not into democracies. States remained strong in relation to civil society. And economies based on oil rather than manufacturing industry left states with substantial wealth for buying off potential challengers, while leaving little room for the emergence of autonomous social groups. If the trickle-down of wealth failed to placate any aspiring democrats, ample coercive resources were available (see especially Brynen, Korany, and Noble 1998: 267–278; and Kamrava 2001: 187–216.) The external pressure for democracy is also missing, as the oil-producing countries are less likely to be dependent on Western aid or the demands for good governance that go with it.

The Bases of Democracy on Three Continents

We return to the main question of whether the nature and existence of democracy are best understood by looking at the distinctive nature of each continent. We shall skate around the pedantic point that some of the Middle East is actually in Africa and some is in Asia, as there are ample precedents for treating it as an entity in its own right. We shall also omit any discussion of the island states in the Caribbean and Pacific, though in Chapter 6 we noted that democracy was more likely to flourish in small states.

Of the three continents colonized by Europe, Asia has the strongest claim to a distinctive culture that sets it apart from its colonial masters. Long before the arrival of Europeans, Asia enjoyed complex administrative structures that exercised a broader and deeper control over their territories than anything comparable in precolonial Africa or Latin America. Asia also had widely followed philosophers and religious prophets, as well as works of art, literature, and technology, which had few parallels on the other continents. The timing of colonization varied between different Asian countries, but most of it was earlier than the nineteenth-century scramble for Africa. As we saw in Chapter 3, this meant that much of the technology that helped to subordinate Africa, including the railway, the steamship, the telegraph, and the Maxim gun, was not yet available, and deals had to be struck that left substantial autonomy with indigenous leaders. As a result, much more of the indigenous culture was left intact, including Asian religions, social structures, educational systems, and languages that continued to enjoy official status. Within the sweep of such a history, in which European penetration was relatively brief and shallow, Asians may claim that any democracy they now enjoy can and should be infused largely by Asian cultures and values rather than by universal democratic values that some people in the West claim ought to prevail. One implication of this claim to authenticity is that the word "cultures" has to be used in the plural. India, Indonesia, and South Korea may all claim distinctive Asian identities, yet the differences between the three countries are much greater than one would normally find in comparing African countries and much greater than one would find within Latin America. This makes generalizing about Asian democracy difficult; hence, I will simply suggest some broad outlines, while leaving room for the possibility of numerous exceptions to any suggested "rules."

Latin America occupies the opposite pole to Asia on the diversity/ homogeneity scale. We can admire the evidence of precolonial civilization unearthed by archaeologists, but there are few threads to link such civilization with postcolonial Latin America. Most of the continent shares a common heritage of Iberian conquest, language, religion, and culture, and substantial European settlement. Every country has been ruled largely by men of European descent. This does not mean that uniform cultures, institutions, and values have emerged, but it does make the countries of Latin America more alike than those of Africa and Asia (see especially Diamond et al. 1999: 32). Such diversity as exists has less to do with ancient cultures or ethnic differences than with the different relationships between various social groups that emerged with economic change and industrialization in the nineteenth century (see especially Stephens 1989: 281–352). While claims are frequently made for distinctively African or Asian forms of democracy, whether as an ideal or as a justification for existing practices, there are few advocates of a distinctively Latin American version. Democracy tends to be seen more in instrumental terms than as a reflection of indigenous culture or timeless values. It rests more on the need for accommodation between conflicting social groups, with periodic adjustments as the powers and resources of different groups wax and wane.

Africa occupies an intermediate position. Nineteenth-century colonial penetration, aided by new technology and the ideological imperative of a European "civilizing" mission, was much deeper than in Asia or Latin America. Fewer indigenous institutions were left intact, as European administrative structures, religions, languages, and educational systems provided a new framework. But this did not produce uniformity, if only because the number of colonizing powers was much greater than in Latin America. (The focus in this chapter is on sub-Saharan Africa. Much of North Africa belongs to, or has common ground with, the Middle East.)

There is also, in contrast to Latin America, the more peripheral role of European settlement, which was confined mainly to the highland areas and the more temperate countries of the south. By the 1980s only Namibia and South Africa were ruled by Europeans, and by the end of the twentieth century government by Africans was universal. This meant that, for all the European institutions inherited from colonial rule, the pattern of politics was likely to reflect the diversity of African cultures. Kenya with its warrior tradition and its small number of dominant ethnic groups is clearly different from Tanzania, where the existence of a large number of small groups leads to a search for consensus. Both are different from Ghana, in that the traditional role of the chieftaincy in the latter country remains a powerful element in politics. The ending of colonial rule is sufficiently recent to have left its mark on present-day politics. Countries that gained independence through armed struggle, such as Zimbabwe, may be less tolerant of opposition than those where there was a more peaceful transfer of power, and countries experiencing a relatively long period of preparation for independence, such as Ghana and Nigeria, may have developed more durable institutions than those experiencing a hurried handover, such as the Congo and Guinea.

Yet Africans, to a much greater extent than Latin Americans, do make much of their distinctive common culture, from ruling politicians like Nelson Mandela, Julius Nyerere, and Léopold Senghor, through political scientists like Claude Ake, Ali Mazrui, and Celestine Monga, to novelists and poets such as Wole Soyinka. Like those who claim a distinctive Asian culture, they play down the European emphasis on the rights of the individual in favor of the collective rights of the community, though they also emphasize the search for consensus rather than mere majority rule. Whether Africans practice what they preach is another matter, but the myth of the palaver tree can be invoked to justify what is seen as the African way. President Benjamin Mkapa of Tanzania invoked it to explain the apparent resolution of the conflict between government and opposition in Zanzibar.

> The only miracle option I had was to revert to African traditions and ways of resolving conflicts, under which even before colonialism, our elders, when confronted with a major crisis, used to "sit under a tree," discuss, listen to each side, weigh each argument, without regard to how long it took to reach agreement. The overriding objective was to reach a consensus . . . a consensus in which there are no winners and no losers . . . because each side considers itself part of the process and of the agreement reached. (*Tanzanian Affairs,* 2002, January–February: 10)

I have attempted to sketch out what is said to be distinctive about Africa, Asia, and Latin America; our focus now turns to the extent to which each continent provides any distinctive means of consolidating democracy or suffers any distinctive handicaps that stand in the way of such consolidation. Table 10.2 lists four variables: (1) the extent of consensus on the nature and conduct of democracy, (2) the effectiveness and capacity of political institutions, (3) the depth and cohesion of civil society, and (4) the

Table 10.2 The Prospects for Democratic Consolidation on Three Continents

Variable	Africa	Asia	Latin America
Extent of consensus on the nature and conduct of democracy	Most transitions were dominated by elites who did not seek consensus with opposition groups or civil society	Most transitions were government controlled but responded to civil society pressures; often there was consensus that authoritarianism had served its purpose	Greater involvement of opposition groups and civil society in transition; broader and deeper consensus
Effectiveness and capacity of political institutions	Very limited; paucity of resources encourages patronage rather than competing policies	Ruling parties are often strong and provide coherence	Elected presidents and armies are often strong; danger of arbitrary rule
Depth and cohesion of civil society	Deep colonial penetration and poverty have kept society weak; wealth and status in society depend heavily on control over, or access to, the state	Many societies are strong and autonomous but often remain aloof from politics (i.e., much of society is not "civil" society)	Relatively strong civil societies though weakened by postindustrialism and the decline of corporatism; important role of churches
Democratic culture and values	Myth of the palaver tree but difficult to relate to modern conditions; experience of the second wave; emphasis on collective rather than individual rights	Emphasis on distinctive Asian values rather than individual rights; many countries missed the second wave	Many democratic settlements reached by elites and counterelites by early twentieth century; experience of second, and sometimes first, waves; competing ideologies may enhance or overstretch democracy

nature of democratic values. We shall look at these variables in relation to each continent.

An African Model?

One might expect democracy to fare better if it has been launched, or has evolved, on the basis of *consensus* between government and opposition and between elites and masses. Any such consensus may fall well short of perfection, but some are more imperfect than others. In Africa there is a wide disparity between the myth of the palaver tree and the processes by which transitions to democracy have been engineered. Few transitions outside South Africa have been based on pacts between governments and other groups. Transition has sometimes been preceded by a national conference or constituent assembly that attempts to include representatives of the opposition and civil society, but we have seen that the conferences generally produced winners and losers rather than consensus. Authoritarians did not willingly give up the benefits derived from controlling the machinery of state or offer to share the benefits with others, though public pressure forced some of them to go unwillingly. As for constituent assemblies, these might give voice to a variety of demands, but any prudent government ensured that the majority of assembly members were people who would follow its own line or that it had power to veto any initiatives it disliked. In many cases, the formality of a conference or assembly was dispensed with, and the rulers simply decided what minimal concessions to democracy they needed to make to avoid rebellion at home or loss of aid from abroad. None of this suggests a recipe for consensual democracy. Opposition parties are told, in effect, that they may contest elections, but on terms dictated by their masters. Civil society, for all its growing importance in social and economic life, is similarly told to know its place when it comes to constitutional matters. Some nongovernmental organizations may enjoy influence in high places, but virtually all are required to register their existence, as if groups in society gain their legitimacy from the state rather than the other way around.

Political institutions in Africa are generally limited in their resources and capacity. This is partly a reflection of the poverty of much of Africa, even in comparison with the rest of the third world, which leaves states with weak tax bases and, partly, as we saw in Chapter 9, a reflection of the reluctance of institutions to perceive their role as one of sustaining development rather than safeguarding their own interests. There is a paucity of resources that governments might use in the pursuit of distinctive policy objectives, such as extending social welfare or building economic infrastructures. Unable to maintain power by winning electoral support for distinctive policies, governments are tempted instead to maintain support by disbursing benefits to favored groups through systems of patronage. These arrangements mean that ruling politicians and their clients will go to considerable lengths to avoid losing elections and thus losing the mutual benefits.

The greater depth of colonial penetration in Africa is said to have left *civil society* weak. Indigenous institutions and values were stunted, calling to mind Agyeman-Duah's observations about everything beginning and ending with the state (see Chapter 5). Civil society is visible enough, but those citizens who want to enjoy wealth and status within it have limited resources unless they enjoy adequate access to the state—whether at an individual level of obtaining a job, a contract, or a place in a school or at the communal level of obtaining adequate roads, drinking water, or medical facilities.

The curtailment of much state provision with economic liberalization has thrown communities back more on their own resources, and this may augur well for democracy in the future. There have also been cases where elements in civil society have challenged authoritarian tendencies in government, but civil society's role is generally seen to have diminished when one moves from challenging authoritarianism to consolidating democracy. This is a trend in much of the third world, but it is particularly marked in Africa where the links between civil society and formal institutions are more tenuous. Political parties are exceptionally shallow, and most civil society groups are more concerned with self-help than with articulating political demands.

It is when we move on to the extent to which *democratic cultures and values* exist that the prospects for consolidation in Africa look more promising. The gulf between the myth of the palaver tree and the actual behavior of many African politicians appears to be a wide one, with poverty, weak civil societies, and brittle institutions all standing in the way of democracy. Yet notions of how one ought to behave, whether in politics or religion, may still be important even if the precepts are ignored more frequently than they are followed.

Although we have suggested that the late arrival of colonialism in Africa was exceptionally destructive of indigenous society, because it was able to employ late nineteenth-century technology, it was also brief. Many Africans lived long enough to see the first colonial governor arrive and the last one depart. The values of precolonial times were not therefore the stuff of ancient history, as in much of Asia and Latin America. If precolonial times are not within the memory of any Africans living today, they were at least within the memory of many of their grandparents. This is not to suggest the existence of some precolonial democratic utopia, and values obviously varied between different areas, but few Africans would deny that there was a tradition within many communities of seeking consensus. This was helped by relatively fluid class structures, compared with the other continents. Chiefs were superior to their subjects, but there were not the inequalities based on caste or ownership of plantations, mines, or factories; even chiefs were subject to removal if the consensus of the community required it.

Again, without over-romanticizing African society, it does seem that when a new problem or challenge arises, the reaction is to seek a consensus unless there are pressures that push the decisionmaking process in other directions. Unfortunately for democracy, the frequency of such pressures is so great that consensus politics can be submerged for long periods— hence long periods of authoritarian rule, bureaucratic arrogance, military force, and the purchase of influence through bribery. But when the tide recedes, the democratic values are still there. How else could one explain the reconciliation in South Africa after apartheid, the growth of local community participation in Uganda after years of authoritarianism and civil war, or the restoration of pluralist politics in Ghana after military governments had plundered state coffers and shot their opponents? Empirical observation suggests that whether it is in running a student amateur dramatic society, deciding if a chief has discharged his duties correctly, deliberating within a constituent assembly, or even resolving a disputed election in Zanzibar, the African has a preference for democratic consensus. This does not guarantee that all existing authoritarian practices or the resort to violence will be abandoned, but it might suggest that appeals to African values will exert a pull that cannot always be resisted.

An Asian Model?

The sheer diversity of Asia might tempt one to abandon any search for an Asian model. Even if we exclude China, North Korea, the former Soviet Republics, and possibly Indochina from the discussion—on the grounds that they are not members of the third world but remnants of the second— we are still left with variations stretching from the prosperity of South Korea to the poverty of Afghanistan and from the stability of Singapore to the threatened disintegration of Indonesia. Yet many Asians still insist that there are distinctive Asian values that transcend these differences. Political analysis might suggest that two of the keys to Asian distinctiveness are (1) the strength of political institutions and (2) the extent to which democratization, where it has occurred, has been based on a broad consensus that authoritarianism has outlived whatever usefulness it had.

In Asia, as in Africa, most transitions to democracy have been government controlled. At first glance there does not appear to have been any attempt at a *consensus* to incorporate opposition groups or civil society. Yet transition frequently involved more than a government seeking the legitimacy of electoral support while making minimal constitutional changes. In Indonesia, the Philippines, and South Korea, democratization was hastened by extensive riots, which suggested that pressure came from large segments of the population and not merely from a small number of intellectuals or defectors from the government. National conferences, constituent assemblies, and formal negotiations between government and opposition have generally been absent, yet one can detect a consensus in the sense that government and opposition alike seek to prevent violent confrontation from destroying the nation. There may also be a consensus that authoritarianism, whatever its achievements in the past, has outlived its usefulness. This was especially obvious in the cases of the "tiger" economies of South Korea and Taiwan, where authoritarians might take the credit for rapid economic development but might offer fewer justifications for remaining in power once the economic miracle has been achieved. The growing middle class and working class that they had helped to create were now strong enough to voice democratic demands that could not be ignored. It may be stretching the concept of consensus if one is looking for a detailed constitutional settlement that government, opposition, and civil society could all accept, but there was agreement across most of society and the polity that electoral competition (which had not been eliminated to the same extent as in Africa) should be conducted more fairly and that civil rights should be protected more rigorously. Democracy has been tested to the extent that it has survived the peaceful transfer of power to former opposition groups in Bangladesh, South Korea, Taiwan, the Philippines, Indonesia, and Pakistan, though with a subsequent authoritarian restoration in Pakistan.

The strength of *political institutions* in Asia could be used to explain both the distinctiveness of Asia from Africa and the greater diversity within Asia compared with Africa. Institutional strength in Asia has been helped by a longer postindependence history and in the case of South Korea and Taiwan by economic prosperity that has enabled governments to deliver more benefits to their citizens. In many of the Asian countries, the exigencies of the Cold War led to the building up of substantial armies. In India, Malaysia, Singapore, and Taiwan, ruling parties have built up forms of organization and support that have few parallels in Africa. Whether all these developments are good for democratic consolidation is another matter.

There is the immediate question of whether the institutions are themselves democratic or seek to promote democracy. Strong armies in Indonesia, South Korea until the 1980s, and Myanmar (Burma) were not great promoters of democracy, and even the most charitable view of the Pakistan Army would suggest that it has set democracy back by not allowing civilian groups to resolve political crises. Political parties present a more varied picture. The ruling party in Singapore has turned any attempt at constitutional opposition into a hazardous activity, and the ruling coalition in Malaysia sees opposition as little more than a necessary evil. In contrast, the Congress Party is praised for broadening and deepening democracy in India, and the Kuomintang in Taiwan eventually permitted free elections and a peaceful transfer of power. Although much may depend on the benevolence or otherwise of the leaders of these institutions, there is also the question of whether any authoritarian tendencies could be moderated by the counterweights of other institutions or by civil society.

The Congress Party, as we saw in Chapter 6, could not easily have destroyed democracy without destroying India as a nation, and too many people had an interest in preserving the nation to permit that. The army in South Korea and the political party created by the army in Indonesia faced so much violent resistance, actual and potential, from dissident groups and urban mobs that an orderly retreat seemed prudent. The contrast between countries where powerful institutions come face-to-face with "someone their own size" and countries where they do not is brought out by the experiences of Pakistan and Bangladesh. The armies of both countries came from the same cultural stable, but the Pakistan Army had acquired a privileged position, which meant that it had much to lose from democratization, whereas the Bangladesh Army acknowledged its limitations and calculated that it would survive better as an institution if it withdrew from politics (Wilkinson 2000: 203–226). All these experiences might suggest that the strength of institutions in Asia, compared with Africa, can lead to more durable forms of authoritarianism but that strong institutions with strong counterweights may be able to produce more sustainable democracies than most of Africa has enjoyed.

Civil society in Asia appears to possess advantages over Africa if it can trace its lineage back to Buddha or Confucius. As mentioned previously, it was difficult to achieve high social status in Africa unless one could tap into the resources of the state. The necessary conspicuous expenditure can usually be traced back to the prestigious post, the contract, or even the bribe rather than solely to inherited family wealth or to enterprise independent of state patronage. Many Asians also owe their wealth to state patronage, but the state is a smaller fish in a bigger pond. Princes, landlords, monks, and philosophers have all seen different governments come and go, and states did not generally throttle society in the way that they did in late-nineteenth-century Africa.

Difficulties arise when we begin to think about civil society rather than society in general. Societies may flourish, but they may see participation in politics as peripheral to their interests, leaving a vacuum to be filled by the political entrepreneur who knows more about how to win power than about why to win it. Our examples from South Korea and Thailand have shown how political conflict is generally bereft of ideology. In these cases, political parties with meager public support subsist on the contributions of wealthy donors. Where society does exert an influence, our examples from India suggested that it was often in the direction of protecting privileged groups at the expense of the "modern" sector, leaving the poorest sections of society with even less influence. If one regards civil society as important for democracy because it can prevent the state from monopolizing every aspect of life, then Asia enjoys certain advantages. But if one expects civil society to imbue people with democratic values and to inspire participation in democratic institutions, there appears to be fewer grounds for optimism.

Turning directly to *democratic values*, we return to the discussion in the previous chapters of whether Asian values can be seen as adding a distinctive flavor to democracy or as a pretext for governments to preserve their authoritarian and intolerant ways. Few would dispute Chan's assertion that one can be a democrat and still subscribe to beliefs embedded in much of Asian culture with regard to family and communal values, religious practices, marriage rights, the death penalty, homosexuality, abortion, and freedom of expression in the nonpolitical sphere (Chan 1998: 28–41). Even if one has a preference for legalized abortion and homosexuality, liberal divorce laws, and unlimited freedom to attack accepted religious beliefs and practices, one can presumably accept that the majority of people in other societies have a right, through the representative process, to frame laws that reflect a different set of preferences and beliefs. One could also accept Diamond's argument that it is possible to have a form of liberal democracy with greater emphasis on the rights of the community rather than the individual and on the social obligations of the individual (Diamond 1999a: 15).

Can we go still further and accept that democracy is compatible with the Confucian values enumerated by Shin, including the rejection of individual freedom, human rights, and the rule of law, in favor of the rule of man, the supremacy of the group over the individual, family over community, duties over rights, and personal wisdom over impersonal law (Shin 1999: 254)? Much would probably depend on the extent to which these values were embedded in the law of the land and not merely accepted as guiding principles within society, though even here it is difficult to envisage a democratic society that rejects individual rights and the rule of law entirely. There is also the question of whether laws or constitutions based on allegedly nondemocratic values are imposed by an unrepresentative minority or in response to populist demands, or whether they have evolved in response to widely held, enduring values. The Islamic law imposed in Iran fits the former category, and the upholding of Muslim values in Malaysia is closer to the latter.

Another distinctive feature of much of Asia is the limited extent to which it was involved in the second wave of democratization. India, Pakistan, and Sri Lanka gained independence at the beginning of that wave, and Malaysian independence in 1957 might be regarded as part of it, but democratization in most of East and Southeast Asia was confined to the third wave in the late 1980s and 1990s. It is probably too early to judge the significance of this for the effectiveness of democratic consolidation, but nonparticipation in the second wave, when South Korea, Taiwan, the Philippines, and Indonesia were still under authoritarian rule, means that experience of democracy is more limited than in much of Africa. There has not been the same process of trial and error that may enable democrats to spot authoritarian threats, especially from the army or the ruling party, or to strengthen democratic safeguards, such as freedom of the press and the careful monitoring of elections. The chronological difference also means that the late democratizers are coming into a postindustrial world in which political participation is at a low ebb, as compared with the days of mass party membership and of extensive governmental roles in social and economic provision in response to mass demands. Postindustrialization has, of course, engulfed Europe and Latin America as well as Asia, but many Asian political institutions do not even have roots in the earlier era to provide a legacy of democratic values and expectations. Perhaps a slimmed-down version of democracy, with fewer expectations of state provision, a more consumer-oriented society, and a more skeptical attitude toward the desirability of political participation will serve Asia better than a folk memory of earlier times. But if that is to be Asia's fate, it suggests that any democratic advance will not be on a wave of enthusiasm. In some countries the balance of power between different institutions, aided by a favorable international climate, may help to keep authoritarianism at bay, but there lies ahead the task of evolving a more democratic culture.

A Latin American Model?

Latin America appears to enjoy several advantages over Africa and Asia in attempting to achieve democratic consolidation. Many of the Latin American republics were involved in the first and second waves of democratization, as well as the third, so there is no shortage of democratic experience. Few of the national frontiers are in dispute, and there are few distractions in the form of separatist groups challenging the existence of nation-states. State institutions have proved their strength, yet civil societies have also proved their resilience, especially in the years of authoritarian rule. Given all these advantages, we might need to ask why democracy has not advanced much further, instead of being plagued by presidents wielding excessive power, military vetoes, declining political participation, and governments unable to deliver material benefits.

Consensus on the nature and conduct of democracy has not been universal, but there have been several cases of opposition and civil society

groups being involved in the process of transition, whether directly as nego-
tiators or indirectly as forces whose strength and legitimacy are acknowledged. Outgoing military rulers recognized that they could not simply withdraw from politics on their own terms, and in many countries they had to
accept the election of politicians who would not have been their own first
preference. Authoritarian governments had fewer achievements to their
credit than in Asia, although a case has been made that the regimes in
Brazil and Chile, for all their brutality, were necessary to achieve economic
and political stability. Elsewhere, there were few people outside the army or
narrow elites who mourned the passing of the authoritarians.

As in Asia, there has been no shortage of strong *institutions*. The problem has again been one of the adequacy of counterweights to the institutions. The tradition of presidential constitutions makes for strong executives, often made stronger by the weaknesses of legislatures and political
parties. Armies remain influential, and if Latin America has a longer history
of democracy than the other continents, it also has a longer history of military intervention and a greater expectation that the military will be able to
extract favors from elected governments. The apparent imbalance between
the power of executives and the military, at the expense of representative
institutions and public opinion, has led to some pessimism about the
prospects for democracy, and much that happens between elections might
suggest survivals from earlier times, though with many fewer human rights
abuses. But what does seem to have been consolidated effectively in most
countries is electoral democracy. There may still be question marks in
Nicaragua, with excessive U.S. influence, and in other parts of Central
America, where ruling elites are difficult to dislodge. Yet the frequency
with which incumbents have been defeated over much of the continent suggests a development that will not be reversed easily.

Civil society appears to have proved its strength during the years of
authoritarian rule, both in helping everyday survival and ultimately in challenging authority, but we must recall the pessimism of democrats who regret
the inability of civil society to connect adequately with the new democratic
governments. This is at a time when the old corporate structures, which once
facilitated participation and representation, have been weakened or destroyed
in the wake of postindustrialization and economic liberalization. Although
such trends no doubt make for a wider democratic deficit, we must not forget
that much of the literature is comparing today's Latin America with yesterday's Latin America and not with Africa and Asia. Compared with those continents, civil society appears to be much better organized than in Africa,
given the longer experience of democracy, and more politically engaged than
in Asia, where indigenous culture provides many more diversions.

When it comes to *democratic values,* Latin Americans spend less time
talking about distinctive Latin American values than Africans and Asians
do in talking about the distinctive values of their continents. But there is

an almost unspoken acceptance that the democratic arena now provides the only effective means of resolving political conflicts. Latin American values may not be paraded as the basis for any particular type of ideology, but particular ideologies figure more strongly than in Africa or Asia. The ending of the Cold War has blunted many groups on the left, and some ideological rhetoric is more an echo of past battles and loyalties than present reality, but we can still use the words "left" and "right" to describe political conflict in Latin America in a way that would not be appropriate on the other continents. The scope for radical reform may be limited in an era of globalization and structural adjustment, yet a long history of class conflict has left its mark. We have noted assertions about recent elections being more concerned with personalities than policies, but it is common to refer to social democratic politicians in Chile, Peronists in Argentina, and former Marxist radicals in Central America when one would have much greater difficulty in describing the ideological affiliations of politicians in India, Nigeria, or South Korea.

The ideologies themselves do not necessarily give a high priority to pluralist democracy, but the fact that a multiplicity of them may exist in any one country means that nonviolent means have been sought to regulate political competition. Whether we look at the bargaining between social groups in nineteenth-century Chile or at the settlement between the elites and Marxist guerrillas in El Salvador in the 1980s, the extension of democracy was seen as the best means of resolving political crises. It would be foolhardy to predict the consolidation of a permanent democracy in view of Latin America's long history of alternation between authoritarianism and democracy, but for the foreseeable future it is difficult to envisage who would be able or willing to restore authoritarian government.

Many armies suffered a loss of professional cohesion as a result of being in government and would be reluctant to intervene again, and few civilians would support them in view of their past records. One-party rule has never been a feature of Latin American politics, as no single party could span the class divides. This leaves the possibility of creeping presidentialism, with executives taking more and more power into their own hands. The presence of weak legislatures and political parties, and diffuse civil societies, may encourage such a trend, but the experiences of Guatemala and Peru suggest that there is a limit beyond which it is dangerous for presidents to go, and that the democratic forces will eventually reassert themselves.

Conclusion

The observations in this chapter suggest that democracy and democratization can take on distinctively African, Asian, and Latin American flavors. This does not mean that we ignore the diversity within each continent, especially in the case of Asia, or that we do not allow for the possibility of one country having more in common with another country on a distant shore than with its immediate neighbors. And, there are certain common influences within each continent that exert a pull of their own.

In Africa there is the weakness of civil society, resulting largely from the depth of nineteenth-century colonial penetration. By default, this leaves much power, though not necessarily capacity, in the hands of those who control the state, and makes the practice of opposition politics a barren experience. Those controlling the state have generally made few concessions to opposition groups or civil society when making the transition to democracy. Thus, there is little consensus on the rules of the democratic order. Yet the lateness of colonial rule, compared with Asia and Latin America, has also meant that the myth of a precolonial democratic order is more alive and can be invoked to show the superiority of African values over alien values that see democracy more in terms of winners and losers. Democrats may regret that this myth has been invoked only infrequently, but its existence may provide a degree of hope on a continent where optimism is in short supply.

In the case of Asia, the main grounds for optimism among democrats appear to be the relative strength of political parties in some countries (especially India and Taiwan) in providing a balance between stability and participation and the heterogeneity of many societies that makes authoritarian control difficult. No autocrat has been able to control India since independence, none has done so in Thailand for any length of time, and the prospect of anyone doing so again in Indonesia or the Philippines seems remote. Society may turn its back on the state to a greater extent than on the other continents, but it may also set limits to state interference in areas where this is deemed illegitimate. Against this, Asia contains many more countries that have so far resisted democratization. Strong institutions can provide a democratic framework if there is a balance between them. But without such a balance, an army in Myanmar or a ruling party in Singapore can block attempts at democratization. Asia's experience of democracy has in many cases been patchier than Africa's, with many countries unaffected by the second wave; Asian values frequently place a greater emphasis on order and hierarchy than participation. In a way we have a mirror image of Africa, with the prospects for consolidation not helped unduly by indigenous culture or previous democratic experience but aided by a balance of power between institutions and by the limited ability of governments to penetrate or coerce society.

Latin America presents a more familiar picture to anyone with knowledge of the evolution of democracy in Europe. There is little attempt to invoke any myth of precolonial democratic values, and society does not remain aloof from the state as it does in much of Asia. Democracy emerged largely from the dynamics of economic change, which produced new groups that were able to strike bargains with incumbent elites. None of the democratic settlements survived permanently, but each episode of democracy added to the store of experience that could be utilized whenever the pendulum swung away from authoritarianism. Democracy was enriched by a much greater clash of social groups and ideologies than in Africa or Asia, though sometimes it proved too rich for the polity to digest. Elites feared for the loss of their privileges, the United States sometimes feared for the loss of right-wing allies, and the military suspended democracy. With at least nominal democracy restored in most countries after the ending of the Cold War, a key question is whether either the weakened corporate and participatory foundations on which democracy was originally built, or the subsequent rise of social movements, will provide a sufficient basis for the consolidation of democracy.

We are left with a fascinating balance of cultural, structural, and historical forces that are shaping or retarding democracy. In Africa, the issue is whether a half-buried culture of democratic consensus (the myth of the palaver tree) can overcome the structural obstacle of states that are strong enough to overpower civil society. In Asia, the structural advantage of strong political parties has to be balanced against the structural handicap of dominant parties and armies and the historical lack of experience of democracy over much of the continent. Conversely a long, if interrupted, history of democracy is an asset in Latin America, but the decline of corporatism and the institutions of mass participation have made for structural handicaps. It is not the function of the political scientist to predict which sets of assets and liabilities will be most conducive to democracy in the future, but future analysts will enjoy the challenge of plotting the varied routes to democratic success and failure.

11

Conclusion

On the whole Western man has justified the hopes of eighteenth century
democrats: the people, it has turned out, can be trusted. . . . The world outside Europe has learnt to handle our machines; it has still to be won for
our ideas. At the very least, this task will provide some interest and occupation for the next fifty years. Better that than emulate medieval man,
waiting for the end of the world in AD 1000 and sit in helpless contempla-
tion of the universal catastrophe that may well have come before AD 2001.
(Taylor 1950: 8)

British historian A. J. P. Taylor, writing in 1950, contemplated winning the
world outside Europe for "our ideas" over the ensuing fifty years. Attempting to win the third world for democracy has certainly provided "interest
and occupation" for many politicians and academics, but not all of them
would take such a Eurocentric view of "us" and "them." In most parts of
the world, there are both democratic and authoritarian elements in indigenous culture as well as individuals who are willing to fight for both democratic and authoritarian causes. Democracy had triumphed, or was well on
the way to triumphing, in most Western countries by the early twentieth
century. But this did not prevent Western countries from imposing or supporting authoritarian regimes in many other parts of the world. African and
Asian nationalists like Gandhi, Nehru, Nkrumah, and Nyerere saw themselves as democrats and the Europeans as authoritarians. They invoked precolonial indigenous culture, especially in the case of Africa, as the basis of
democracy, yet when it came to building modern nation-states they could
hardly ignore the democratic models that had emerged in the West. If
an indigenous culture that was favorable to democratic values existed or
could be revived, that was a major asset. But when it came to creating
actual structures, Western experience of democracy could not easily be
ignored, nor could Western limitations to the democratic process if would-
be rulers wanted to temper democracy with order and stability. Knowledge

of constitutional provisions for declaring a state of emergency, mobilizing the police during a strike, or operating an electoral system that could give the government an inflated majority could all be useful.

Democratic values and practices have not remained static since 1950. For nationalist leaders in the mid-twentieth century, democracy was equated largely with freedom from foreign control. Elections by universal suffrage were important in giving independent governments a mandate to pursue the elusive goal of development, but there was no great preoccupation with procedures for constraining or ultimately removing governments, except among impotent opposition politicians. By the 1980s and 1990s, people who had experienced decades of authoritarian rule were more concerned with accountable government, human rights, and the autonomy of civil society. With the hoped-for development turning out to be an illusion, there was no longer any case for preserving authoritarian government to pursue this unattainable end.

Democratic aspirations in the West had also changed by the late twentieth century. Voters were less inclined to judge governments by their ability to provide generous social welfare and full employment, as these objectives were increasingly deemed to be impracticable or undesirable. Sexual, racial, and religious equality had become more important, but not social equality or the ability of elected governments to control the economy in the perceived public interest. Individual and communal participation in politics had declined, and much of the gap was filled by corporate sponsorship. Where this has not involved outright corruption, it has made politicians increasingly subservient to business interests. As societies became more nonegalitarian and fragmented, crime and terrorism grew, and this raised questions about the balance between civil liberties and public order. In many respects Western liberal democracy became more liberal but less democratic. There were fewer restrictions on drinking, gambling, divorce, abortion, homosexuality, and even drug taking, but governments increasingly insisted that the public sector should retreat, leaving more decisions in the hands of private individuals, private business, and the voluntary sector.

External Pressures and Constraints

Democrats in the third world are not simply the passive recipients of whatever the current notion of democracy happens to be in the West. What seems more likely is that the Western conception of democracy will set limits to what third world countries are able to do. It may also have a detrimental effect by projecting an image of democracy that either conflicts with indigenous values in many countries or enables third world authoritarians to justify their actions on the grounds that they are behaving no differently than Western governments. The Western insistence on a free market economy and a slimmer state immediately narrows political choice by ruling out social democratic alternatives. This might be seen as making a virtue (or vice?) out of a necessity, given the limited capacity and resources of most third world governments, but it also limits the scope for serious debate on questions such as whether there should be comprehensive national policies for education and health provision rather than reliance on the diffuse activities of various nongovernmental organizations. Any debate on the merits of developing the indigenous economy by restricting the inflow of imports or of global capital is likely to be given even shorter shrift, given the current Western ideological climate.

In the case of the Western "permissive society," much of which is now sanctioned by more liberal laws, no one is trying to impose this directly on the third world, but it may affect the image that countries have of the West and create a fear that greater democratization will mean greater permissiveness. Even Fukuyama, one of the leading apostles of the universality of Western democracy, is concerned with the contrast between the Asian enthusiasm for the American model of the 1950s and 1960s, and the Asian dislike of today's individualism and self-indulgence in the West: "Many Americans see their own contemporary culture as being as problematic as Asians regard it. If they succeed in making it more appealing to themselves, its appeal in Asia will succeed as well" (Fukuyama 1998: 227).

Flanagan and Lee also see dangers in libertarian beliefs and behavior and the pursuit of self-interest as undermining society and the democratic polity, with tolerance as the only value (Flanagan and Lee 2000: 656). Kausikin speaks of many people in the West perceiving the dangers of an overemphasis on liberal values and individual rights, and the erosion of legitimate authority, in contrast to the greater Asian emphasis on order (Kausikan 1998: 24).

Right-wing Christian sects, most of them based in the United States and with branches in much of the third world, offer a somewhat different perspective. They preach "family values" rather than permissiveness, but they have little to say on democracy, social justice, or the power of big business. While many Anglican and Catholic priests have shown courage in campaigning on matters such as human rights and the plight of the poor, the right-wing sects are more concerned with spiritual self-gratification, just as free market fundamentalists are concerned with material self-gratification.

While some of the "liberal" aspects of liberal democracy are regarded as unappetizing in much of the third world, the inadequacy of the "democratic" aspects in the West poses additional problems. Diamond is concerned about the widening gap between rich and poor and the "raw purchase of political influence." He argues that if the growth of democracy in the third world is to continue, it must continue to do so "in the most economically advanced countries" with a greater emphasis on civic obligation and citizens participating as political equals (Diamond 1999a: 273–274). Peeler draws parallels between the retreat of democracy in the face of big business in both the United States and Latin America. Governments in both hemispheres have taken the line of least resistance and accepted "that property yields political power, that policy must serve the interests of the capitalist system, and that popular participation in decision-making must be kept within limits that do not threaten these interests" (Peeler 1998: 196–197).

The combination of growing business influence and declining popular participation, and indeed public interest in politics, is likely to mean that behavior previously regarded as improper or corrupt will either become socially acceptable or will be condemned by sections of the media and the "chattering classes" for a few days and then be forgotten or go unpunished. Britain's connivance in the sale of arms to Iraq and U.S. support for terrorists in Nicaragua are two cases in point. This is not to argue that Western politicians did not do reprehensible things in the more distant past, but they were probably more constrained by actual or potential public protest. In Britain, widespread protests against the Suez invasion in 1956 and against human rights abuses in British colonies such as Cyprus and Kenya all met with widespread public condemnation, as did U.S. conduct of the war in Vietnam, and it is arguable that democratic protest eventually produced changes of policy. It is doubtful whether comparable actions would produce such widespread protests today.

The impact of changing Western values, standards, and behavior is not easy to gauge, but it can hardly avoid presenting third world politicians with justifications for any antidemocratic tendencies they may have. Corrupt deals, encroachments on civil liberties, and indifference or hostility to extending political participation can all be presented as little different from the practice of politics in the West. Even the sanctity of the electoral process came into question when the allegedly rigged election in Zanzibar in October 2000 was followed a few weeks later by the vote counting in Florida that decided the outcome of the U.S. presidential election. Some Western commentators still expressed misgivings about the Zanzibar election, but democrats who live in glass houses may be reluctant to throw stones. This is not to argue that deviations from the democratic path in the West are necessarily comparable with the behavior of the most authoritarian or corrupt rulers in the third world but simply to note that the image presented by the West is a more ambiguous one than at the time of the second wave of democratization. Western democratic initiatives may be pursued with greater vigor, with aid dependent on "good governance," and with Western diplomats breathing down the necks of erring third world politicians. But the version of democracy peddled appears to rule out extensive welfare provision or control over the economy, while it sanctions the sacrifice of the public interest to business interests, and possibly to the interests of politicians who have a close relationship with business.

Internal Dynamics of Democratization

One of the paradoxes running through this book has been the contrast between the unexpected ease with which democracy has been established in the third world and the greater difficulty in transforming political systems into much more than electoral democracies. While virtually all of Latin America and the vast majority of countries in Africa and Asia are now living under elected governments, breadth has been achieved but not depth, quantity but not quality, transition but not consolidation. This should not detract from the importance of achieving any democratization at all. If it turns out that the democratic bus terminates at electoral democracy rather than the distant destinations of participatory democracy or social democracy, this would still be a significant achievement. Far fewer people are now imprisoned, tortured, or executed for their political beliefs; there is much more freedom for people in civil society to pursue a wide range of political activities; and most armies have influence but only a few wield power. Unpopular politicians are still not easy to displace, but many have departed with a minimum of violence, and many of the most degrading forms of obsequience to authority are no longer necessary. Critics can point out that poverty, inequality, corruption, incompetent administration, and ethnic and religious conflict continue to flourish, yet there is little reason to believe that continued authoritarianism would have made the situation any better, except perhaps by keeping the lid on some of the conflicts.

Attempts to explain and understand the process of transition to democracy are therefore worthy exercises in themselves. One of the lessons of the past half-century has been that apparently entrenched regimes can crumble remarkably quickly. When Taylor was writing about "the world outside Europe" in 1950, most of the British Empire was still intact, except for the Indian subcontinent (Taylor 1950: 8). Within two decades little remained except a few small islands. Much of what was by then called the third world was under authoritarian rule in the early 1980s, but barely a single decade elapsed before multiparty competition was restored in most countries. In 1961 the construction of the Berlin Wall seemed to symbolize the impregnability of the Soviet authoritarian fortress. Nineteen ninety-one saw the final collapse of that fortress as Red Army soldiers surrendered to the power of unarmed civilians.

Although some authoritarian regimes were replaced with near anarchy, as ill-organized warring factions plundered what was left of the state and the economy, it is possible in the vast majority of cases to trace a transition not to chaos but to democracy. We have considered some of the reasons for this, and the reasons why the transitions took the varied forms that they did. People living under authoritarian regimes in the twentieth century were aware of the existence of democratic systems in other countries in a way that people in earlier times had not been aware. Not only did more democratic countries exist, but modern means of transport and communication meant that opposition leaders and members of counterelete groups could visit democratic countries, and populations could be exposed to information that their rulers did not want them to receive. The nature and effectiveness of the different transitions might vary according to the skills and behavior of individual actors, and some of the advances toward democracy were the result of political pressures that had other immediate objectives, such as relieving food shortages or ending the domination of a particular ethnic group, but few of those who challenged authoritarian governments were positively hostile to a democratic settlement. If democracy was not yet the only game in town, alternative games based on replacing one set of authoritarians with another, imposing a theocracy based on fundamentalist religion, or giving free rein to rival armed factions did not have a lot of adherents. The ending of the Cold War and subsequent Western pressure for good governance gave the democratization process a greater impetus, but the process was already under way by the early 1990s.

The speed with which authoritarian rule has been toppled, whether through the dissolution of European empires in the third quarter of the twentieth century or through the third wave at the end of the century, has been remarked on, in contrast to the survival of authoritarian regimes for several centuries in earlier times. This can be attributed partly to the factors already mentioned, such as modern communications and external pressures, but what also seems important is the fragile legitimate base on which the recent authoritarian regimes appear to have rested. Many rulers in earlier times claimed the right to rule on the basis of divine right, social superiority, or simply tradition, and they were not held responsible for the performance of the economy or the adequacy of social provision. Third world authoritarians sometimes claimed to be wielding power in the pursuit of some higher moral or ideological purpose, or in keeping with some indigenous tradition, and they might sometimes surround themselves with activists and sycophants to try to give credibility to their claims. But if the markets began to run out of food, or public employees could no longer be paid regularly, people took less interest in whatever ideological or traditional clothes the naked emperor was supposed to be wearing.

This overview provides the more obvious explanations of the undermining of authoritarian rule, the reasons why it was replaced with democracy, and the reasons why the transition was so rapid in most countries. If we measured the success of democracy in the third world by the ability of countries to achieve transitions to democracy, we could conclude that since the early 1980s, and especially in the 1990s, there has been considerable success. Not only have most third world countries arrived at the democratic destination, but it is difficult to envisage the majority of them reverting to the previous authoritarianism, given the climate of both internal and external opinion. Yet the consolidation, or further advance, of democracy is another matter.

Consolidation does not imply the achievement of a democratic utopia. It does not necessarily imply the achievement of a more participatory, egalitarian society. One could argue that Britain enjoyed a consolidated democracy in the late eighteenth century in the sense that governments were established, functioned, and were removed by a set of generally accepted norms, even if later generations might deplore the narrowness of the franchise, the corruption, and the lack of concern for the poor. Conversely, democracy has not been consolidated in contemporary Zimbabwe, despite the existence of a constitution granting universal suffrage, because there is little consensus on the way in which elections should be conducted, the human rights that people should enjoy, or the ways in which the government should be held accountable. The problem in many third world countries is not the failure to achieve utopia but the failure to achieve a consensus on the basic workings of a democratic system. This is not to say that progress has not been made. Many countries can point to the conduct of relatively orderly elections that have achieved peaceful changes of government, to armies that interfere much less in the political process, to misbehaving rulers being removed, to governments held more accountable for their actions, and to much greater respect for human rights. Yet it is significant that, beyond the small number of countries that have enjoyed continuous democracy since independence, experts have difficulty in naming more than one country that they regard as a consolidated democracy in the third world. That country is Uruguay, and Uruguay is exceptional in that its experience of authoritarian rule was brief and had been preceded by a long period of stable democracy. For the remaining countries, particular aspects of democracy have been consolidated, but they are not regarded as adding up to a consolidated whole. Disqualifications from membership of the consolidated club include the rigging of elections, the subservience of judiciaries and bureaucracies to incumbent governments, lack of accountability, excessive political patronage and corruption, failure to curb the excesses of the army and police, the smothering of civil society, and the inability of governments to translate policy decisions into action.

External and Internal Forces Meet

These inadequacies might be regarded as little more than teething troubles in countries that have undergone rapid transitions. Should we not admire their achievements in shaking off authoritarianism rather than carping about their failure to achieve what it took the West several generations to achieve? A similar plea was sometimes made when the anticipated economic development did not materialize in the 1960s and 1970s—countries need more time to shake off the effects of authoritarian rule. But if we can find only one country in the third world that has unambiguously made a transition from authoritarianism to democracy, and then consolidated that democracy, it might seem that the problem is more acute than it appears at first sight. It may be more than a matter of individual political actors blocking the emergence of a democratic consensus through their own willful behavior.

The argument in this book is that consolidation has been made difficult by a range of internal and external factors and by the interaction between the two. Internally, the democratic transition occurred at a time when already impoverished countries were suffering economic decline, in contrast to the earlier democratizations in Europe during periods of rising prosperity. Newly elected governments were therefore unable to deliver many material benefits in return for votes, and the poorest groups in society had generally been excluded from the negotiations over the terms of the transition. Although they might prefer poverty with freedom to poverty with arbitrary arrest, torture, and imprisonment, there were no obvious reasons why they should feel any great stake in the political system. At an institutional level, representative institutions such as political parties, legislatures, and trade unions found it difficult to generate support or to articulate public opinion. In Latin America this could be attributed to the effects of deindustrialization in weakening mass movements that had previously provided a bridge between government and governed, and in other regions there had not been a process of industrialization in the first place to stimulate such developments. While representative institutions have remained weak, the civil and military bureaucracies have retained substantial influence and have often made only minor adjustments to meet the requirements of a democratic order. All this leaves post-transition rulers with substantial power in day-to-day politics, even if the boundaries of their discretionary powers are more visible than they were formerly.

Of the external factors, the most obvious constraints on democratic consolidation are manifested through the structural adjustment programs, which transfer much control over policy from elected governments to nonelected international financial institutions in Washington. Individual Western governments and the European Union add to the constraints by setting their own terms for aid, not just in specifying the purposes for which aid should be used, but in laying down detailed administrative prescriptions. Yet beyond these clearly visible external constraints are the more subtle ones to which we referred at the beginning of this chapter. Western governments may have a genuine desire to promote democratic consolidation, but they are doing so at a time when they themselves are being carried along by forces that have narrowed the scope for democracy. Here, too, deindustrialization and globalization may be offered as explanations. The breakup of traditional industries, the weakening of trade unions, and the growth of consumer societies in which life offers many diversions other than politics have all altered the balance of political forces. Mass movements and political parties have lost much of their membership and influence, global business has gained a tighter grip by threatening to move elsewhere if its demands are not met, and declining political participation has made it more difficult for governments to be held to account. This lack of accountability applies not just to inadequate policies but to behavior that sails close to the wind in terms of constitutional propriety and integrity.

Thus, we have three separate but overlapping changes in the West that ultimately affect the shape and scope of democracy in the third world. First, global capital has reduced the opportunities for democratic participation in economic policy, whether by governments, workers, or civil society as a whole. Second, the rise of the consumer society and the atomization that has gone with it have led to pressure on governments to extend individual freedom in the nonpolitical sphere to permit a wide range of whims to be gratified. This may be seen by some people as an overdue recognition that the state has no right to regulate personal morality and by others as the provision of bread and circuses to distract public attention from more serious matters. Third, the combined effects of increased business influence and reduced participation have enabled governments to escape public censure for behavior that would previously have been regarded as corrupt, or at least as contrary to accepted ethics.

For the third world, the first development means that Western governments offering aid are unlikely to permit the recipient governments the sort of freedom that they themselves do not enjoy. In earlier times, third world governments could nationalize foreign firms whose behavior conflicted with their own objectives, or impose controls over their operation. Nationalization would be almost unthinkable today, and exercising even minimal control has become increasingly difficult. Control over economic policy is often limited to the fine detail of negotiating aid packages.

The growth of the permissive society in the West, generally sanctioned and reinforced by legislation, does not necessarily imply any compulsion for third world countries to follow suit. What it may do is to encourage third world politicians with authoritarian tendencies to claim the moral high ground and link Western attempts to impose democracy with moral decadence. For President Robert Mugabe, British demands for greater respect for human rights in Zimbabwe are countered with the argument that a government that contains several homosexuals has no business preaching to Africa. This is obviously not to argue that social legislation in Britain has been the main barrier to democratization in Zimbabwe. But, as Fukuyama hints, trends in the West since the 1950s have made the whole Western model less attractive to Asians, and probably to other parts of the third world (Fukuyama 1998: 227).

Finally, the perceived fall in standards of political integrity in the West may make it more difficult for the West to insist on good governance in the third world. And it is this perception as much as reality that is important. Whether the way in which the Uganda Commercial Bank was privatized was more, or less, reprehensible than the way in which Britain's railways were sold to the private sector for a fraction of their real value is not the important point. As long as Western politicians are seen as pursuing narrow self-interest rather than the public interest, it is difficult for them to lay down any moral code that is likely to be followed in the third world.

These changes in the political processes of many Western countries are not insuperable barriers to democratization in the third world. One could argue that they are more of a pretext for opponents of democratization to drag their feet than a serious handicap. But taken together, reduced ability to control the economy, less clear standards of public behavior, and a fear that greater democratization will lead to greater self-indulgence and the undermining of indigenous values do pose serious problems. When there are additional indigenous problems of widespread poverty and illiteracy, weak representative institutions, weak civil societies, limited government capacity, and unpredictable armies, consolidation is going to be a formidable task.

The number of question marks over the future of democracy in the third world are even greater today than when the authoritarian regimes began to crumble in the late 1980s and early 1990s. The sheer rapidity of the transitions to democracy often meant that many groups, especially the poor and ethnic and religious minorities, were left out of any consensus on the form that democracy should take and the interests it should serve. Alienation and resistance by minority groups continues to be a problem in many countries, with violent resistance providing a pretext for responses that go beyond democratic norms. The poor have yet to find an effective voice in most countries, with the decline or nonemergence of mass movements, but we cannot be sure that they will accept their plight indefinitely, or that any challenge to authority will necessarily be within a democratic framework. A return to the authoritarianism of the 1970s and 1980s seems unlikely, partly because memories of brutal regimes would provoke resistance, partly because both armies and erstwhile single parties are so discredited, and possibly because Western countries would not tolerate authoritarianism. The prospects for extensive democratic consolidation in the foreseeable future seem equally implausible. It is not just that third world countries are unlikely to copy any Western model but that any consensus on how the democratic process should work is difficult to achieve. Again, this is partly because some significant groups are not even invited to join in any search for a consensus. Even if they were, there would still be the imbalance between weak representative institutions and powerful executive institutions. A set of rules of the game is difficult to establish if many people can see little value in the game itself. The combined effects of widespread poverty, limited governmental capacity, and external constraints on what governments are able to do may mean that casting a vote has little impact on the distribution of resources.

In the early 1990s there were suggestions that democratization in the second and third worlds was a manifestation of the "end of history," with all the world moving toward liberal democratic politics and free market economics because no alternative was feasible. The false gods of totalitarianism and the command economy had been exorcised for good (Fukuyama 1991: 659–663). Today such assertions seem not so much incorrect as unhelpful. Being a nonauthoritarian and a nonadvocate of a centrally planned economy still leaves one with a wide range of positions that can be occupied. Indeed, the economic fundamentalists who favor granting almost unlimited power to global capital probably have more in common with erstwhile communists who favored unlimited power for the state than they have with liberals who have always favored a diffusion of power between a variety of groups. The market can be accepted as a driving force that largely determines the distribution of resources, but there is room for a variety of policies to harness that force to serve the democratic will of the people. As regards democracy itself, it could be regarded not so much as the only game in town but as a series of games varying from those with clearly codified and accepted rules to games in which the winners put a very different interpretation on the rules from the losers, and games in which the uninitiated may find it difficult to discover any rules at all. Even to characterize the majority of third world democracies as unconsolidated is to overlook wide variations in which institutions and practices have, or have not, been consolidated. The features that contribute to lack of consolidation include various permutations of disputed elections, weak institutions to articulate and represent public aspirations, limited public participation, limited scrutiny of the executive, limited state willingness or capacity to respond to public demands, and the continued internal violence on the part of national armies and rebel groups.

But we need to emphasize not only the word "unconsolidated" but the word "democracy." The fact that there is at least some electoral competition, some process of representation and accountability, and some protection of civil liberties that constrains those wielding the means of coercion points to the contrast between democracy, however limited, and authoritarianism. There are democratic deficits, often extensive ones, but the democratic account remains open. We have seen in the course of this book how some of these deficits have been reduced or eliminated: a more impartial administration of elections here, an agreement to reduce the political role of the army there, or a genuine attempt by politicians somewhere else to relieve poverty rather than line their own pockets. In an environment of continued poverty in the third world, and continued dependence on an outside world whose commitment to democracy is at best ambiguous, the task of moving from consolidating particular parts of the democratic process, to achieving a consolidated whole, is not going to be easy. The setting is certainly a very different one from the setting of rising prosperity, expanding education, and a secure sense of nationhood that provided the background to democratization in the West. The end of history looks much further away than it did a decade ago. For much of the third world, history has only just begun.

Bibliography

Abrahamsen, R. (2000) *Disciplining Democracy*. London: Zed Books.

ACP (African, Caribbean and Pacific) Group of States. (1999) *The Santo Domingo Declaration*. Brussels: ACP.

Aguero, F., and J. Stark., eds. (1998) *Fault Lines of Democratization in Post-Transition Latin America*. Miami: North-South Center Press.

Agyeman-Duah, B. (1987) "Ghana, 1982–6: The Politics of the PNDC," *Journal of Modern African Studies* 25 (4): 613–642.

Ake, C. (1996) *Democracy and Development in Africa*. Washington, D.C.: Brookings Institution Press.

Alam, M. B. (1986) "Democracy in the Third World: Some Problems and Dilemmas," *Indian Journal of Politics* 20 (1 and 2): 53–68.

Allison, L. (1994) "On the Gap Between Theories of Democracy and Theories of Democratization," *Democratization* 1 (1), Spring: 8–26.

Almond, G. A., and S. Verba, eds. (1963) *The Civic Culture*. Princeton: Princeton University Press.

Amin, S. (1987) "Democracy and National Strategy in the Periphery," *Third World Quarterly* 9 (4): 1129–1156.

Amsden, A. H., and Y-D Euh. (1993) "South Korea's 1980s Financial Reforms: Good-bye Financial Repression (Maybe), Hello New Institutional Restraints," *World Development* 21 (3): 379–390.

Amundsen, I., et al. (2001) *Political Institutions in Africa—The Quest for Democratic Accountability in South Africa and Zambia*. Paper presented at the European Consortium for Political Research Conference, Canterbury, England.

Apter, D. (1961) *The Political Kingdom in Uganda*. Princeton: Princeton University Press.

Arnstein, S. (1969) "A Ladder of Citizen Participation in the USA," *Journal of the American Institute of Planners,* July: 216–224.

Arts, K., and J. Byron. (1997) "The Medium-Term Review of the Lome Convention: Heralding the Future," *Third World Quarterly* 18 (1): 73–97.

Austin, D. (1964) *Politics in Ghana, 1946–60*. Oxford: Oxford University Press.

———. (1993) "Reflections on African Politics: Prospero, Ariel and Caliban," *International Affairs* 69, (2): 203–221.

Azarya, V., and N. Chazan. (1989) "Disengagement from the State in Africa: Reflections on the Experience of Ghana and Guinea," *Comparative Studies in Society and History* 29 (1): 106–131.

Baker, B. (2000) "Can Democracy in Africa Be Sustained?" *Commonwealth and Comparative Politics* 38 (3), November: 9–34.

———. (2001) "Democratisation in Sub-Saharan Africa," in J. Haynes, ed., *Towards Sustainable Democracy in the Third World.* Basingstoke, England: Palgrave, pp. 83–112.

Baker, B., and A. Hughes. (2000) "Introduction," *Commonwealth and Comparative Politics* 38 (3), November: 1–8.

Baloyra, E. A., ed. (1987) *Comparing New Democracies: Transitions and Consolidation in Mediterranean Europe and the Southern Cone.* Boulder: Westview Press.

Barkan, J. D. (2000) "Protracted Transitions Among Africa's New Democracies," *Democratization* 7 (3), Autumn: 227–243.

Belloc, H. (1970) *Complete Verse.* London: Duckworth.

Bequele, A. (1983) "Stagnation and Inequality in Ghana," in D. Ghai and S. Redwan, eds., *Agrarian Politics and Rural Poverty in Africa.* Geneva: International Labour Organisation, pp. 219–247.

Berg-Schlosser, D. (1985) "Elements of Consociational Democracy in Kenya." *European Journal of Political Research* 13: 95–109.

Bermeo, N. (1990) "Rethinking Regime Change," *Comparative Politics* 22 (3): 359–377.

Binder, L., et al., eds. (1971) *Crises and Sequences in Political Development.* Princeton: Princeton University Press.

Booth, M. (1999) "Costa Rica: The Roots of Democratic Stability," in L. Diamond et al., eds., *Democracy in Developing Countries: Latin America.* 2nd ed. Boulder and London: Lynne Rienner, pp. 429–468.

Boron, A. A. (1998) "Faulty Democracies: A Reflection on the Capitalist 'Fault Lines' in Latin America," in F. Aguero and J. Stark, eds., *Fault Lines of Democratisation in Post-Transition Latin America.* Miami: North-South Center Press, pp. 41–65.

Bradshaw, Y., and S. W. Ndegwa, eds. (2000) *The Uncertain Promise of Southern Africa.* Bloomington: Indiana University Press.

Bratton, M. (1999) "Second Elections in Africa," in L. Diamond and M. Plattner, eds., *Democratization in Africa.* Baltimore and London: Johns Hopkins University Press, pp. 20–31.

Bratton, M., P. Lewis, and E. Gyimah-Boadi. (2001) "Constituencies for Reform in Ghana," *Journal of Modern African Studies* 39 (2): 231–259.

Bratton, M., and N. van de Walle. (1997) *Democratic Experiments in Africa.* Cambridge, England: Cambridge University Press.

Brautigam, D. (1999) "'The Mauritian Miracle': Democratic Institutions and Economic Policy," in R. Joseph., ed., *State, Conflict, and Democracy in Africa.* Boulder and London: Lynne Rienner, pp. 137–162.

Bretton, H. (1973) *Power and Politics in Africa.* Chicago: Aldine Atherton.

Brynen, R., B. Korany, and P. Noble. (1998) "Conciliation, Democratization, and Arab Experiences," in B. Korany, R. Brynen, and B. Noble, *Political Liberalization and Democratization in the Arab World.* Boulder and London: Lynne Rienner, pp. 267–278.

Burgess, A. (2001) "Universal Democracy, Diminished Expectation," *Democratization* 8 (3), Autumn: 51–74.

Burnell, P. (1998) "Arrivals and Departures: A Preliminary Classification of Democratic Failures and Their Explanation," *Commonwealth and Comparative Politics* 36 (3), November: 1–29.

Burnell, P., and A. Ware, eds. (1998) *Funding Democratisation.* Manchester, England: Manchester University Press.

Cameron, G. (2001) "The Tanzanian General Elections in Zanzibar," *Review of African Political Economy* 88 (28), June: 282–286.

Cameron, M. A. (1998) "Latin American *Autogolpes*: Dangerous Undertows in the Third Wave of Democratisation, *Third World Quarterly* 19 (2): 219–239.

Cammack, P. (1991) "Democracy and Development in Latin America," *Journal of International Development* 3 (5): 537–550.

———. (1985) "The Political Economy of Contemporary Regimes in Latin America: From Bureaucratic Authoritarianism to Restructuring," in P. O'Brien and P. Cammack, eds., *Generals in Retreat: The Crisis of Military Rule in Latin America.* Manchester, England: Manchester University Press, pp. 1–36.

Cammack, P., D. Pool, and W. Tordoff. (1988) *Third World Politics,* Basingstoke, England: Macmillan.

———. (1993) *Third World Politics,* 2nd ed. Basingstoke, England: Macmillan.

Campbell, D. (2001) "Getting the Right Result," *The Guardian,* 7 November: 17.

Carothers, T. (1999) *Aiding Democracy Abroad.* Washington, D.C.: Carnegie Endowment for International Peace.

Chadda, M. (2000) *Building Democracy in South Asia.* Boulder and London: Lynne Rienner.

Chalmers, D. A. (1977) "The Politicized State in Latin America," in J. Malloy. ed., *Authoritarianism and Corporatism in Latin America.* Pittsburgh: University of Pittsburgh Press, pp. 38–60.

Chan, J. (1998) "Asian Values and Human Rights: An Alternative View," in L. Diamond and M. Plattner, eds., *Democracy in East Asia.* Baltimore and London: Johns Hopkins University Press, pp. 28–41.

Chazan, N. (1988) "Ghana: Problems of Governance and the Emergence of Civil Society," in L. Diamond et al., eds., *Democracy in Developing Countries.* Vol. 2, *Africa.* London: Adamantine Press.

———. (1989) "Planning Democracy in Africa: A Comparative Perspective on Nigeria and Ghana," *Policy Sciences* 22: 325–357.

Chazan, N., et al. (1999) *Politics and Society in Contemporary Africa,* 3rd ed. Boulder: Lynne Rienner.

———. (1992) *Politics and Society in Contemporary Africa,* 2nd ed. Boulder: Lynne Rienner.

———. (1988) *Politics and Society in Contemporary Africa.* Boulder: Lynne Rienner.

Close, D. (1988) *Nicaragua.* London: Pinter.

Cockcroft, J. D. (1990) "Latin America: The New Politics of Challenge," *New Politics* 3 (1): 16–31.

Cohen, Y. (1987) "Democracy from Above: The Political Origins of Military Dictatorship in Brazil," *World Politics* 40 (1): 30–54.

Collier, D., ed. (1990) *The New Authoritarianism in Latin America.* Princeton: Princeton University Press.

Collier, R. B. (1999) *Paths Toward Democracy: The Working Class and Elites in Western Europe and Latin America.* Cambridge, England: Cambridge University Press.

Crook, R. (1983) "Bureaucratic Politics in Ghana: A Comparative Perspective," in P. Lyon and J. Manor, eds., *Transfer and Transformation: Political Institutions in the New Commonwealth.* Leicester: Leicester University Press, pp. 185–213.

Crowder, M. (1988) "Botswana and the Survival of Liberal Democracy in Africa," in P. Gifford and W. R. Lewis, eds., *Decolonization and African Independence.* New Haven: Yale University Press, pp. 461–476.

Cruz, R. C. (1996) "Political Parties and Party Systems," in R. Sieder, ed., *Central America: Fragile Transition*. Basingstoke, England: Macmillan, pp. 15–24.

Currie, B. (1996) "Governance, Democracy and Economic Adjustment in India: Conceptual and Empirical Problems," *Third World Quarterly* 17 (4): 787–807.

Dahl, R. A. (1971) *Polyarchy*. New Haven: Yale University Press.

Daudelin, J., and W. E. Hewitt. (1995) "Churches and Politics in Latin America: Catholicism at the Crossroads," *Third World Quarterly* 16 (2): 221–236.

Davidson, B. (1988) "Conclusion," in P. Gifford and W. R. Lewis, eds., *Decolonization and African Independence*. New Haven: Yale University Press, pp. 505–514.

Deegan, H. (2001) *The Politics of the New South Africa*. Harlow, England: Longman.

Diamond, L. (1989) "Beyond Authoritarianism and Totalitarianism: Strategies for Democratization," *The Washington Quarterly* 12 (1): 141–163.

———. (1999a) *Developing Democracy*. Baltimore and London: Johns Hopkins University Press.

———. (1999b) "Introduction," in L. Diamond and M. Plattner, *Democratization in Africa*. Baltimore and London: Johns Hopkins University Press, pp. ix–xxvii.

Diamond, L., and B. K. Kim, eds. (2000) *Consolidating Democracy in South Korea*. Boulder and London: Lynne Rienner.

Diamond, L., J. Linz, and S. M. Lipset, eds. (1989) *Democracy in Developing Countries*. Vol. 3, *Asia*. London: Adamantine Press.

———. (1988) *Democracy in Developing Countries*. Vol. 2, *Africa*. Boulder: Lynne Rienner.

Diamond, L., and M. Plattner, eds. (1998) *Democracy in East Asia*. Baltimore and London: Johns Hopkins University Press.

———. (1999) *Democratization in Africa*. Baltimore and London: Johns Hopkins University Press.

Diamond, L., et al., eds. (1999) *Democracy in Developing Countries: Latin America*. 2nd ed. Boulder and London: Lynne Rienner.

Dicklitch, S. (2000) "The Incomplete Transition in Uganda," in R. B. Kleinberg and J. A. Clark, eds., *Economic Liberalisation, Democratisation, and Civil Society in the Developing World*. Basingstoke, England: Macmillan, pp. 109–128.

Dodd, C. H. (1979) *Democracy and Development in Turkey*. Beverley, England: Eothen Press.

Drake, P. W. (1994) *International Factors in Democratization*. Working paper, Center for Advanced Study in the Social Sciences, Madrid.

Dunn, J., and A. F. Robertson. (1973) *Dependence and Opportunity: Political Change in Ahafo*. Cambridge, England: Cambridge University Press.

Edie, C. J. (1991) *Democracy by Default: Dependency and Clientelism in Jamaica*. Boulder and London: Lynne Rienner.

Espindola, R. (1997) *Parties and Electoral Processes in Latin America's New Democracies*. Paper presented at the Political Studies Association Conference, Belfast.

Etzioni, A. (1996) "Positive Aspects of Community and the Dangers of Fragmentation," *Development and Change* 27 (2): 301–314.

Ferdinand, P. (1998) "Building Democracy on the Basis of Capitalism: Towards an East Asian Model of Party Funding," in P. Burnell and A. Ware, eds., *Funding Democratisation*. Manchester, England: Manchester University Press, pp. 180–201.

Fieldhouse, D. (1988) "Arrested Development in Anglophone Black Africa," in P. Gifford and W. R. Lewis, eds., *Decolonization and African Independence*. New Haven: Yale University Press, pp. 135–158.

Finer, S. E. (1962) *The Man on Horseback.* London: Pall Mall Press.

Fitch, J. S. (1998) *The Armed Forces and Democracy in Latin America.* Baltimore and London: Johns Hopkins University Press.

Flanagan, S. C., and A-R. Lee. (2000) "Value Change and Democratic Reform in Korea," *Comparative Political Studies* 33 (6), June: 626–659.

Flint, J. (1983) "Planned Decolonisation and Its Failures in Africa," *African Affairs*: 389–411.

Frank, A. G. (1984) *Critique and Anti-critique: Essays on Dependency and Reformism.* Eastbourne, England: Praeger.

———. (1991) "No Escape from the Laws of Economics," *Review of African Political Economy* 50: 21–32.

Freedom House. (2001) *Freedom in the World.* Online at: http:/www.freedomhouse. org/research/freeworld.2001table1.htm.

Fukuyama, F. (1998) "The Illusion of Asian Exceptionalism," in L. Diamond and M. Plattner, eds., *Democracy in East Asia.* Baltimore and London: Johns Hopkins University Press, pp. 224–227.

———. (1991) "Liberal Democracy as a World Phenomenon," *PS* 24: 659–663.

Furley, O. (2000) "Democratisation in Uganda," *Commonwealth and Comparative Politics* 38 (3), November: 79–102.

Galtung, J. (2000) "Alternative Models of Global Democracy," in B. Holden, ed., *Global Democracy.* London: Routledge, pp. 143–161.

Garrard-Burnett, V. (1996) "Resacralising the Profane: Government, Religion and Ethnicity in Modern Guatemala," in D. Westerlund, ed., *Questioning the Secular State.* London: Hurst, pp. 96–116.

Ghai, D., and S. Redwan, eds. (1983) *Agrarian Politics and Rural Poverty in Africa.* Geneva: International Labour Organisation.

Ghana. (1997) *Report of the Ad Hoc Committee on Union Government.* Accra: Ghana Publishing Corporation.

Gifford, P., and W. R. Lewis, eds. (1988) *Decolonization and African Independence.* New Haven: Yale University Press.

Giliomee, H. (1999) "South Africa's Emergent Dominant Party Regime," in L. Diamond and M. Plattner, eds., *Democratization in Africa.* Baltimore and London: Johns Hopkins University Press, pp. 140–154.

Gillespie, C. G. (1989) "Democratic Consolidation in the Southern Cone and Brazil: Beyond Political Disarticulation?" *Third World Quarterly* 1 (2): 92–112.

———. (1990) "Models of Democratic Transition in South America," in D. Ethier, ed., *Democratic Transition and Consolidation in Southern Europe, Latin America and Asia.* Basingstoke, England: Macmillan, pp. 45–72.

Githongo, J. (1997) "Civil Society, Democratization, and the Media in Kenya," *Development* 40 (4): 41–45.

Glickman, H. (1988) "Frontiers of Liberal and Non-liberal Democracy in Africa," *Journal of African and Asian Studies* 23 (3–4): 234–254.

Glickman, H. S., ed. (1995) *Ethnic Conflict and Democratization in Africa.* Atlanta: African Studies Association Press.

Green, D. M. (1999) "The Lingering Liberal Moment: An Historical Perspective on the Global Durability of Democracy After 1989," *Democratization* 6 (2), Summer: 1–41.

Grugel, J. (1991) "Transitions from Authoritarian Rule: Lessons for Latin America," *Political Studies* 39 (2): 363–368.

Gupta, A. (2000) "India: Democracy and Dissent," in M. O'Neill and D. Austin, eds., *Democracy and Cultural Diversity.* Oxford: Oxford University Press, pp. 181–188.

Gyimah-Boadi, E. (1999) "Ghana's Elections, the Challenges Ahead," in L. Diamond and M. Plattner, eds., *Democratization in Africa*. Baltimore and London: Johns Hopkins University Press, pp. 105–121.

Hagopian, F. (1998) "Democracy and Political Representation in Latin America in the 1990s: Pause, Reorganization, or Decline?" in F. Aguero and J. Stark, eds., *Fault Lines of Democratization in Post-Transition Latin America*. Miami: North-South Center Press, pp. 99–143.

Harbeson, J. W. (1994) "Civil Society and the Study of Politics in Africa: A Preliminary Assessment," in J. W. Harbeson, D. Rothchild, and N. Chazan, eds., *Civil Society and the State in Africa*. Boulder and London: Lynne Rienner, pp. 285–300.

———. (1999) "Rethinking Democratic Transitions: Lessons from Eastern and Southern Africa," in R. Joseph, ed., *State, Conflict, and Democracy in Africa*. Boulder and London: Lynne Rienner, pp. 39–55.

Harbeson, J. W., and D. Rothchild, eds. (1994) *Africa in World Politics*. Boulder: Westview.

Hargreaves, J. D. (1979) *The End of Colonial Rule in West Africa*. Basingstoke, England: Macmillan.

Haugerud, A. (1997) *The Culture of Politics in Modern Kenya*. Cambridge, England: Cambridge University Press.

Hawthorn, G. (1993) "Liberalization and 'Modern Liberty': Four Southern States," *World Development* 21 (8): 1299–1312.

Haynes, J. (1997) *Democracy and Civil Society in the Third World*. Cambridge, England: Polity Press.

———. (1999) "The Possibility of Democratic Consolidation in Ghana," *Democratization* 6 (1), Summer: 105–122.

Haynes, J., ed. (2001a) *Democracy in the Developing World*. Cambridge, England: Polity Press.

———. (2001b) *Towards Sustainable Democracy in the Third World*. Basingstoke, England: Palgrave.

Hearn, J. (2000) *Foreign Aid, Democratisation, and Civil Society in Africa: A Study of South Africa, Ghana, and Uganda*. Brighton: Institute of Development Studies. Online at: http://nt1.ids.ac.uk/eldis/hot/civsoc.htm.

Heavey, J. F. (1991) "Land Policy and the Economics of Colonial Exploitation," in R. Noyes, ed., *Now the Synthesis*. London: Shepheard-Walwyn, pp. 136–151.

Heper, M. (1991) "Transitions to Democracy Reconsidered," in D. A. Rustow and K. P. Erikson, eds., *Comparative Political Dynamics*. London: HarperCollins: pp. 192–210.

Herbst, J. (1994) "The Dilemmas of Explaining Political Upheaval: Ghana in Comparative Perspective," in J. A. Widner, ed., *Economic Change and Political Liberalization in Sub-Saharan Africa*. Baltimore and London: Johns Hopkins University Press, pp. 182–198.

Hewison, K., ed. (1997) *Political Change in Thailand*. London: Routledge.

Hewitt, V. (1990) "The Congress, the Opposition and the Transfer of Power in India." Paper presented at the Political Studies Association Conference, University of Durham, England.

Hojman, D. E., ed. (1985) *Chile After 1973: Elements for the Analysis of Military Rule*. Liverpool: Centre for Latin American Studies, University of Liverpool.

Holden, B., ed. (2000) *Global Democracy*. London: Routledge.

Holm, J. D., and S. Darnoff. (2000) "Democratizing the Administrative State in Botswana," in Y. Bradshaw and S. N. Ndegwa, eds., *The Uncertain Promise of Southern Africa*. Bloomington: Indiana University Press, pp. 115–150.

Hooper, J. (1990) "The Spanish Connection," *The Guardian*, 22 March: 21.

Hunter, W. (1998) "Civil-Military Relations in Argentina, Brazil, and Chile: Present Trends, Future Prospects," in F. Aguero and J. Stark, eds., *Fault Lines of Democratization in Post-Transition Latin America*. Miami: North-South Center Press, pp. 299–322.

Huntington, S. P. (1991–1992) "How Countries Democratize," *Political Science Quarterly* 106 (4): 579–616.

———. (1968) *Political Order in Changing Societies*. New Haven: Yale University Press.

———. (1991) *The Third Wave: Democratization in the Late Twentieth Century*. Norman: University of Oklahoma Press.

———. (1984) "Will More Countries Become More Democratic?" *Political Science Quarterly* 99 (2): 193–218.

Huntington, S. P., and J. M. Nelson. (1976) *No Easy Choice: Political Participation in Developing Countries*. Cambridge, Mass.: Harvard University Press.

Hurrell, A., and N. Woods, eds. (1999) *Inequality, Globalisation and World Politics*. Oxford: Oxford University Press.

Hyslop, J., ed. (1999) *African Democracy in the Era of Globalisation*. Johannesburg: Witwatersrand University Press.

Im, H. B. (1987) "The Rise of Bureaucratic Authoritarianism in South Korea," *World Politics* 39 (2): 231–257.

———. (2000) "South Korean Democratization in Comparative Perspective," in L. Diamond and B. K. Kim, eds., *Consolidating Democracy in South Korea*. Boulder and London: Lynne Rienner, pp. 21–52.

Inglehart, R. (1977) *The Silent Revolution*. Princeton: Princeton University Press.

Jackson, R. (1990) *Quasi States*. Cambridge, England: Cambridge University Press.

Jeffries, R. (1993) "The State, Good Government and Structural Adjustment in Africa," *Commonwealth and Comparative Politics* 31 (1): 20–35.

Jenkins, R. (1999) *Democratic Politics and Economic Reform in India*. Cambridge, England: Cambridge University Press.

Jonas, S. (1990) "Contradictions of Guatemala's Political Opening," in S. Jonas and N. Stein, eds., *Democracy in Latin America*. London: Bergin and Garvey, pp. 65–83.

———. (1989) "Elections and Transitions: The Guatemalan and Nicaraguan Cases," in M. Booth and M. A. Seligson, eds., *Elections and Democracy in Central America*. Chapel Hill: University of North Carolina Press, pp. 126–157.

Jonas, S., and N. Stein, eds. (1990) *Democracy in Latin America*. London: Bergin and Garvey.

Joseph, R., ed. (1999) *State, Conflict, and Democracy in Africa*. Boulder and London: Lynne Rienner.

Kamrava, M. (2001) "The Middle East and the Question of Democracy," in J. Haynes, ed., *Towards Sustainable Democracy in the Third World*. Basingstoke, England: Palgrave, pp. 187–216.

Kamrava, M., and F. O. Mora (1998) "Civil Society and Democratisation in Comparative Perspective: Latin America and the Middle East," *Third World Quarterly* 19 (5): 893–516.

Karl, T. (1990) "Dilemmas of Democratization in Latin America." *Comparative Politics* 23 (1): 1–21.

Kausikan, B. (1998) "The 'Asian Values Debate': A View from Singapore," in L. Diamond and M. Plattner, eds., *Democracy in East Asia*. Baltimore and London: Johns Hopkins University Press, pp. 17–27.

Kim, B. K. (1998) "Korea's Crisis of Success," in L. Diamond and M. Plattner, eds., *Democracy in East Asia*. Baltimore and London: Johns Hopkins University Press, pp. 113–132.

Kivumbi, M. (1999) "Cultural Traits and the Congolese Conflict," *Sunday Observer*, 29 August, Dar es Salaam: 7.

Kleinberg, R. B., and C. A. Clark, eds. (2000) *Economic Liberalisation, Democratisation and Civil Society in the Third World*. Basingstoke, England: Macmillan.

Korany, B. (1998) *Political Liberalization and Democratization in the Arab World*. Boulder and London: Lynne Rienner.

Kraus, J. (1985) "Ghana's Radical Populist Regime," *Current History* 84 (501): 164–168, 186–187.

Larbi, G. A. (1998) "Institutional Constraints and Capacity Issues in Decentralizing Management in the Public Services: The Case of Health in Ghana," *Journal of International Development* 10: 377–386.

Lee, J. (2000) "Political Protest and Democratization in South Korea," *Democratization* 7 (3), Autumn: 181–202.

Legon Observer Ghana (1980). Interview with President Hilla Limann, 21 November: 290.

Lehmann, D. (1990) *Democracy and Development in Latin America*. Cambridge, England: Polity Press.

Levine, D. H. (1988) "Paradigm Lost: Dependence to Democracy," *World Politics* 40 (3): 377–394.

Lewis, P. G., and D. C. Potter, eds. (1973) *The Practice of Comparative Politics*. Harlow, England: Longman.

Liebenow, J. G. (1985) "The Military Factor in African Politics," in G. Carter and P. O'Meara, eds., *African Independence: The First Twenty-five Years*. London: Heinemann, pp. 126–159.

Linz, J. J., and A. Stepan. (1996) *Problems of Democratic Transition and Consolidation*. Baltimore and London: Johns Hopkins University Press.

Lipset, S. M. (1959) "Some Social Requisites for Democracy: Economic Development and Political Legitimacy," *American Political Science Review* 53 (1): 69–105.

Loveman, B. (1988) "Government and Regime Succession in Chile," *Third World Quarterly* 10 (1): 260–281.

Low, A. (1988) "The End of the British Empire in Africa," in P. Gifford and W. R. Lewis, eds., *Decolonization and African Independence*. New Haven: Yale University Press, pp. 33–72.

Lowe, C. (1999) "Civil Society, the Domestic Realm, History, and Democracy in Southern Africa," in J. Hyslop, ed., *African Democracy in the Era of Globalisation*. Johannesburg: Witwatersrand University Press, pp. 414–440.

Luckham, R. (1995) "Dilemmas of Military Disengagement and Democratization in Africa," *IDS Bulletin* 26 (2): 49–61.

———. (1996) "Faustian Bargains: Democratic Control over Military and Security Establishments," in R. Luckham and S. White, *Democratisation in the South*. Manchester, England: Manchester University Press.

Luckham, R., and S. White. (1996) *Democratisation in the South*. Manchester, England: Manchester University Press.

Ludwig, F. (1996) "Is Religious Revival a Threat to Tanzania's Stability?" in D. Westerlund, ed., *Questioning the Secular State*. London: Hurst, pp. 216–236.

Lyon, P., and J. Manor, eds. (1983) *Transfer and Transformation: Political Institutions in the New Commonwealth*. Leicester: Leicester University Press.

MacAskill, E., and R. Norton-Taylor. (2001) "Global Conflict," *The Guardian*, 3 October: 3.

MacDonald, S. B. (1986) *Trinidad and Tobago: Democracy and Development in the Caribbean*. London: Praeger.

McCargo, D. (1997) "Thailand's Political Parties," in K. Hewison, ed., *Political Change in Thailand.* London: Routledge, pp. 114–131.

McGreal, C. (2001) "Leaders Back 'Marshall Plan for Africa,'" *The Guardian,* 24 October: 19.

Mainwaring, W. (1988) "Political Parties and Democratization in Brazil and the Southern Cone," *Comparative Politics,* October: 91–120.

Malan, M. (2000) "Civil-Military Relations in Africa: Soldier, State and Society in Transition," in H. Solomon and I. Liebenberg, eds., *The Consolidation of Democracy in Africa.* Aldershot, England: Ashgate, pp. 139–170.

Malloy, J., ed. (1977) *Authoritarianism and Corporatism in Latin America.* Pittsburgh: University of Pittsburgh Press.

Manor, J. (1990) "How and Why Liberal and Representative Politics Emerged in India," *Political Studies* 38 (1): 20–38.

Mauceri, P. (1997) "Return of the *Caudillo:* Autocratic Domination in Peru," *Third World Quarterly* 18 (5): 899–911.

Menda, A. (1999) "Firms Withdraw from Dar Waste Management Services," *Business Times,* Dar es Salaam, 20 August: 9.

Miliband, R. (1973) *The State in a Capitalist Society.* London: Quartet Books.

Mitra, S. K. (1992) "Democracy and Political Change in India," *Journal of Commonwealth and Comparative Politics* 30 (1): 9–38.

Monga, C. (1996) *The Anthropology of Anger: Civil Society and Democratization in Africa.* Boulder and London: Lynne Rienner.

Mohiddin, A. (1998) "Partnership: A New Buzz-Word or Realistic Relationship," *Development* 41 (4): 5–16.

Moore, B. (1967) *The Social Origins of Dictatorship and Democracy.* London: Allen Lane.

Muller, E. N. (1985) "Dependent Economic Development, Aid Dependence on the United States, and Democratic Breakdown in the Third World," *International Studies Quarterly* 29: 445–469.

Munck, R. (1989) *Latin America: The Transition to Democracy.* London: Zed Books.

Mung'ong'o, C. G., and V-M. Loiske. (1995) "SAPs and Peasant Responses in Tanzania," in D. Simon et al., eds., *Structurally Adjusted Africa.* London: Pluto Press, pp. 159–183.

Munslow, B. (1983) "Why Has the Westminster Model Failed in Africa?" *Parliamentary Affairs* 38 (2): 218–228.

Noyes, R., ed. (1991) *Now the Synthesis.* London: Shepheard-Walwyn.

Nyong'o, P. A. (1992) "Democratisation Process in Africa," *Review of African Political Economy* 54: 97–102.

O'Brien, P., and P. Cammack, eds. (1985) *Generals in Retreat: The Crisis of Military Rule in Latin America.* Manchester, England: Manchester University Press.

O'Donnell, G. (1986) "Introduction to the Latin American Cases," in G. O'Donnell, P. Schmitter, and L. Whitehead, eds., *Transitions from Authoritarian Rule in Latin America.* Part 2. Baltimore: Johns Hopkins University Press, pp. 3–18.

———. (1993) "On the State, Democratization, and Some Conceptual Problems: A Latin American View with Glances at Post-Communist Countries," *World Development* 21 (8): 1355–1369.

———. (1990) "Tensions in the Bureaucratic Authoritarian State and the Question of Democracy," in D. Collier, ed., *The New Authoritarianism in Latin America.* Princeton: Princeton University Press, pp. 285–318.

O'Donnell, G., P. Schmitter, and L. Whitehead, eds. (1986) *Transitions from Authoritarian Rule in Latin America*. Part 2. Baltimore: Johns Hopkins University Press.

Olsen, G. R. (2001) "Europe and Africa in the 1990s: European Policies Toward a Poor Continent in an Era of Globalization," *Global Society* 15 (4): 325–343.

O'Neill, M., and D. Austin, eds. (2000) *Democracy and Cultural Diversity*. Oxford: Oxford University Press.

Oquaye, M. (2000) "The Process of Democratisation in Contemporary Ghana," *Commonwealth and Comparative Politics* 38 (3), November: 53–78.

Payne, T. (1988) "Multi-Party Politics in Jamaica," in V. Randall, ed., *Political Parties in the Third World*. London: Sage, pp. 135–154.

Pearce, R. (1984) "The Colonial Office and Planned Decolonisation in Africa," *African Affairs*: 77–93.

Peeler, J. A. (1998) *Building Democracy in Latin America*. Boulder and London: Lynne Rienner.

Petras, J. (1990) "The Redemocratisation Process," in S. Jonas and N. Stein, eds., *Democracy in Latin America*. London: Bergin and Garvey, pp. 85–100.

———. (1989) "State, Regime, and the Democratization Muddle," *Journal of Contemporary Asia* 19 (1): 26–32.

Philip, G. (1990) "The Political Economy of Development," *Political Studies* 38: 485–501.

Pinkney, R. (1988) "Ghana: An Alternating Military/Party System," in V. Randall ed., *Political Parties in the Third World*. London: Sage, pp. 32–56.

———. (2001) *The International Politics of East Africa*. Manchester, England: Manchester University Press.

———. (1990) *Right-Wing Military Government*. London: Pinter.

Pool, D. (1991) "Democratisation and Its Limits in the Middle East." Paper presented at the Political Studies Association Conference, Lancaster, England.

Price, R. M. (1975) *Society and Bureaucracy in Contemporary Ghana*. Berkeley: University of California Press.

Przeworski, A., et al. (2000) *Democracy and Development*. Cambridge, England: Cambridge University Press.

Putnam, R. (2000) *Bowling Alone*. London: Simon and Schuster.

Randall, V., ed. (1988) *Political Parties in the Third World*. London: Sage.

Ravenhill, J. (1994) "Dependent by Default: Africa's Relations with the EU," in J. W. Harbeson and D. Rothchild, eds., *Africa in World Politics*. Boulder: Westview Press, pp. 95–123.

Riley, S. P. (1992) "Africa's 'New Wind of Change,'" *World Today* 48 (7), July: 116–119.

Rizvi, G. (1985) "Riding the Tiger: Institutionalising Military Regimes in Pakistan and Bangladesh," in C. Clapham and G. Philip, eds., *The Political Dilemmas of Military Regimes*. London: Croom Helm, pp. 201–236.

Rothchild, D., and N. Chazan, eds. (1988) *The Precarious Balance: State and Society in Africa*. Boulder: Westview Press.

Rustow, D. A. (1990) "Democracy: A Global View," *Foreign Affairs* 69 (4): 75–91.

———. (1973) "How Does Democracy Come into Existence?" in P. G. Lewis and D. C. Potter, eds., *The Practice of Comparative Politics*. Harlow, England: Longman, pp. 117–132.

———. (1970). "Transition to Democracy," *Comparative Politics,* April: 337–363.

Sandbrook, R. (2000) *Closing the Circle: Democratisation and Development in Africa*. London: Zed Books.

———. (1988) "Liberal Democracy in Africa: A Socialist-Revisionist Perspective," *Canadian Journal of African Studies* 22 (2): 240–267.

Schmitter, P. C. (1995) "Transitology: The Science and Art of Democratization," in J. S. Tulchin and B. Romero, eds., *The Consolidation of Democracy in Latin America*. Boulder and London: Lynne Rienner, pp. 11–41.

Share, D. (1987) "Transition to Democracy and Transition Through Transaction," *Comparative Political Studies* 19 (4): 525–548.

Sharma, S. D. (1999) *Development and Democracy in India*. Boulder and London: Lynne Rienner.

Shin, D. H. (1999) *Mass Politics and Culture in Democratising Korea*. Cambridge, England: Cambridge University Press.

Sieder, R., ed. (1996) *Central America: Fragile Transition*. Basingstoke, England: Macmillan.

Simon, D., et al., eds. (1995) *Structurally Adjusted Africa: Poverty, Debt, and Basic Needs*. London: Pluto Press.

Sklar, R. L. (1983) "Democracy in Africa," *African Studies Review* 26 (3/4): 11–24.

———. (1987) "Developmental Democracy," *Comparative Studies in Society and History* 29 (4): 686–714.

Solomon, H., and I. Liebenberg, eds. (2000) *The Consolidation of Democracy in Africa*. Aldershot, England: Ashgate.

Southall, R. (2000) "The State of Democracy in South Africa," *Commonwealth and Comparative Politics* 38 (3), November: 147–170.

Southall, R., and G. Wood. (1998) "Political Party Funding in South Africa," in P. Burnell and A. Ware, eds., *Funding Democratisation*. Manchester, England: Manchester University Press, pp. 202–228.

Steinberg, D. I. (2000) "Continuing Democratic Reform: The Unfinished Symphony," in L. Diamond and B. K. Kim, eds., *Consolidating Democracy in South Korea*. Boulder and London: Lynne Rienner, pp. 203–238.

Stephens, E. H. (1989) "Capitalist Development and Democracy in South America," *Politics and Society* 17 (3): 281–352.

Steves, F. (2001) "Regional Integration and Democratic Consolidation in the Southern Cone of Latin America," *Democratization* 8 (3), Autumn: 75–100.

Stockton, H. (2001) "Political Parties, Party Systems, and Democracy in East Asia," *Comparative Political Studies* 34 (1), February: 94–119.

Sunar, I., and S. Sayari. (1986) "Democracy in Turkey: Problems and Prospects," in G. O'Donnell et al., eds., *Transitions from Authoritarian Rule in Latin America*. Baltimore: Johns Hopkins University Press, pp. 165–186.

Tangri, R., and A. Mwenda. (2001) "Corruption and Cronyism in Uganda's Privatization in the 1990s," *African Affairs* 100 (938): 117–133.

Tanzanian Affairs. (2002) "Zanzibar: A Comprehensive Agreement," January–February: 10.

Taylor, A. J. P. (1950) "The Turn of the Half Century," *The Guardian*, 30 December: 8.

Thompson, M. R. (1996) Late Industrialisers, Late Democratisers: Developmental States in the Asia-Pacific," *Third World Quarterly* 17 (4): 625–647.

Tindigarukayo, J. K. (1989) "The Viability of Federalism and Consociationalism in Cultural Plural Societies of Post-Colonial States: A Theoretical Exploration," *Plural Societies* 19 (1): 41–54.

Tornquist, O. (1999) *Politics and Development*. London: Sage.

Tripp, A. M. (1997) *Changing the Rules: The Politics of Liberalization and the Urban Informal Economy in Tanzania*. Berkeley: University of California Press.

Tulchin, J. S., and B. Romero, eds. (1995) *The Consolidation of Democracy in Latin America*. Boulder and London: Lynne Rienner.

Turner, M., and D. Hulme. (1997) *Governance, Administration and Development*. Basingstoke, England: Macmillan.

UNDP (United Nations Development Programme). (2000 and 2001) *Human Development Reports*. Oxford: Oxford University Press.

Valenzuela, A. (1978) "Chile: The Chilean Military, the 1973 Election, and Institution Breakdown," in J. J. Linz and A. Stepan, eds., *The Breakdown of Democratic Regimes*. Baltimore: Johns Hopkins University Press, pp. 81–110.

———. (1999) "Chile: Origins and Consolidation of Latin American Democracy," in L. Diamond et al., eds., *Democracy in Developing Countries: Latin America*. Boulder and London: Lynne Rienner, pp. 191–247.

Waisman, C. H. (1996) "Argentina: Capitalism and Development," in L. Diamond et al., eds., *Democracy in Developing Countries: Latin America*. Boulder and London: Lynne Rienner, pp. 71–130.

Wallerstein, I. (1974) "Dependence in an Interdependent World," *African Studies Review* 17 (1).

Watt, D., R. Flanary, and R. Theobald. (1999) "Democratisation or the Democratisation of Corruption: The Case of Uganda," *Commonwealth and Comparative Politics* 47 (3): 37–64.

Weiner, M. (1987) "Empirical Democratic Theory and the Transition from Authoritarianism to Democracy," *PS* 20 (4): 961–966.

———. (1971) "Political Participation: Crisis of the Political Process," in L. Binder et al., eds., *Crises and Sequences in Political Development*. Princeton: Princeton University Press, pp. 159–204.

Weiss, T. G., and L. Gordenker. (1996) *NGOs, the United Nations, and Global Governance*. Boulder and London: Lynne Rienner.

Westerlund, D., ed. (1996) *Questioning the Secular State*. London: Hurst.

Whitehead, L. (1993) "Introduction: Some Insights from Western Social Theory," *World Development* 21 (8), August: 1245–1261.

———. (1985) "Whatever Became of the Southern Cone Model?" in D. E. Hojman, ed., *Chile After 1973: Elements for the Analysis of Military Rule*. Liverpool: Centre for Latin American Studies, University of Liverpool, pp. 9–28.

Widner, J. A., ed. (1994) *Economic and Political Liberalization in Sub-Saharan Africa*. Baltimore and London: Johns Hopkins University Press.

Wilkinson, S. I. (2000) "Democratic Consolidation and Failure: Lessons from Bangladesh and Pakistan," *Democratization* 7 (3), Autumn: 203–226.

Willsher, K. (2001) "Mauritanians Rue EU Fish Deal with a Catch," *The Guardian*, 9 November: 15.

Wiseman, J. (1990) *Democracy in Black Africa*. New York: Paragon House.

———. (1999) "The Gambia: From Coup to Elections," in L. Diamond and M. Plattner, eds., *Democratization in Africa*. Baltimore and London: Johns Hopkins University Press, pp. 216–227.

Wood, E. J. (2000) *Forging Democracy from Below*. Cambridge, England: Cambridge University Press.

World Bank. (1993) *Uganda: Growing out of Poverty*. Washington, D.C.: World Bank.

———. (1998) *World Development Indicators*. Washington, D.C.: World Bank.

Wyatt, A., and K. Adeney. (2001) "Democracy in South Asia: Getting Beyond the Structure-Agency Dichotomy." Paper presented at the European Consortium for Political Research Conference, Canterbury, England.

Young, C. (1988) "The African Colonial State and Its Legacy," in D. Rothchild and N. Chazan, eds., *The Precarious Balance: State and Society in Africa*. Boulder: Westview Press.

———. (1994) *The African Colonial State in Comparative Perspective*. New Haven: Yale University Press.

Index

About the Book

Thoroughly updating his widely acclaimed book on third world democracy, Pinkney incorporates provocative explorations of the influences of external forces, the roles of the state and civil society, and the varying trajectories of democratic consolidation (and decay).

Robert Pinkney is research fellow in politics at the University of Northumbria at Newcastle.